MAP
LIBRARIANSHIP

MAP
LIBRARIANSHIP

Harold Nichols MA FLA

CLIVE BINGLEY
LONDON

LINNET BOOKS
HAMDEN · CONN

FIRST PUBLISHED 1976 BY CLIVE BINGLEY LTD
16 PEMBRIDGE ROAD LONDON W11
SIMULTANEOUSLY PUBLISHED IN USA BY LINNET BOOKS
AN IMPRINT OF THE SHOE STRING PRESS INC
995 SHERMAN AVENUE HAMDEN CONNECTICUT 06514
SET IN 10 ON 11 POINT BASKERVILLE
PRINTED AND BOUND IN THE UK BY
REDWOOD BURN LTD TROWBRIDGE AND ESHER
COPYRIGHT © HAROLD NICHOLS 1976
ALL RIGHTS RESERVED
CLIVE BINGLEY ISBN: 0–85157–204–9
LINNET ISBN: 0–208–01530–2

Library of Congress Cataloging in Publication Data

Nichols, Harold.
    Map librarianship.

    Bibliography: p.
    Includes index.
    1. Map collections. I. Title.
Z692.M3N52 1976   025.17'6   75-40141
ISBN 0-208-01530-2 (Linnet)

Contents

Introduction

The literature of map librarianship has grown considerably in recent years but mainly in the form of periodical articles. It is intended that this book will bring together basic principles of librarianship as applied to maps, and, where controversial, stimulate ideas on the development of map libraries. Whilst it is hoped that all map curators and anyone with an interest in map collections will find much to interest them, the book is primarily directed to those librarians in general public, university and college libraries, with no special education in map librarianship, who have a responsibility for current maps or maps in a local studies department, and the curators in university geography departments who probably have had no education in librarianship. I am indebted to many curators and librarians of map collections who have allowed me to examine their collections and who have always spent a lot of time explaining the methods in use. There are too many to name, I hope all will accept my grateful thanks expressed here.

Parts of the book are of a bibliographical nature and full references are given in the text for works noted or described, at least at the first mention. Elsewhere the works are noted in the text by a capitalised abbreviation, usually author's surname, and the reading list at the end of the volume provides full citations for the works used arranged alphabetically by the abbreviation. Should a reader wish to know the books etc used in a single chapter, there is at the end of each chapter a set of 'chapter references' which notes them by abbreviation only.

1

The content of the map collection, current maps

Some years ago a large van stopped in a minor Nottingham street, the driver obviously looking for someone to direct him. A passer-by was nevertheless rather surprised to be asked 'Am I all right for London, mate?' One can only presume the driver had no map and managed to find his way normally by the usually efficient direction marking on British roads. Road signs in the last two or three decades have changed considerably to accommodate the increased speed of car travel and the increased numbers of road users, including those from other countries. To do this the traditional British signpost was scrapped. In shape and size it had lasted for centuries, apparently originally designed to be most clearly visible to a man on horseback. Much larger signs were introduced to be seen at speed, using stylised symbols to give the necessary information at a glance and with internationally accepted graphics. With these signs far more information began to be communicated by the road signs than the routes and distances of earlier signs. In some degree the development of maps through the centuries can be likened to the more recent development in road signs. No doubt in ancient Egypt a visitor having visited the temple at Karnak and been ferried to the west bank of the Nile would have asked someone the way to the Valley of the Kings and his informant might have drawn a simple map in the sand. Today governments try to ensure that road signs are intelligible to road users, and general education attempts to provide educated man with at least an elementary knowledge of map reading and the use of maps. Success however is not always achieved and it might be said that the van driver was ungraphicate, a word for which I am indebted to the writings of Patricia Alonso, Map Librarian of the State Library of Victoria, Australia, and which means lacking familiarity and skill in reading graphic material such as maps.

There is no doubt however that people who have some understanding of maps and who use them as necessary, are growing in number every year and now form a large majority of the population, at least in Great Britain, and are an even larger proportion of the users of public libraries and of the students and staff of universities. Twenty five years ago it was unusual to see an Ordnance Survey map in a home-reading library in England, but now even very small branch libraries in rural areas have their shelves of folded and cased copies of the OS 1 inch to 1 mile scale, or the 1:50,000 sheets for the country. Apart from those universities containing specialist map libraries of very long standing, university map collections in the western world were very sparse before the second world war and commonly recognise the beginnings of their development to gifts from government sources after that war. In any library the provision of the right material has to be made before it attracts users; library users are rather passive in their acceptance of the absence of forms of material from their chosen library. Only when the material is provided, in anticipation of largely unexpressed user requirements does the reader make his needs known and the use of the material develop, be it of maps or any other form of record. For most British libraries the collections of modern maps are still at the stage where they are only beginning to make their presence felt on the potential readership, and indeed to some extent on librarians.

Two articles in the *Cartographic journal* in recent years have reported research studies on the use of maps and on user requirements. These were designed to be of value to the map publisher as a market study. The surveys were conducted among private households in regard to the maps in a family's possession. DREWITT (1973) summarised her findings as 'For maps as a whole most reasons for reference were connected with motoring including day trips, long distance motoring and making holiday plans. Also important were finding the way/ sightseeing in towns (it is thought that many respondents treated this as two separate activities so that finding the way was related to motoring generally and not specifically to town use), general interest, business and professional use, walking in the country and study'. KIRBY (1970) made a survey partly among people who might be expected to be map users, eg members of the Ramblers' Association, surveyors etc. and they were found to possess many copies of maps such as the 1:63,360 Ordnance Survey sheets. Both surveys noted the expressed need for more plotting of amenities on general maps, to locate bus stations, public lavatories, post offices and provide landmark guidance by the locating of such features as very tall blocks of flats. It seems that map-makers must pay more attention to the representation of the details of urban topography. Obviously other users in almost any library are students of geography and many other disciplines where maps are regularly needed. These surveys do not help librarians

10

directly but they might be thought to confirm observations. Student needs are comparatively well-known, their course requirements are publicised, but it must be realised that not all student use of maps is for geographical study. It is not so straight forward with the general reader. If maps of one's own country at scales suitable for walking are in three-fifths of households, they are popularly needed, and two-fifths of the population will find it necessary to visit a library now and again to see such maps. Business interest suggests maps of all parts of the world, particularly in connection with exporting firms. Firms like these will probably possess atlases, so it is necessary for public libraries to be able to provide maps of any country on a scale significantly larger than is possible in an atlas.

What is the potential readership? To many, the associated idea growing from the concept of maps in libraries is the study of geography. This is an obvious source of much of the use of maps in general and is the basis of a need for a collection of maps in a university or other educational institutions. The historical omission of current maps in a university main library has meant that a university map collection is frequently part of the department of geography or of earth sciences, where one had to be developed for the immediate needs of the student geographer. In time this departmental collection has by its existence, attracted users from other departments of the university. Again new disciplines such as urban and regional planning have developed and in them also maps and plans are necessary tools for their work. The geography departmental collection may have widened its scope to cater for the needs of the historian, the sociologist, the agriculturalist, the planner, the geologist etc, or small more specialist collections may have proliferated. In some universities this development, the natural widening of the use of a departmental collection to one for the university as a whole, has led to the university library administering the map library with the map curator a member of the library staff. Usually however the primary need of geographers has been accepted and the collection has remained physically within the geography department. Depending upon the campus geography and the relative positions of the main library and the map collection, this can mean that the value of the maps to students and staff in other departments is somewhat reduced, the saying 'out of sight, out of mind' reflects a normal aspect of human psychology. And it has a double effect, the comparative lack of map users from other departments which will result to some extent from departmental isolation, is reflected in the map curator's selection of material to be added, because known users have a greater 'points value' than potential users, and so there is less attraction for other departments, and the cycle continues.

11

HAGEN (1970) has made a survey of the users of maps at the UCLA Map Library which is within the Geography Department and rather awkwardly situated for the campus as a whole. The results of the survey lead him to conclude that 'in a large university the map library serves the needs of the entire campus community. Therefore such a library should be administered by a campus wide facility such as a library system which functions to serve the need of the entire campus. The map library should also be centrally situated.' He had found that there was extensive use by the School of Architecture and Urban Planning, and that 'the most challenging requests do not generally come from the geographers, geologists and other earth science users but they come from industrial users and from users not generally associated with maps, such as people in the biological sciences, economics, fine arts or physical sciences'. Hagen feels that departments of geography and geology should have their own collections of national topographical maps and of the world on a small scale, but these should, in the main, be duplicating part of the holdings in the main map library. These departments should also be providing maps in accordance with the specialist interests emphasised in their courses, and as required for field work and in multiple copy sets for laboratory use. These considerations will, for example, lead a map curator to acquire map coverage in depth for a part of a foreign country with maps of a larger scale than would otherwise be the case.

Once the map library is recognised as a resource serving the needs of the entire university, it is apparent that maps will be required which are not particularly relevant to academic study in geography or any related subjects but have a useful function in any community of thousands of people. Road maps will, among other uses, allow the better planning of field studies undertaken by many different groups, plans of cave systems will be of value to the speleologists club, and other types of maps and atlases will strengthen the collection over and beyond the academic requirements which are nevertheless the overriding primary responsibility of the library in map provision.

Within the public library the potential users of maps form an even broader group. At present they are less well catered for than in a university because of the absence of an easily identifiable group demanding maps, such as the geography staff and students in universities. Actually there is a rather amorphous group recognised in public libraries, the recreational traveller, but to some extent the group's needs are met by guide books, a book form of provision which perhaps to many librarians is more easily provided and thus the possible demand tempered. The 1974 reorganisation of local government in England and Wales has meant that all public libraries outside London are

12

serving very large populations, Kent County for example serves a population of 1,400,000. London boroughs, whilst generally being very much smaller, serve concentrated urban populations and therefore demand is concentrated on comparatively few service points, which tends to provide a similar rate of demand on depth and variety of resources. Service to populations of this size obviously means that there is a considerable latent need for sheet maps in every library area, far beyond the now obvious and accepted set of folded and backed medium scale sheets in home-reading libraries. The reader accessible general map room, or map area, is still rare although some new library buildings such as that of Birmingham Central Library, England are noteworthy examples. Yet local maps have always been accepted as an important section of a public library department of local history.

A public library can not dilute its services to all the citizens of a community by over emphasising services for students who already have access to their university or college library as primary source of materials, but there are many public library users of maps and atlases for purposes of geographical study, not necessarily of a formal nature and they are found to be particularly interested in aspects of physical geography. The university student will naturally use these facilities as additional to his other resources in term and in vacation. The public library will then cater in general terms for the needs of the groups identified as using university map collections, although the public library might be expected to be more concerned to reflect the actual demands of such students who are users rather than the potential demand of students, which must be left to the care of the university or college libraries.

The many ways in which maps are used in public libraries for purposes other than geographical study can perhaps be illustrated best by some examples, commencing with the common and obvious. Many enquirers can be categorised as requiring information on routes and locations, but the forms this type of enquiry can take is very varied. A prospective holiday maker wishes to know the location of a camping site in southern Italy, its relationship to the coast and its accessibility for other places he may wish to visit. He may then plan a route from his home in England to the camp site, a route evolved from an examination of maps on which he can locate other camp sites from a camping directory and make a choice of which to use depending on their position and such personal matters as desired sightseeing. Once the choices have been made, the holiday traveller will then buy his own maps for the trip, not necessarily the ones used in the library, but in some cases less detailed road maps for which he

13

seeks the bibliographical advice of the staff regarding availability and prices. The increasing use of maps in travel and the popularity of map buying for holiday touring is recognisable from the large number of sales outlets for commercial and, to a lesser extent, official maps. They occupy an increasing proportion of general booksellers' shelves and can be found quite liberally represented in Automobile Association shops and the like. Newspapers like *The guardian* and *The observer* occasionally include a useful survey of map series in their travel pages. Planning tours to drive through Europe is commonplace, including the countries of Eastern Europe and the Soviet Union, but other road travellers can be much more adventurous and it is not unknown for drivers to plot a route to South East Asia, sometimes on rather inadequate atlas information. The Royal Geographical Society Map Room and Library, whose map room is open to the public, has a prepared reading list to help answer this request which is apparently more common than one would imagine. Sometimes considerations other than recreation affect the planning of a route, as in the case of a policeman who had to escort a prisoner to Italy by the shortest railroute and hand his prisoner over to the Italian police at the first possible railway station—a route dictated by allowable expenses. That was fact, but fiction calls for maps too as in the case of the British author, his personal library containing many maps, who nevertheless, in writing a thriller concerning an American private detective, needed a street plan of San Francisco to estimate the time it would take to walk from one identified city address to another.

Of more obvious community value is the assistance given by public library information services to industrial and commercial firms who in their exporting activities often require map aids. This broad group of user interest is recognised in some metropolitan areas by the map collection being situated in the commerce library of the public library. The division of Germany into different Occupied Zones for some time after 1945 was only the first since that date of many instances where exporters have needed to know the effective authority occupying a part of a country, so that necessary documentation and addressing of goods can be properly completed. Unfortunately, there have been many occasions where boundaries have been altered, sometimes only temporarily, as a result of war or internal conflict and, at least for the perimeter zones of such areas, it can be very difficult to discover a location in respect of the appropriate new authority. But commerce has other needs not arising from such man-induced difficulties, the need to know of road and rail communications in developing countries, and to discover, possibly with the assistance of thematic maps, information on climate which can effect packaging, lubrication of

14

machines etc, and the insurance premiums to be paid by someone going to live in the tropics. Experience in a public library information service will soon produce many more different examples of the role of maps, both national and foreign—general, topographical, thematic, and using sheet maps, atlases, and maps within books.

It is possibly the most important duty of a map curator to ensure that the maps which are going to be needed are acquired and are made available. Financial considerations, and sometimes space limitations, may inhibit the acquisition of maps but this only makes the task of selection more important and more difficult. The curator or map librarian must establish the known requirements of the map users and this may not be easily done. At its simplest, a university map curator can discover the probable map needs of the various courses to be taught in geography and other map-using studies during each year, what field trips are planned, etc, but as has been shown this is only part of the need. A public librarian can also discover from appropriate heads of department in the various educational institutions which make some use of the central library services, what students will be expected to use on formal courses including adult education and other part-time classes. Beyond the provision for known courses the position is rather more tenuous. HAGEN (1970) survey, already mentioned, is very helpful, but any survey of users can only provide information on those who are using the map collection, whereas potential users may not be using the map collection because the maps they would require are not obviously present. Within a university the presence of the university map library within the geography department tends to suggest a limitation of use to geographers, and to perpetuate the position whereby other possible users are not present, because their maps are not acquired, because there is no expressed demand for them. It is therefore vitally necessary for the map curator to know his clientele, particularly the stranger to the map room and to know how the collection has satisfied his requirements or in what way the necessary information is lacking. But so often the librarian has to foresee, from his knowledge of maps and his experience of the use made of those that are in stock, that maps of different types will be used if they are available. He should aim to provide not only coverage in the sense of region or a particular subject, but also the best type of map in the most appropriate scales for the anticipated use. If a university map curator, she must not be inhibited in selection by being financed departmentally. The map librarian must be as economical as possible and make every purchase 'pay its way'. There is no point in buying sheet maps for a country when there are maps of that country on the same scale in an atlas in the library. There

15

may not be much point in spending money on a new national atlas because it is a very good one, if the record of consultations of other national atlases already in the library are so few as to suggest that the readers do not often find a need to use them, or perhaps they are not sufficiently exploited by the map library. But there may be good reasons for buying that national atlas other than for immediate use. For example, it is good sense to build up the map collection to a position of excellence in depth for a chosen field. This can only be done when the basic day to day needs of the collection have been fully and properly met, but the steady accumulation of suitable maps within a narrow field will begin to attract use because of the range and value of the maps provided, and will be of significance to appropriate users over an area much greater than the usual general catchment area of the library. A field of special coverage must not be chosen arbitrarily but show regard to the conditions of the parent institution, as in the obvious example of the maps of the region for a public library, or elsewhere to build upon a specialist collection received as a donation from a geographer.

Whatever guidelines might be given as to the selection of maps, plans and atlases for a library collection, must always be assessed in the light of the needs of a particular library, now and in the future, as recognised by successive map curators. In Britain the RSI Section of the Library Association has prepared *Standards for reference service in public libraries*, approved 1969, which includes a section on maps and plans. The level of suggested provision is divided into four grades according to the population covered by the library authority, but as all public library authorities in England and Wales now generally exceed the minimum 300,000 population for the top grade this is the only grade relevant. The suggestions for populations in lower grades can of course be used as suggestions for the requirements of district information centres within the library system. The top grade must now be regarded as less than the minimum requirements for most libraries as many library authorities serve a population several times larger than 300,000. The RSIS *Standards for reference service in public libraries* note that maps and plans should be provided, in Great Britain, as follows:

Great Britain   All 2½″, 1″ and smaller scale Ordnance Survey maps;
All 6″ and 50″ Ordnance Survey maps for own region;
Geological Survey 6″ maps for region;
Soil Survey and Land Utilisation maps, complete sets;

16

Foreign	Ordnance Survey historical maps.
	1:1,000,000 for the World
	1:200,000 for Western Europe
	1″ for Ireland
	Town plans for the major towns of the world

These *Standards* . . . are now several years old and there is no doubt that RSI Section would now wish to revise them, for the introduction of metrication of some scales cited, and particularly in the light of the reorganisation of local authority boundaries, but they can still be used as a starting point.

One would expect that any map collection would have a need for every scale of Ordnance Survey map or plan for the region selected as covered by the collection, which would mean at least the addition of the 1:2500 scale to the list suggested by the *Standards* . . . . Similarly a much wider view of the term region should be understood than might be implied in the *Standards* . . . , city libraries have not found it un-reasonable to provide 1:10,000 (6″ previously) sheets for the whole of their country, eg England, and the new local authority libraries ought to offer at least comparable resources as part of their general infor-mation services. Similarly all the different scales available of Geologi-cal Survey maps of the region must be provided as well as those of other subject interests, as the Soil Survey, Second Land Utilisation Survey, Agricultural Land Classification maps, etc. Again one might reasonably expect geological maps for a much larger area than appears to be suggested by the term 'region'. Certainly a student of geography has probably more interest in geological maps of areas of geological interest or of areas endowed with economic minerals than with the geology of the local region. Administrative maps on all scales published by the Ordnance Survey must be mentioned, and possibly interest in them has revived since the creation by acts of parliament of new local authorities whose boundaries are mapped on the 1:100,000 scale.

The *Standards for reference service in public libraries* seem to ignore the value of the commercially produced maps of the country in which the library is situated, yet these productions seek to provide mapped in-formation which official surveys have tended to exclude. This is par-ticularly true in relation to recreational maps, road maps, and those specially designed for marketing purposes. The Ordnance Survey has entered the field of recreational interest and advertises the 1:25,000 scale maps as 'the map for fishing, walking, climbing, orienteering' and the possibility at one time, that this series might cease publication aroused widespread unrest. In the series *Outdoor leisure maps* of the same scale, which commenced in 1972 and in which maps covering

17

national parks and popular recreational centres are published, the Ordnance Survey has produced well-conceived maps including information on camp sites, picnic sites, viewpoints, youth hostels and on the four sheets of *English lakes* has identified the field boundaries which are dry-stone walls for the benefit, primarily, of the walker. Commercial publishers attempt to satisfy similar and related interests and in *Bartholomew's half-inch series* provide a scale for tourist and others which covers the whole country. The other main strength of commercial publishers of maps is the wide variety of road maps, differing in style and coverage from publisher to publisher, providing a series not recognised by the *Standards . . .* which, even if it is thought that the sheet maps of this type were more appropriately bought by the private individual, should recognise the need for such maps of local conurbations in the library and for the regular library use of national road atlases.

The main difficulty in using *Standards for reference service in public libraries* however is in determining the library's 'own region'. It is implied that it is an area greater than the area of the local authority for a public library, but this is a principle which has to be decided for a university map collection also. The natural hinterland of a city or the region of geographical unity gives some guidance but the real issue is the recognition of that area for which the users of the map collection might reasonably expect larger scales of maps to be provided and to some extent this requires a knowledge of the existence of other map collections and their holdings. For a public library it also implies an understanding of the attraction of readers to the central information library from a wide area, not of equal radius in all directions and formed by other influences ranging from major shopping facilities to the catchment area for hospitals. In many cases where the library is fairly centrally situated the 'own region' should cover a substantial part of the area of the Regional Board but taking into account the existence of other libraries within the region. Where the map collection or public library reference/information centre is not central a similar size of area should be considered but taking in its bounds parts of more than one region. In universities less attention might be given to actual administrative boundaries but on the perimeter of the university's local interest the presence or absence of interesting geographical or other phenomena may decide the extent to be covered.

It might be thought useful to consider a more rule-of-thumb guide, and, in Britain, base the coverage of large scale plans on a segment of the National Grid. The Ordnance Survey publishes index diagrams for the large scale National Grid plans, each page of the index covering one quarter of a 100 Km square on the National Grid. As an example, two such pages of index, the SE and SW quarters of the 100 Km square SK, covering approximately an area bounded by Grantham, Lincolnshire in the E, Leicester and Walsall (Warwickshire) in the S, Leek (Staffordshire) in the W, Ripley (Derbyshire) in the N, and covering the S half of Nottinghamshire, Loughborough being approximately central in the area chosen, shows a little under 2000 sheets of the 1:2500 plan, as published in May 1974. Assuming all the sheets were available in the 2 Km x 1 Km format, this coverage would have cost £3,370 at that date. This is possibly prohibitive for any one library, but the area described contains the major portions of five public library systems, and part of a sixth, as well as three universities and two polytechnics, and cooperative purchase to avoid unnecessary duplication and to achieve complete coverage at this large scale, 1:2500, should be possible. Another probability is that a library would have commenced buying sheets of this scale when the 1:2500 plan began publication as sheets in the metric edition in 1969, and it will not be completed for the country as a whole for a number of years, thus the cost quoted above would be spread over several years. The 1:2500 OS plan, not noted in *Standards . . .* is a set which should be available in libraries open to the public, hopefully for the whole country on a cooperative basis because this set has a quality not present in other maps of Great Britain in that areas of parcels of land are calculated and recorded, in hectares and acres in the metric edition, together with the identifying parcel numbers. It is the nearest British equivalent to a cadastral map and is a map which is often required for property enquiries, although it must be conceded that the enquirer is more likely to require a sheet of an area outside the 'local region' than within it.

The position with regard to the 1:10,000 (previously 1:10560) OS map is less difficult. To cover the same area as outlined above would require some 200 sheets at a cost of £172. The map user might reasonably expect a much larger area to be covered by his library at this scale and some university and public libraries are providing sheets for the whole country, and others should follow. The Ordnance Survey *Map catalogue 1975* states 'There were 2017 1:10,000 sheets in publication during the summer of 1974 but it will be many years before the whole series (coverage, Great Britain) of some 10,500 maps at this scale is published'. A useful aspect of this map is that it contains the names of all streets and can be useful for this purpose for enquiries regarding areas not covered in the library by commercially produced town plans, although there is no street index for a 1:10,000 OS map.

1:1250 scale (50" plans in the *Standards . . .*) is currently the largest OS scale and covers urban areas with populations above 20,000. They

19

should be bought, where available, for the whole of a local authority area, by a public library, and for any additional adjacent urban areas with which users in the local public library or university library might be assumed to have some connection.

General maps of foreign countries are a separate consideration and the *Standards* . . . recommends that British libraries buy maps of western Europe on a scale of 1:200,000 and cover the rest of the world at 1,000,000. Ireland is treated separately, being within the British Isles, and the value of a collection of town plans is noted. To examine the position with regard to town plans first; there is little that can be suggested as to what the major towns of the world which should be represented by town plans, might be. All map librarians would obviously select the outstanding ones such as Paris, Rome, Leningrad, Singapore, Vancouver and many others, but it must be mainly on the score of personal knowledge of the general users connections as tourists, exporters, etc that would guide a buyer as the area of less obvious choices began to be reached. In many circumstances it would be advisable to be aware of the availability of reasonably satisfactory and up-to-date town plans in copies of guide books before individual plans were bought for towns of less obvious interest, and the possibility of obtaining free maps from foreign government tourist offices might also be explored for those towns which have a tourist interest. No guideline regarding the size of population is of value for buying town plans, plans of some quite small towns in Europe may be of much more use in a British library than plans of some towns, considerably more populous, elsewhere in the world. To commence a collection of foreign town plans it would be advisable not to compile initially a list of towns to be represented in the collection but to examine what is readily obtainable from a good map dealer by examining publishers' catalogues, and select from what can be supplied. Many city libraries have established very extensive town plan collections where, at least for Europe, all available plans are obtained. Duplication by different publishers' street maps of the same town must of course be avoided. When the collection has been formed a list of desiderata can be compiled from any omissions of significance that are discovered, and efforts made to trace such plans if published, most probably by seeking the assistance of an agency situated in the country concerned.

Sheet maps of foreign countries should be of a greater scale than maps of those countries which are available as plates in the atlases in the library. In general, atlases for use in British libraries will reflect the thoughts of the compilers of the *Standards for reference service in public libraries* in that maps of, say, France will be of a larger scale than the

20

maps of S E Asia but one atlas *The international atlas*, London, George Philip and Son; Chicago, Rand McNally, 1969, attempts to move away from this bias of supposed national interest and 'In this atlas the space allotted to each region reflects its relative economic and cultural significance on the world scene as well as its total population area', Introduction. However in practice this has resulted in more equality of scales used throughout the world coverage rather than increasing the scale of maps in more distant parts of the world. It is of interest to compare the scales used in this atlas and in two other good atlases well represented in British libraries, for selected countries, to demonstrate the need for larger scale sheet maps being available in the library for many countries of the world.

The Times	*Atlas of the world*	Mid-century ed
The Times	*Atlas of the world*	Comprehensive ed 1972
Philip	*The international atlas*	1969

Country	*Mid-century*	*Comprehensive ed*	*International*
Switzerland	1:550,000	1:550,000	1:1M (Zurich-Geneva-Strasbourg)
Zambia (N. Rhodesia)	1:5M	1:5M	1:6M
Peru	1:5M	1:5.1M	1:6M
Khmer Rep (Cambodia)	1:4M	1:5M	1:6M
Ohio (USA)	1:2.5M	1:2.5M	1:300,000 (Cleveland region)

It would be a significant advance on such scales if the *Standards for reference service in public libraries* are followed in a library by providing coverage for the world at 1:1M and, in Britain, for Western Europe at 1:200,000, at least for those areas not covered by larger scale sets. In public libraries some regions, not necessarily a whole country, need to be treated as liberally in scale as is suggested for Ireland at 1:63,360. Brittany, for example, is a very popular part of France for the British tourist and the British camper, one would imagine that it attracted more English tourists than Ireland, and so it should be an area for which 1:50,000 sheets are available.

In university collections maps on these medium scales must be

21

provided for a region which is emphasised in geography and other courses and the regions to be treated at these larger scales are not necessarily situated in western Europe. Truly large scale plans are not normally of interest to the geographer, but they may be selectively, for other academic purposes in the university. These considerations are outside the area of choice for the map librarian but are part of her primary duty in providing those sheets which are expected to be required for the use of an academic course. The map librarian however may also be building up a research collection based upon a reasonable assumption that it will become of major value when the desired coverage is obtained. Such a research collection might have had as its nucleus a donation of a substantial collection of maps from a government map library or a military department. If all map librarians could build small special collections in depth, not duplicating one another, these, publicised, would be a great asset to the wider community, particularly for areas away from the national specialist map collections.

Maps on a scale of 1:200,000 of western Europe would usually be road maps, but for small scale maps of the rest of the world of the order of 1:1M there are several choices. C B Muriel Lock *Modern maps and atlases* London, Clive Bingley; Hamden, Conn, Linnet Books 1969 will be noted later, but it should be stated at this point that the work provides overall information on the current map publishing of the countries of the world both official and private, and including small scale world maps.

John Bartholomew and Son Ltd, Edinburgh, publish a *World travel map* series, currently of 25 maps which covers the land areas of the world but the maps are not uniform in size of area covered, nor of scale, and the variety of scales used from 1:350,000 for Israel with Jordan to 1:10M for North America means that the maps are not necessarily an advance on the scales of the atlas maps available in the library. Perhaps more frequently used in libraries is the *World map (Karta mira)* on a scale of 1:2.5M produced cooperatively, 1964–74, by the official surveys of Bulgaria, Czechoslovakia, German Democratic Republic, Hungary, Poland, Roumania and USSR. The various surveys take responsibility for different sheets, the National Office of Lands and Mapping, Hungary preparing those for North America, and the Main Administration of Geodesy and Cartography, USSR deals with most of the oceans of the world. The text of the maps is in Russian and English, roman lettering is used on the map for placenames etc, other scripts being transliterated. Sandor Rado, World maps, scale of 1:2,500,000, *International yearbook of cartography* VI (1966) is an account of this map. Pergamon Press is agent in Britain for this map but it is available also through map dealers, the 234 sheets being variously priced according to content. *The international map of the world 1:1M* (IMW) is a map conceived at the end of the last century to be published in conformity with an internationally agreed format and produced cooperatively by official map agencies of the world which take responsibility for the sheets covering their own area. Although publication commenced in 1913 it is not yet quite complete in the first edition as contemplated. The IMW is now produced under the auspices of the UN, Department of Economic and Social Affairs which has published reports on *International map of the world on the millionth scale.* The latest full report seen was for 1969, published 1970, and it included an index map and a 'Table of published sheets' which lists:

    a) Sheet reference as it appears on the map
    b) Special (local) series title, if any
    c) Designation. (The name of the main place
    contained in the sheet, eg Lhasa.)
    d) Publishing country
    e) Year of publication
    f) Remarks on the edition

A UN document (ST/ECA/SER D/15) dated 11 June 1974 supplements this report but only gives an index map to show the state of publication of IMW sheets as at 31 January 1972 from which it can be seen that the map is complete with a few exceptions, most of Canada, three sheets for parts of USA and some sheets which would map parts of Namibia, Botswana and S Africa. Some of the sheets have appeared in several editions and some areas are covered by maps in the same style produced however as the *International map of the world 1:1,000,000; Series 1301* by the Directorate of Military Survey, Ministry of Defence, United Kingdom and the Army Topographic Command in the USA. The American Geographical Society produced, in 107 sheets, the *Hispanic America Series, 1:1M* to provide the maps in the uniform style to cover South America. These good maps are not as commonly seen to provide for world coverage in British libraries and map collections as one might expect. It would seem that maps currently appearing as a result of more recent and more advertised publishing programmes have been bought as the map holdings were developed in the last two or three decades. The Directorate of Military Survey, UK also produces an *International topographic map of the world*, identified as Series 1404, on a scale of 1:500,000, which is to be found in a number of libraries to provide coverage for the world or for Europe on this scale.

    Aeronautical charts published by military services are used sometimes by both university and public libraries to provide general world coverage or for selected areas only where the larger scales of official surveys are not needed. The aeronautical chart exhibits a different emphasis on the land features to be shown compared with the usual topographic maps. Place-names are generally less frequent, whilst spot heights for high ground are more frequent. That aeronautical charts emphasise the portrayal of relief is however welcomed by many users in geography departments, and in public libraries where a knowledge of the physical geography of an area is a common requirement.

The International Civil Aviation Organisation (ICAO), Montreal, Canada, produce *World aeronautical charts* (WAC) on a scale of 1:1M;

The Directorate of Military Survey, Ministry of Defence, UK, and the Defense Mapping Agency, St Louis, USA produce *Operational navigation charts* (ONC), scale 1:1M; and *Tactical pilotage charts* (TPC), scale 1:500,000.

It is interesting to compare the maps of world coverage above, on the scale of 1:1,000,000 and 1:500,000 taking as an example a sheet for an area which should be represented on scales of this order in any library. The chosen area is that around Kiev, Ukraine, USSR. Comparing the two sheets at the scale of 1:500,000: Directorate of Military Survey, *Series 1404*, sheet 233B, (Kiyev), Edition 1, 1958; and Directorate of Military Survey, *Tactical pilotage chart*, E-3c, Edition 2, 1971; one immediately notices the comparative lack of detail in the Series 1404 sheet. This is particularly obvious in the recording of towns. Series 1404 marks towns conventionally with a circle, not graded, except for the very largest cities, whilst the TPC sheet provides an actual outline block area coloured red for every town of any size. There are some differences in place names, presumably the 1971 TPC is the more accurate, because more up-to-date, in this respect but the Series 1404 sheet has some place names not noted on the TPC sheet which, as an aeronautical chart, has less need to record the names of smaller places. For the same reason the TPC sheet provides an emphasis on relief information, showing six elevation tints with 500 ft interval contours well marked, with auxiliary contours at lower levels. The Series 1404 sheet gives some spot heights but, on this sheet, no relief colouring or contours. Both sheets provide similar information on boundaries, railways and classes of roads, whilst waterways and woodlands are more easily seen on Series 1404 because of the absence of information about relief. The TPC series naturally provide a great deal of additional information for air navigation and includes aerodrome runway patterns and heights of vertical obstructions which may be unnecessarily obtrusive to some non-aeronautical users. There are many gaps in the world coverage of TPC sheets.

24

The Kiev sheets of the 1:1M world maps are: Directorate of Military Survey, Ministry of Defence, London, UK, *Series 1301*, Sheet NM-36 (Kiyev), Edition 6, 1960; and Defense Mapping Agency, St Louis, USA, *Operational Navigation Chart*, Sheet E-3, Edition 6, 1973. Defense Mapping Agency cartographic publications are made available to the public through the National Ocean Survey, Distribution division C44, Riverdale, Md, 20840, USA. The ONC sheet, which covers a substantial portion of the western USSR and most of Poland, Czechoslovakia, and small areas of Austria and Hungary, is basically a relief map with elevation tints and shading in mountainous areas, water features, city outlines with some towns and villages marked conventionally. Not many place-names are recorded even when a town outline is shown. Naturally there is a great deal of other information for aircraft navigation purposes. The Series 1301 sheet is considerably more valuable for place-names, probably as good as the larger scale map of Series 1404. Towns, in five grades of importance are indicated by varied typography and conventional signs. Boundaries, railways, roads and water features are well represented but the representation of relief is a weak spot. This may be due to a lack of information on this area at that date, 1960, because contour lines at 100 ft intervals for the lower heights and spot heights elsewhere should be provided.

The *Karta mira* is, at 1:2,500,000, on a much smaller scale than any of the above but sheet 54 (Sofia), prepared by the Military Topographic Direction, Bucharest, Rumania in 1968 shows it to be a rather good general map, relief well delineated and a reasonable number of place-names, but of course the scale is no bigger than that of many atlas plates.

The sizes of the sheets described above are as follows:

Series 1301	1:1M	Sheet NM-36	71 × 56 cm
ONC series	1:1M	Sheet E-3	106 × 146 cm
Series 1404	1:500,000	Sheet 233-B	62 × 74 cm
TPC Series	1:500,000	Sheet E-3c	106 × 146 cm
Karta mira	1:2.5M	Sheet 54	74 × 100 cm

Size should not affect the purchase of a particular series from the point of view of storage, but the limitations of furniture or reading space might in certain libraries make a map sheet of the size 106 × 146 cm an embarrassment to librarian and user. The two sheets of this size are in fact published folded, providing a convenient storage size of 27 × 37 cm.

25

World maps of this nature are required by map librarians every-where. Larger scale maps are needed for some countries also and a variety of scales, including the largest published, are needed for the country of the library. In this chapter the national maps have been considered on the basis of Great Britain, in other countries similar considerations will have to be taken into account relevant to the size and geography of the country, which affects the proportion of the area of the country which can be served by the purchase of the different scale maps published. Standards may be suggested for libraries else-where. One excellent guide is by Patricia A G Alonso, the Map Libra-rian of the State Library of Victoria, Australia, entitled 'Map collections in public libraries: starting, building, maintaining them', Library Council of Victoria, Public Libraries Division *Technical bulletin* 1/73, January, 1973. Mrs Alonso makes recommendations for map buying by libraries in Victoria and in a series of five appendices lists recommended maps and Australian sources. The maps are all Australian, and the article could be useful for map librarians else-where who may have a special interest in Australian maps. E F Kunz, Maps for small and medium size municipal and shire libraries, *Austra-lian library journal* 9 (April) 1960, 56–60 was an earlier guide in the same field. A library needs to buy maps of other countries selectively, in Britain the interest is primarily on European countries but connec-tions with Commonwealth countries, particularly in Africa it seems, are also represented, as is the United States. The absence of maps of areas outside Australia in Mrs Alonso's list, except for the very small scales available in atlases, is possibly due to the budget limitations suggested, but no doubt it also reflects the geographical position of Australia and this type of consideration would need to be present in any suggested standards for the map holdings of general libraries in any country.

Chapter references:
ALONSO 1973–1; DREWITT; HAGEN 1970; IMW; KIRBY; KUNZ; LOCK; RADO; STANDARDS.

2

Aids for tracing and buying modern maps

In the previous chapter comment was made on the variety of users of modern maps in libraries, in a later section the use of early maps in libraries will be considered. The map curator must select and obtain the maps which will satisfy best the needs of the enquirers in his library and which will develop the map collection so that it will become of greater use to more people. The curator is limited at any one time by some financial restriction, sometimes by space difficulties, and often in general libraries, it seems, by lack of knowledge of the full extent of the cartographic materials available for acquisition. This knowledge must come from two sources, one from bibliographical records of map publication and the other a full appreciation of the variety of cartographic techniques, with a flexibility of mind that will permit the curator to make an objective selection of new maps in the light of his understanding of their probable value and use to readers some of whom will have little or no cartographical knowledge. G R P LAWRENCE has written, 'It is therefore necessary to be able to assess the value of any given map in a fair and as objective a manner as possible. This assessment is variously regarded as "appreciation" or "critical appraisal" or "critique" of the map. The chief dangers in making such an evaluation are those of subjectivity and intolerance bred from years of habitual use of maps of a limited range of types'. LAWRENCE continues by developing suggestions for the assessment of a map which can be briefly summarised by this list which he gives—

    a) The overall features of the map. (This includes such facts as the scale, and date of survey).
    b) Methods utilised for presenting the mapped data.
    c) Suitability of mapping techniques.
    d) Adequacy of detail depicted for map purpose.
    e) Aesthetic considerations.

The necessity for a map curator to make a critical appreciation of maps before buying them and to appreciate the use and qualities, good and bad, in the library's collection, is perhaps exaggeratedly demonstrated by the more wilder comments of some passionate users in Great Britain of the Ordnance Survey *One inch to one mile* map when the *1:50,000 first series* sheets were introduced.

The curator needs the knowledge to buy the best maps for his collection and for the very important task of interpreting the maps in the collection for the expressed requirements of an enquirer in the library. The enquirers will, in a well-founded map library, come from many backgrounds and only a small minority can be expected to have cartographic knowledge. The librarian must be sympathetic in understanding their needs, which are probably not purely geographical, as well as the needs of her geography orientated users so that the best material can be produced for them and if the readers needs are not adequately met this must be appreciated by the librarian and her selection of maps to be purchased modified or enlarged accordingly. This communication and feedback between librarian and reader is absolutely essential in any dynamic library, one properly useful and economical for the community it serves. The staff of a map library, either university or public, consists of very few people and normally the librarian or curator will be responsible for the selection of all acquisitions. This must be, but the curator should seek the views of her assistants who have possibly more contact with the users than the curator and therefore a more down-to-earth knowledge of how the collection answers the needs of those who visit the library. But the assistants must also be expected to learn the qualities of the maps in the collection and being added to it, an education process which should be regularly conducted by the curator. It is of little value for the curator to introduce a fresh range of maps into the collection if the staff is not aware of the cartographic qualities which led to the new series or set being bought to satisfy present or potential needs.

Current selection

The bibliographical records which are required in a library so that it is possible for the curator to have an adequate field of choice for buying suitable maps, are very varied and not always as well represented within the map library as one would hope they should be. As in the selection of any printed records for a library, map buying can be divided into current and retrospective selection. Current selection refers to the curator examining the records of the current output of all types of map publisher and selecting those new maps or new editions which are thought to be of value for her particular collection. In a map library a large proportion of purchases will be of maps consisting of many sheets which will be issued over a period of time. These sheets of the map will not be selected and ordered individually as they are currently issued. When the map was initially selected a standing order should have been placed with the publisher or the dealer, for all the sheets in the set, if that is what is required, or all the sheets pertaining to an accurately defined region if the whole set is not to be bought. In most cases the sheet numbers will be identifiable before publication and if only the sheets for a particular region are to be bought it will be possible to provide the dealer with a list of wanted sheets to be delivered when issued. Bibliographical records of map production will therefore be used in map selection for knowledge of new maps, single or multi-sheet, not for new sheets of a series already commenced. Nevertheless this type of bibliographical record has a part to play for map sets in that, as they record the issue of new sheets, they provide a very necessary check on the receipt of standing orders. All maps produced as sets should be provided in the library with an index map covering the set, or in some cases for large scale maps the part to be bought by the library. The index map may be available from the map publisher or may have to be made within the library. This can be used, by appropriate marking, to record the receipt of the individual sheets. The map librarian can, by examining bibliographical records of current map publications, check if newly published sheets have been received and, if the sheets are delivered in batches by the dealer, can, by judiciously used marking, record on the index map the publication of sheets which have not yet been received, as a check for receipt in the near future.

Retrospective selection
Not all additions to the map library will be made however when the map is newly published. For a number of reasons a decision to buy a particular map may be made when that map is some years old, or when a large number of sheets in a map set have already been published. This is normal particularly as a library is developing. The curator discovers that she has a potential clientele for a certain map or type of map which is not in the collection. At its most simple this could be due to the announcement of a new course in a university or college. The curator must then discover what maps have been published, and are in print, which will be useful for this course. It would be possible for the curator to search back through serially produced bibliographies recording current map production and sometimes this has to be done, but it is helpful if retrospective bibliographies are available which record the whole of the available publications in the particular

29

cartographic field, or at least cumulations of current bibliographical records into sequences covering a substantial period of time.

Often these records must be consulted to identify a specific single map or a number of sheet maps as when the reader requires a town plan and it is not in the library, or a naturalist requires a walking map of an area in the Italian Alps which is not available, and consideration leads the map librarian to believe that this request which has come to her notice is the tip of an iceberg of unexpressed requests which, if the plans or maps were bought, would represent a greater number of satisfied clients. HAGEN (1971) when reporting as a consultant on the requirements for a map library in a newly developing university in California, recommended the formation of a 'Map information file' which, whilst being necessary to assist the librarian in tracing maps to be purchased, would be the type of resource which the map library requires to deal immediately with the type of reader enquiry just noted.

These examples are reader-initiated retrospective purchases but in other cases they could be library-initiated in anticipation of reader requirements. A review of a new map, a visit to another map library, an article in a journal or newspaper, or just a fresh general awareness of a public interest, may stimulate the map curator or member of her staff to think that the supply of a type of map not previously available in the collection, it may be different in subject or purpose or scale or region, may provide a development in the useful growth of the collection. Perhaps it is a realisation that the library does not provide coastal charts, yet sailing in coastal waters is a popular activity. Charts from official hydrographic surveys or from commercial concerns, have to be identified, evaluated in the light of the anticipated library interest, and selected. The librarian could make a mistake of course and too enthusiastic a development in a new direction might not find a reader response commensurate with the costs involved. So perhaps the librarian will buy somewhat tentatively at first, make enquiries as to what is the favourite sailing coast for the part of the country where the library is situated and select from what has been published for that coastal area alone and develop the chart collection when users respond. New purchases must be given a fair trial and every effort made to publicise them among users of the library generally and among the potentially interested members of the community who are not necessarily library users, in this case local sailing clubs. The sailing clubs would no doubt welcome an approach from the map librarian at an earlier stage and have been willing to discuss the possible use of types of chart by sailing enthusiasts in the map library, just as appropriate lecturers would be approached for comment on the addition of a new type of map in a university map collection.

30

Bibliographical buying aids

There are a variety of types of bibliographical aids for map identification. They have varied and overlapping uses and some are
designed for a purpose different from assistance for librarians in map
identification for purchases. Because of the obvious international
nature of maps and of the subjects which can be well illustrated in cartographic form, no library can afford to be parochial in its purchasing
any more than in its geographical coverage. Some bibliographical
aids do provide extensive international coverage and they are very
valuable, but it is necessary for any map library to be aware of the
greater possibility of comprehensiveness in a national map bibliography or listing, for that country's cartographical output. If the
library gives a particular emphasis to a foreign country or region, it
will be necessary to receive bibliographies, trade catalogues etc which
emanate from that country, and sometimes have a supplier there, or
one specialising in that area. Even as a tourist visiting a foreign
country one can observe the greater abundance of town plans, touring
maps, as well as guide books, for that country which are available
there, compared with the records of them available in your own
country's bibliographical publications. These locally produced plans,
road-maps etc are probably more accurate and up-to-date than their
equivalents, if they exist, which are published by major international
map publishers. The same applies to the cartographic productions of
local geographical and specialist institutions, although the foreign
official survey should be well known. There may sometimes be a language difficulty, Russian town plans on sale in Moscow shops are not
in English, and if, say, in Middle Eastern countries the text is translated into English it is often of a type which seems a trifle eccentric,
but this is not usually a major problem with cartographic publications. Cartographic publications of importance from any part of the
world can be expected to be recorded eventually, but it may be some
considerable time before they appear in an international bibliography.

Basic bibliographies of maps in print

Faced with the problem of commencing a map collection, or more
usually starting a collection for a new area or a new subject, where
does one begin? How does one know what might be available, and
from which sources? Unfortunately all literature guides gradually
become out-of-date, but at the time of writing the map librarian has
the opportunity to consult with profit a very helpful guide to cartographic work generally, map series, map publishers etc.

    C B Muriel Lock *Modern maps and atlases, an outline guide to twentieth century production* London, Clive Bingley; Hamden, Conn, Linnet Books, 1969. Dr Lock's work provides, in narrative form, information on important topographic maps and atlases, and thematic maps and atlases. This information is recorded for topographic maps, in an arrangement of sections for the world, continents divided into regions, subdivided by countries, and for thematic maps under the headings—geomorphology, climatology, oceanography, natural vegetation, soil, agriculture, economic resources, biogeography, population, settlement, health and disease, history. It has been suggested that it is not possible for one person to be sufficiently informed to undertake the task which Dr Lock set herself, and no doubt specialists may find omissions in their field, but there is no other cooperative venture which has attempted this work and map librarians will find it very helpful when needing a background knowledge of what might be available for a particular area or theme. It is therefore possible for a map librarian to consult LOCK and see the paragraphs which, for example, refer to Alaskan maps and find that the US Geological Survey is responsible for mapping that American state, but at the time of publication 'The whole country (USA) is covered by the small-scale series, with the exception of Alaska'. The US Geological Survey, Map Information Office publishes index maps showing the state of topographic mapping at all scales and for Alaska a geological map index prepared by E H Cobb has been published by the survey. Elsewhere, and through the aid of the book index, it is stated that the *Ice atlas of Arctic Canada* compiled by C M W Swithinbank (Canada Defence Research Board) 1960 includes the north coast of Alaska. Consulting a book, or bibliography, for a region of a country, as in this case Alaska, one must always remember, like the map library user, that the greater geographical or political area, in this case the United States, will have publications which include the region. For major nations LOCK gives several pages of bibliographical description of the mapping services of a country. Thus Germany has a main section of seven pages, with additional important references on other pages.

Inevitably in any bibliographical work unless it is of a serial nature, as time passes some of the information becomes out-of-date, but once the map curator has, from this work, obtained a good understanding of the basic pattern of map provision in a country or subject it is comparatively simple to take steps to ensure that later changes in this information are discovered. For Zambia LOCK notes only one atlas, Collins-Longmans *Primary atlas* for schools together with *Atlas of Rhodesia and Nyasaland* (now Rhodesia, Zambia and Malawi) in nineteen sheets, 1960–1962, published by the then Federal Department of Trigonometrial and Topographical Surveys. Since the appearance of LOCK there have been—*Atlas of Zambia* Lusaka, Surveyor General, 1969; D Hywel Davies *Zambia in maps* London, ULP, 1971. These later works can be discovered in map bibliographies, the value of LOCK is now in providing the general background.

From LOCK the map curator will turn to a fine up-to-date international bibliography of maps and atlases—Kenneth L Winch *International maps and atlases in print* London, New York, Bowker Publishing Co, 1974. This is a systematic listing of maps and atlases in print and for sale, and since its publication must be regarded as the main buying guide, at least in the English-speaking world. Kenneth Winch is principal cataloguer of Edward Stanford Ltd, London, the international map retailers, and he previously produced *Stanford's reference catalogue*, a map dealer's catalogue of comprehensive coverage in a loose leaf format, which is now superseded by the publication of this bibliography. It is hoped that new editions of the bibliography can be published at regular intervals to keep it reasonably up-to-date. The new carto-bibliography is an independent work but it can be assumed that the maps listed are available for sale through Stanford's International Map Centre, 12/14 Long Acre, LONDON. WC2E 9LP, Great Britain. Maps are listed under world, continents, and countries, arranged according to the notation of the Universal Decimal Classsification. Space and moon maps are included but not marine or aeronautical charts, nor petrol company road maps or other publications available for free distribution; facsimiles of early maps are included. Within each country maps are arranged under the following divisions:

A1	General maps—roads
A2	General maps—local
B	Town plans
C	Official surveys
D	Political and administrative
E1	Physical—relief
E2	Physical—land features
F	Geology
G	Earth resources
H	Biogeography
J	Climate
K	Human geography
L	Economic
M	Historical
N	Mathematical (Geodetic, triangulation and levelling data).

The same arrangement is followed for atlases with the addition of:

01	National atlas—reference
02	National atlas—school edition
W1	World atlas—reference
W2	World atlas—school edition
W3	World atlas—local edition

The entry for each map or atlas gives all the necessary bibliographic information and where relevant includes reference to the appropriate index map. Some 400 index maps, reproductions of those issued by the map publishers, are included, gathered together in groups after each continental section. A minor but very useful feature of the entries under a country is that reference is made to the sheets of a world or international map which cover the country. Full bibliographical details are not given in these entries but can be readily obtained in the main entry. Thus the division for Zambia, 689.4 and C—official surveys includes the reference:

KARTA MIRA
1:2,500,000
PPWK [Initials of the Polish publisher of the sheet]
2 sheets, to cover Zambia, 134, 154
See WORLD 100c and index 100/2

and similar entries for a US Army Map Service World map and the *International map of the world* 1:1M

It is said that *International maps and atlases in print* contains 8,000 entries from about 700 publishers. It should answer the bibliographical questions about maps in print and for sale which are likely to be asked in any library. Without it, or dealers' catalogues, the map librarian would not have the means to see at a glance all the map resources covering a particular country. In one section for FRANCE, A1 General maps—Roads, maps from sixteen publishers are listed. Because of this work the map librarian is aware of the variety of readily available road maps of France, without it she would be aware only of some by examining different map publishers' catalogues which might be available in the map library. For most purposes the *International maps and atlases in print* obviates the need for a map curator to collect the catalogues of individual publishers, unless it proves to be commercially impossible to publish it at fairly regular intervals, a possibility which is basically the responsibility of all libraries and map collections who may, or may not, buy each new edition. If a map library has a need to buy the maps of a particular area, or a particular subject, in depth it is still desirable to have the catalogues of the appropriate publishers since they provide more information than the listing of sheets available. Similarly if for any reason it is desirable to know the variety of maps produced by one publisher, this can only be seen from the publisher's catalogue. Perhaps more importantly a library on a publisher's mailing list receives prompt information about new maps and atlases as soon as they appear, probably in publicity material format not as a catalogue.

Geo Center *Geo Katalog* 2v Annual. Geo Center is an international map selling firm at D7000 Stuttgart 80 Vaihingen, Honigwiesen Str 25, Postfach 80 08 30, Germany. Formed by the amalgamation of two firms, Reise-und Verkehrsverlag of the Stuttgart address above, and Zumstein's Landkartenhaus, Munich. *Geo Katalog 1974*, Geo Center's catalogue of maps for sale is the 11th edition of the previously entitled *Zumstein Katalog*.

In a more restricted manner, and primarily by the very much briefer bibliographical descriptions for each entry, it offers the same function to the map librarian as the *International maps and atlases in print*. There are differences which make it desirable for the English speaking map librarian, the entries are in German, to have a copy as a supplement to *International maps and atlases in print*. *Geo Katalog* includes aeronautical charts and provides the necessary information for a map librarian interested in buying the sheets of the *Tactical pilotage chart* (incorectly named Topographical pilotage chart in *Geo Katalog*), *Operational Navigation Chart*, and the ICAO *World Aeronautical Chart*.

There appears to be a good coverage of recreational maps for skiing, canoeing and commercially produced charts of coastal seas and inland waterways. It does not appear to be as comprehensive for thematic maps, except possibly for geology. One small feature is the existence of a number of page advertisements for commercial map publishers and these are indexed, to provide for the map librarian a possibly useful, if rather sketchy, guide to the publications of a particular publisher.

The arrangement of *Geo Katalog* shows its German origin by beginning with the maps of Germany, followed by Alps, Europe, Asia, Australia, Africa, Americas, Polar regions and oceans, world and space, followed by a thematic appendix. This latter mainly consists of aeronautical charts, recreational maps and geological maps and atlases, but other thematic maps such as population and climate appear in the arrangement under each country. A subject index refers not only to pages for a country section, but also to town, national parks etc which are named as map titles. Some index maps appear at the end of the text catalogue volume but others to which references are made in the entries appear in volume two, the latest of which is scheduled to appear in loose-leaf format at the beginning of 1975 and will consist of index diagrams. Not all map sets are represented by index maps, for example there are none for any geological sets for Great Britain. *Geo Katalog* also contains entries for guide books, handbooks for climbing, walking, sailing etc, hotel directories, camping guides, dictionaries and globes.

Current international map bibliography
Bibliographie cartographique internationale. Publiée par le Service de Documentation et de Cartographie Geographiques (CNRS), avec le concours de l'Union Geographique Internationale (UNESCO).

The first annual volume was published 1949, listing maps published in 1946 and 1947 in eight collaborating countries. The 1970 volume was published in 1973 and has a world coverage, but of varying value for different countries. Western European countries and Poland appear to be well represented; African maps are almost entirely represented by the publications of the Department of Overseas Surveys, Tolworth, Surrey, for British Commonwealth countries, by the Institut Geographique National for ex-colonial territories of France, and by the then Portuguese African colonies. In the Americas, Canada and USA appear to be the only countries comprehensively listed, although the Argentine list would appear to be representative. Asian entries occupy no more than six pages out of 645, whilst Australia and New Zealand appear to be well represented. India provides no list, and the USSR is only represented by a few Polish publications.

Obviously this bibliography has serious limitations in coverage but this is not to suggest that the gaps noted in it are not in the international lists of maps in print described above. The *International maps and atlases in print* and *Geo Katalog* have no listing of maps of the USSR on a scale of more than 1:500,000 except for tourist maps and town plans in Cyrillic, and these cover many years of possible publication. The brief note for the Indian official topographical sets records that although surveys on scales of 1:25,000, 1:50,000 and 1:1,250,000 are being produced there is a ban on the export of these maps.

Bibliographie cartographique internationale is compiled in France with the cooperation of correspondents in other countries. A list of the countries cooperating in this way gives an indication of the strength of the bibliography to which should be added the countries, usually ex-colonial, with which these countries have historical ties: Argentine; Australia; Belgium; Canada; Denmark; Finland; France; Germany; Great Britain; Hungary; Italy; New Zealand; Norway; Poland; Portugal; Sweden; Switzerland; Turkey; United States.

The arrangement is firstly world, followed by the continents commencing with Europe, with countries within each continent arranged

36

in alphabetical order, the language used being French. Thematic maps and atlases of all types are listed, including aeronautical charts, marine charts, and facsimiles of early maps. The 1970 volume had marine charts listed which were produced by the official chart publishers of France; German Democratic Republic; German Federal Republic; Great Britain; United States.

There is a subject index to each volume. The maps and atlases are given a satisfactory bibliographical entry, with a brief annotation noting anything exceptional about the map or an accompanying booklet or the like. Each such entry is numbered and in the case of multi-sheet sets sheets issued in later years are noted with the individual title, sheet number and variant scale, etc but reference is made to the first entry by year and number for a complete bibliographical entry for the map. There are no index maps.

The value of this bibliography to the librarian was probably more obvious before the publication of *International maps and atlases in print* but it is still an essential component among the map librarian's selection aids. It is a current bibliography, though always some three years later than the publication of the maps, and therefore a file from the commencement of publication covers, in greater or lesser degree, the cartographic output of the world for a quarter of the century. It is a true bibliography for those countries which cooperate, in that, unlike a dealer's catalogue, it lists what has been produced whether it is available for sale or not, whether it is still in print or not, and for libraries this can be valuable information. Although it is unlikely that a library can buy an identified map which is out of print, for an enquirer who requires the information which is expected to be on that map, identifying the map is a first step to locating a copy of it in another collection elsewhere. Being an annual there is some useful cumulation of entries when compared with the tedium of conducting a retrospective search through, for example, a library's map additions list which appears monthly, and it is basically for this type of retrospective checking that it is valuable. Nevertheless one can not expect any international dealers catalogue or a bibliography to be completely accurate concerning the millions of sheets of maps which have been printed and it is sometimes the case that a wanted sheet may be discovered here when not found elsewhere. *Bibliographie cartographique internationale* 1970 lists many plans in the series, (Great Britain) *Shopping centre plans* scale 1:1056; London, Charles E Goad, Ltd, which can not be found in *International maps and atlases* 1974. They may no longer be in print, although 309 sheets in the series were published in 1972–3 so that is unlikely, or they may not be available for sale commercially, but they are required by some libraries.

One might expect for certain countries, and for certain map publishers, to be able to see in a file of *Bibliographie cartographique internationale* the whole output of maps from 1946 to date. This can be especially important if coverage in depth is sought by a library for one country or region, and it is assisted by the index of map publishers included in each volume. This index lists under the country of origin, the name of each publisher represented by published maps listed in that volume, with the town of publication. Official surveys are underlined but commercial publishers are also listed. Once the name of the publishing organisation and the town are known it is simple to consult trade directories, national yearbooks, telephone directories etc to find the full address to which application can be made to obtain that publisher's catalogue.

Publishers' catalogues: official surveys
In the modern era of map making, large scale maps and plans are required, based upon an accurate national survey. This implies a national government activity, for the resources required to conduct such a survey, and because of the historical functions of such maps, which are military use and for the effective development and planning of the resources for economic growth in a nation. In European countries particularly, the official mapping agencies began as a military or semi-military activity, sometimes still recognisable by the name of the organisation, as in the Ordnance Survey in Great Britain and Istituto Geografico Militare in Italy. The topographical maps and plans produced by these national surveys, 'official surveys' is the heading in *International maps and atlases in print* and 'amtliche kartenwerke' in *Geo Katalog*, are the basis for the vast majority of published maps in most countries of the world, and they are therefore of particular importance in map libraries not only for the country in which the library is situated but for any other countries where the local map users might be expected to have an especial interest. The term 'topographic map' is well defined in a brochure produced by the US Geological Survey *Topographic maps* 1969, 'A topographic map is a graphic representation of selected man-made and natural features of part of the earth's surface plotted to a definite scale. The distinguishing characteristic of a topographic map is the portrayal of the shape and elevation of the terrain. Topographic maps record in convenient readable form the physical characteristics of the terrain as determined by precise engineering surveys and measurements. They show the location and shape of mountains, valleys and plains; the network of streams and rivers, and the principal works of man.'

The official survey organisations publish catalogues of various types to publicise the scales and the sheets for sale, and in order to give the necessary information for identification of sheets required and for ordering procedure. The names of appropriate national surveys can usually be readily found from LOCK and *International maps and atlases in print*, but not their addresses. Richard W STEPHENSON, Head of the Acquisitions Section, Geography and Map Division, Library of Congress, has published in 1969 a list of 173 names and addresses of map publishers and dealers who had produced recent catalogues. This is very useful, but of course gradually changes have to be made.

Dept of Energy, Mines and Resources, Departmental Map Library. *List of map sources* 3rd ed Ottawa, 1972. Also lists with addresses, 'government mapping agencies' as well as private publishers. This publication has a strong emphasis on Canadian and United States sources, but it is well regarded elsewhere and thoroughly useful in libraries throughout the world.

Most countries have one central survey organisation but in some countries with a federal government and state administrations there is a division of responsibility betwen federal and state surveys, the national survey being responsible at least for the general coordination of all surveying and mapping. In the German Federal Republic, the Länder (provinces) have official map-making and publishing departments in Schleswig Holstein, Niedersachsen, Nordrhein-Westfalen, Hessen, Rheinland Pfalz, Saarland, Baden-Württemberg, Bayern. In Australia, the Department of Minerals and Energy, Division of National Mapping is the Australian Government topographic mapping agency, but each individual state has its own official survey. In cases like these, in order to acquire a full knowledge of the official survey of the country on all scales, it will be necessary to acquire the catalogues of the states as well as of the federal government.

The catalogues of the national topographic surveys vary from quite small folders to substantial volumes or collections of folders, usually reflecting a variety of factors, the development of the country, the mapping activity and the size of the country. They usually contain many index maps or index diagrams, and the smaller sales catalogues almost wholly consist of such indexes. An index map is a means of identifying the boundaries of the individual sheets which comprise a map. A map of a nation on, for example, a scale of 1:100,000 will have to be published by dividing it into a number of sheets. The sheets have some form of reference number and sometimes also bear the name of a prominent place shown on that sheet. A buyer will wish to know which sheet or sheets, within the map of the country on the chosen scale, contain the geographical area he requires. Publishers' catalogues print small scale maps of the country with a superimposed grid corresponding to the sheets of the map at a particular scale, each section of the grid containing the appropriate sheet reference. Sometimes two grids are printed on the index map, or a way is described for dividing the grid sections into smaller divisions to allow the same index map to be used for more than one published scale. The index maps may have further functions, colours or shadings or conventional signs will indicate published sheets if the map has not yet been completely published. Other signs may indicate that particular sheets may be obtained in two different editions, eg in a mountainous region some sheets may also be published in a special edition which contain additional information on ski slopes and ski-lifts.

The New Zealand, Department of Lands and Survey *Maps* is a small sales catalogue and it demonstrates the value of such catalogues if detailed knowledge of the maps of an area is required. Firstly one has a general guide to the publishing of the Department of Lands and Survey in the main series and annotations for specialised maps. One tourist map, Marlborough Sounds, 1:100,000,—NZMS 236, is described as 'a multi-colour map showing topographical features, state forest and scenic reserves, hotels, camping sites and fishing information. Relief shading in grey. Inset of Picton township'. *The international maps and atlases in print* has similar lists of the maps and plans published and indeed for the *NZ cadastral map—town series* it provides a listing of the names of individual sheets and scales which are not in the department's *Maps* although that provides a general description of the series. On the other hand the large scale topographical maps, scale 1:25,000 have the individual published sheets identified on an index map in the *Maps* sales brochure whilst *International maps and atlases in print* can only provide a bibliographical entry for the series as a whole, not identifying sheets.

A similar 1973 sales catalogue *Landeskarten der Schweiz* issued by the Eidgenössische Landestopographie, Berne, Switzerland, shows index maps for the three main topographical series, 1:25,000, 1:50,000, and 1:100,000 as well as providing brief notes on these maps and the small scale maps published. Apart from the notes, the information provided in *International maps and atlases in print* is identical with the official brochure, the same index maps are used, although the *International maps and atlases in print* only prints in black and white unlike most official survey catalogues and when necessary additional marks have to be introduced into the index maps to identify information which was shown in colour on the official catalogue index maps. *Geo Katalog* also uses uncoloured index maps and in this particular example of Switzerland it might lead to some confusion. For the 1:25,000 sheets both the 1973 *Landeskarten der Schweiz* and the early 1974 *International maps and atlases in print* show a number of sheets to be not yet published, the first by colouring the other by shading. *Geo Katalog* has no indication that all sheets are not published, and one suspects that it is because *Geo Katalog* has reproduced the coloured original in black and white and not attempted to make the necessary differentiation in another manner between published and unpublished sheets. On the 1:50,000 scale *Geo Katalog* prints the official index map, without the colouring of the original, yet includes the colour key for 'published sheets' which on the original shows that two half-sheets are not yet published. For this same index map *Geo Katalog* omits a sign which should appear on fifteen sheets shown on the index to indicate that these sheets can be bought with ski-routes overprinted, although these particular sheets are noted without individual identification in the wintersport section of the *Geo Katalog*. On the 1:100,000 scale Swiss maps, *Geo Katalog* does note that some sheets are not published (German = nicht erschienen) by identifying them with black dots.

Publishers' catalogues for several official surveys will be noted in the chapter 'Selected official mapping services', but of course many more are produced. It is hoped however that this section will have shown the importance to a map library of the need to possess the required official survey catalogues to complement other bibliographies and dealers' catalogues. Maps and plans produced by official surveys can be bought from an international map retailer such as Stanford's International Map Centre, London or direct from the sales office of the official survey. It is probably most commonly found that a library ordering a substantial number of maps produced by an official survey, particularly with a standing order, will buy them direct from the survey's sales office. There are occasions however, when an institution's finance department prefers ordering to be dealt with in local currency, and, in the case of a British library, this can be achieved by ordering foreign maps from Stanfords. In some cases, certainly in Great Britain, there exist specialist bookshops which may offer an alternative local source. For example, New Zealand maps, mentioned above, can be obtained from Whitcoulls New Zealand Bookshop, 26 Royal Opera Arcade, London SW1Y 4UY, England, the smaller scales being kept in stock.

The official survey maps of the country of the library are essential requirements in map holdings and a library will normally place a standing order direct. In some countries a liberal selection of public and university libraries are depository libraries for the country's official maps, either for all or part of the various series. In Great Britain educational establishments, schools, colleges and universities, and public libraries, may buy direct from the Ordnance Survey,

Ordnance Survey publications and Geological and Soil Survey maps at special discount rates. Copies bought by public libraries with the 'Educational discount' must be copies required for public reference purposes.

Publishers' catalogues—private firms
In modern times the strength of map publishing by private firms, lies in road maps and maps designed for the use of tourists as well as atlases. Private firms supply the market for maps which emphasise, or indeed introduce to maps, details of interest to tourists, businessmen and others, which have not been the concern of official survey maps. Recently official surveys have in some instances begun to introduce features into their maps, or produce special tourist editions, which also reflect this market.

The bibliography *International maps and atlases in print* appears to provide an adequate coverage for maps produced by specialist map producing firms throughout the world. It is not possible however to obtain a list of the publications of a chosen publisher from this bibliography which, correctly, lists the material included on a regional and country basis. The entries within the section Iran show, among others, the maps of Iran produced by the Sahab Geographic and Drafting Institute, Iran, but one would have to trace through the rest of the full bibliography in order to discover any maps of other countries produced by Sahab, eg of Kuwait, Afghanistan etc. An examination of *Sahab's catalogue of publications 1973–4* shows that some items published have not found their way into *International maps and atlases in print*. *Geo Katalog* appears to have a similar coverage, although as this catalogue, unlike *International maps and atlases in print* is not concerned with providing a fairly detailed bibliographical entry, it is not as readily obvious which sheets of Iran are published by Sahab, which incidentally is entered in the abbreviated form of 'Sa'. *International maps and atlases in print* identifies the publisher, noting the place of publication and name, or an abbreviation to which a key is provided at the beginning of the volume. *Geo Katalog* has one advantage which can prove useful—the volumes have a substantial number of advertisement pages, covering most of the major private cartographic and guidebook publishers in Europe. There is a publisher's name index to these pages and it is possible to see on one or more pages a representative listing of one publisher's current output.

No general bibliography or dealer's catalogue can hope to provide the details of a publisher's various series as fully as the details given in the publisher's own catalogue, although because *International maps and atlases in print* usually provides a short descriptive note as part of the entry, this bibliography makes a worthwhile substitute. Nevertheless for those countries in which a map library has a special interest, or it is conceivable that there can be personal special interests among the users of the library, and for tourism etc, it is advisable for the library to have all the appropriate publishers' catalogues and to be on the mailing list for new editions. As many publishers as possible, official survey or private firm, should be represented for their potential and real value for ordering and selecting by map users as well as the librarian; just as no book order department in a library would be without its publishers' catalogues. It is not always necessary to have the catalogue of some foreign private publishers because they will be found to have an agent publishing firm in the country of the library and that agent will provide the necessary catalogue information and notices of new publications. This is also an advantage for purchasing in that the local agent should have required material in stock and it is bought in local currency. The Sahab Geographic and Drafting Institute of Tehran, Iran used as an example above, has agents, all map dealers, in Afghanistan, Germany, Great Britain (Edward Stanford Ltd), Belgium and USA.

In Great Britain: John Bartholomew & Son Ltd, Edinburgh is agent for—Cappelen maps from Norway; Mair of Stuttgart, European road maps and German town plans.

Geographia Ltd, St Albans, Hertfordshire is distributor for— Kummerley and Frey, Bern, Switzerland; Falk of Hamburg, FDR, town plans; Rand McNally, Chicago, USA. Geographia Ltd, has companies in Australia, New Zealand, South Africa and is represented in sixteen countries where the firm does not have an office.

Johnston and Bacon Ltd, London are distributors for— Ravenstein of Frankfurt.

Collins Publishers, Glasgow are distributors of—Hallwag of Bern, Switzerland.

Such distribution arrangements occur for many countries and agreements are made internationally, so Rand McNally are distributors for Kummerley and Frey, and so on. It must be noted however that whilst an agent or distributor will supply the foreign publishers' maps, sometimes from stock, the whole of the foreign publisher's list is not necessarily given in the agent's own catalogue. *Geographia 1973* catalogue lists sixteen Falk town plans for Germany and twenty town plans, including Moscow, for towns outside Germany, but in the *Falk Preisliste 1974* sixty two German town plans and thirty eight other foreign town plans are named.

STEPHENSON *Published sources of information about maps and atlases* provides a combined list of map publishers and sellers, both official and commercial, which is a guide to the names and addresses of many private map publishers. It is not exhaustive however, the absence of map publishers in Sydney, Australia such as; Gregory's guides and maps; Broadbent's maps and guides is noted. These publishers and all others are noted by the name of the firm and town of publication in *International maps and atlases in print* and so the full address could be ascertained from telephone or trade directories.

National bibliographies listing atlases and maps
The wide variety of publications noted in these pages as providing assistance to the map librarian who wishes to identify maps for adding to the library's collection would not be required to anything like the present degree, if bibliographical control were available with the help of the current national bibliographies of the countries of the world. A number of countries do include the listing of sheet maps in the current national bibliography, or in a regular supplement, but this is not always the case. Entries in national bibliographies, do not completely fulfil the requirements of a map librarian for the selection of a map, but a national bibliography, probably based on legal deposit, does bring together all the maps, both official and private, produced in a country, some of which might never be otherwise noted by the map curator. These maps are often of a very miscellaneous nature and not necessarily published for sale but for semi-private circulation. The map selector might, for a new map set, prefer to see a descriptive note such as might be provided in a review in a cartographic journal, but at least one current national bibliography of maps, National Library of Australia, *Australian maps*, Canberra, 1968—gives a full catalogue entry for each map which contains a list of the contents of the map.

STEPHENSON has provided a list of twenty four national bibliographies, published in twenty three countries, which 'regularly describe at least a few cartographical works', and in his article he makes the point that 'information provided by national bibliographies is particularly useful because they are generally current and accurate and, in most instances, provide the map librarian with the ever elusive price'. One of the duties of UNESCO is to give the peoples of all countries access to the printed and published materials produced by any one of them, and in 1950 UNESCO organised a *General conference on the improvement of bibliographical services*. One of the many resolutions passed by the Conference was that member states should give early consideration to the publication of current national bibliographies, including a bibliography of maps and atlases. Some countries already had a well developed system of national bibliographical control prior to this conference, and many other countries, including

44

new developing countries, have since introduced national bibliographies with the UNESCO recommendations available for their guidance, but sheet maps are frequently omitted. The International Advisory Committee on Bibliography, Documentation and Terminology has arranged that regular surveys of the state of national bibliographical services are published by UNESCO and these reports offer an opportunity to discover which countries, and which national bibliographical publications, list maps and atlases. The reports have been published for the years 1951–1952, 1952–1953 compiled by L N Malcles, for 1950–1959 by Robert L Collison, and for 1960–1964 and 1965–1969 by Paul Avicenne. The latest report by Paul Avicenne *Bibliographical services throughout the world 1965–69* Paris, UNESCO, 1972 is the first to examine for basic information about the existence of national bibliographies of maps in individual countries, and also the work by STEPHENSON. One can expect the UNESCO volume to be repeated at about five year intervals, but the information of amendments and additions to national bibliographical services is, if reported by national correspondents, published in a journal which appears six times per annum. *Bibliography, documentation, terminology* is published by UNESCO and for the purpose of the map librarian, has two main sections. Each issue provides a general review of the national bibliographical services of several countries and in a separate section are reported new or changed bibliographical publications. In both cases reference is occasionally made to maps, in the latter case the mention may refer to a bibliography of early maps, the publication of a map catalogue, or even a new atlas of importance, as well as a current national bibliography of maps.

AVICENNE was compiled during the middle months of 1970 from questionnaires which included the question 'Please state what special bibliographies, lists, catalogues etc have been published during the period 1965–69 concerning any of the following types of material . . . ', and one class of materials listed is maps and atlases. The question is a little ambiguous as it could be thought that if maps were included in the full national bibliography during that period then there was no need to mention them because they were not a special bibliography. Correspondents answered in a variety of ways, some noting if maps were in the national bibliography, others did not. The appropriate entry for the Federal Republic of Germany for example reads as follows: 'Information on maps and atlases is given in the *Deutsche Bibliographie*. The five year summary for the period 1961–65 has appeared.' This confusion in replies no doubt explains why STEPHENSON includes in his list of current national bibliographies covering cartographical works, the bibliographies of ten countries

45

whose entries in AVICENNE make no mention of the inclusion of maps or atlases. No doubt some, if not all, of this information could be obtained by a retrospective search through each of the UNESCO reports on *Bibliographical services throughout the world* since 1950, and the issues of *Bibliography, documentation, terminology*. AVICENNE provides information on nine national bibliographies which are not included in STEPHENSON and the following brief guide is compiled from these lists, (A) referring to AVICENNE, (S) for STEPHENSON, and from the issues of *Bibliographie, documentation, terminologie* (BDT) from 1970 to vol XIV, 3 (May) 1974. In addition to the information about maps included in national bibliographies it is frequently mentioned in BDT if a catalogue of the official survey or of an important map library, has been published.

AUSTRALIA *Australian maps* 1968—Quarterly, Canberra, National Library of Australia. Annual cumulation.

AUSTRIA *Österreichische bibliographie* 1946—Fortnightly, Vienna, Der Österreichischen Nationalbibliothek, Section 16 'Karten, atlanten'.

BELGIUM *Bibliographie de Belgique* 1875—Monthly, Brussels, Bibliothèque Royale. Section 91 includes maps and atlases.

BRAZIL (A) *Bibliografia brasileira mensal* 1967—Monthly, Instituto Nacional do Livro.

(S) *Boletim bibliografico* 1951—Semi-annual, Rio de Janeiro, Biblioteca Nacional. Section 912 'Mapas'

BULGARIA *Bălgarski Knigopis* 1897—Monthly. Sofia, 'Kiril i Metodi' National Library.

BYELORUSSIAN SSR *Belorusskaja SSR v pečati SSR i zarubežnyh stran* 1965—Book Chamber, V I Lenin State Library.

CANADA (S) *Canadiana, 1950*—Ottawa, National Library of Canada. Monthly, annual cumulations. 'Maps and atlases are occasionally listed in Section 1, Class 912'.

CYPRUS (BDT) *Cyprus geographical bibliography* Nicosia, Cyprus Geographical Assoc. Lists books, pamphlets, maps and atlases published in or outside Cyprus on the geography of Cyprus'.

CZECHOSLOVAKIA (A) *Česká grafika a mapy* 1958—Annual (BDT) notes publication of above index of Czech graphics and maps, each year. 1969 volume noted in XIV, 3 (May) 1974.

DENMARK (S) *Det danske Bogmarked* Weekly, Copenhagen, Den danske Forlaeggerforening. Annual cumulation *Dansk bogfortegnelse; årskatalog* lists maps Section 41 'Korg og atlas'.

FINLAND (S) *Suomen Kirjakauppalehti* 1907—Semi-annual. Helsinki, Suommen Kustannusyndistys ja Kirjakauppias liitto.

(BDT) *Suomen Kirjallisuus* 1961–63. 4v Helsinki, University Library 1970. Finnish national bibliography, includes maps.

FRANCE   (S) *Bibliographie de la France* 1811—Weekly, Paris, Cercle de la Librairie. Supp E 'Atlas, cartes, et plans', irregular.

GERMAN DEMOCRATIC REPUBLIC (S) *Deutsche National-bibliographie* 1931—Leipzig, Verlag für Buch-und Bibliothekwesen. In two parts: Reihe A *Neuerscheinungen des Buchandels* Weekly. Commercial map and atlas publications, Sect 16 'Karte, Atlanten'.

Reihe B *Neuerscheinungen ausserhalb des Buchhandels* Fortnightly. Official map and atlas publications, Sect 16 'Karte, Atlanten'.

GERMANY, FEDERAL REPUBLIC *Deutsche Bibliographie* 1947—Weekly. Frankfurt, Buchhändler-Vereinigung GmbH Sect 16 Kartenwerke, inc atlases, Supp C (quarterly) cites maps. Five year summary published.

GHANA   (BDT) *Ghana national bibliography* Accra, Ghana Library Board. Includes maps and atlases.

GREAT BRITAIN   (S) *British national bibliography* 1950—Weekly London, 'Cartographic works are listed in Section 912 "Atlases and maps".'

(A) British Museum. *Catalogue of printed maps in the British Museum: accessions*, annual 1966— Royal Geographical Society *New geographical literature and maps* 1951—Semi-annual.

The diverse nature of the entries for Great Britain in STEPHENSON and AVICENNE underlines the need to use all international lists with discretion. There is no national bibliography for British maps. The *British national bibliography* lists atlases and 'street atlases', that is town plans in atlas form, usually indexed. The Accessions lists for the *British Library Catalogue of Printed Maps* covers all additions from all over the world but does not list individual sheets added in multi-sheet series, British or foreign. The additions to the library of the Royal Geographical Society are published, with books and selected periodical articles, in *New Geographical literature and maps*, and include maps from all countries.

HUNGARY   *Magyar nemzeti bibliográfia* 1946—Fortnightly. Budapest, Kiadja az Országos Széchényi Könyvtar. Inc maps and atlases.

(BDT) *Bibliographica Hungarica 1945–60 Catalogus systematicus mapparum in Hungaria editarum* Budapest 1969.

ICELAND   (A) *Arbók* From 1944 'an index has been kept in *Arbók* of all publications issued in Iceland'. Maps are included in this annual listing.

ITALY   *Bibliografia nazionale italiana* 1958—Monthly. Florence, Biblioteca Nazionale Centrale di Firenze. Part 9 lists geographical maps and atlases printed in Italy.

(BDT) XIII 1 (Jan) 1973 'The annual edition of the Italian National Bibliography has however temporarily suspended publication of indexes relating to geographical maps . . .'

NEW ZEALAND *New Zealand national bibliography* 1967—Monthly. Prepared by Alexander Turnbull Library. Wellington, National Library. Sect II, Maps.

NORWAY *Norsk bokhandlertidende* 1880—Weekly. Oslo, Grøndahl. *Norsk bokfortegnelse* Annual cumulation, includes separate section 'Karter'.

PERU (A) *Anuario bibliográfico peruano* 1943—Annual. Lima; Department of bibliography and printed works, National Library. Heading, 'Maps and atlases'.

POLAND *Przewodnik bibliograficzny* 1946—Weekly. Warsaw, Biblioteka Narodowa. Lists maps and they appear under a separate heading in the annual index of authors.

PORTUGAL (A) *Boletim de bibliografia portuguesa* Annual. Lisbon, National Library. Maps and atlases are listed.

ROMANIA (A) *Bibliografia Republicii Socialiste România* (Series I) Cărţi, Albume, Hărţi. 1952—Fortnightly. Bucharest, Biblioteca Centrala de Stat. Series I covers books, albums, maps. Three year cumulation entitled, *Anurul cărţii din România*.

SIERRA LEONE The text of AVICENNE is possibly open to misinterpretation. The word 'book' is defined in the legal deposit law so as to include maps, but the books listed in *Sierra Leone publications*, 1962—Freetown, Sierra Leone Library Board, are those of the narrower accepted definition and (BDT, XI, 2, March 71) do not include maps.

SINGAPORE (BDT) *Singapore national bibliography* 1967—Annual. Singapore, National Library. Includes maps.

SOUTH AFRICA (S) *South African national bibliography* 1959—Quarterly. Pretoria, State Library. Sect 912. Atlases and maps.

SPAIN *Boletín del depósito legal* 1958—Monthly. Madrid, Dirección General de Archivos y Bibliotecas. Inc maps and atlases. *Bibliografia española* 1958—Annual. Inc maps but is not a cumulation of the above.

SRI LANKA (BDT) *Ceylon national bibliography* 1965—Monthly. Colombo, National Archives Department. Includes atlases but not maps.

SWEDEN (S) *Svenska bokförläggareföreningens* 1952—Weekly. Stockholm, Svensk bokhandel. Inc maps. *Svensk bokförteckning . . . årskatalog*, annual cumulation has additional section 'Kartor'.

SWITZERLAND (A) Das Schweizerbuch/Le Livre Suisse/Il libro Svizzero. 1901—Monthly. Bern, Swiss National Library. Lists maps and atlases.

TANZANIA (BDT) 'The national bibliography based on legal deposit material, at the National Central Library and Dar es Salaam University includes maps and atlases.' BDT XII 2 (Mar) 1972 Annual.

TURKEY (S) *Türkiye bibliyoğrafyasi* 1928—Quarterly. Istanbul, Milli Egitim Basimevi. 'Maps (Haritaler)' are listed following Section 910 'Coğrafya Turizm'.

USSR (A) *Kartografičeskaya Letopis* USSR All-Union Book Chamber. (HARRIS), Kartografičeskaya letopis; organ gosudarstvennoi bibliografii SSSR. Annual. Moscow: Vsesoiuznaia Knizhnaia Palata.

USA (A) *Catalog of copyright entries: Part 6, Maps and atlases* Series 3, 1947—2 pa. *National Union catalog* 1952—9 pa with cumulations *Library of Congress catalog*—books, subjects 1950—Q, and annual supplements.

YUGOSLAVIA *Bibliografija Jugoslavija; Knjige brošure i musikalije* 1950—Fortnightly. Belgrade, Jugoslovenski Bibliografski Institut. Includes maps, Section 912 'mape'.

It should be noted that AVICENNE and BDT provide information on map bibliographies of a retrospective nature, usually early maps of the country, sale catalogues of official surveys and publication of the catalogues of map libraries. It would be necessary to check every report *Bibliographical services throughout the world*, and later issues of *Bibliography, documentation, terminology* to know all those publications recorded since 1970.

Accessions lists of map libraries of national importance
Probably the most valuable type of publication to provide the map librarian with an awareness of current publishing over the widest range of maps, both official and commercial, national and international, is the record of the additions to the map collection of a major library. The libraries which are depository libraries under a legal deposit law will offer in their additions list, even if only a selection of additions is given, an opportunity to know of many items from publishers perhaps not usually associated with maps which otherwise could easily be missed. The briefest examination of such lists shows the multiplicity of street maps, tourist maps, local authority maps, and maps of specialist commercial or industrial interest, some of which will be of interest to an individual map library. The same is true of course of any national bibliography which fully records maps and atlases, but library additions lists may provide an alternative where

49

there is no appropriate bibliography, or publish the information earlier, and of course they publish additions from all other countries in the world.

Map additions lists were originally produced for the benefit of the users of that library and this is probably still their primary function. The type of library which issues additions lists has a wide range of users some of whom come from far afield, as in a government departmental map library serving a number of departmental locations and as a specialist map library for the needs of other government departments. In these circumstances the map additions list is not published for sale and is only available for limited circulation and can not be expected to be made available for distribution to libraries at large.

The map libraries in university libraries or university geography departments and in public libraries should now be at a stage where the map, atlas, and appropriate book, additions are in sufficiently significant numbers to provide interest for other libraries of similar status if not for national or important specialist map libraries. David A Cobb 'Selection and acquisition of materials for the map library' *in Drexel library quarterly* 9 (4 October) 1973, 15–25 gives the names and addresses of sixteen libraries issuing additions lists of which seven are universities in the USA and four are Canadian universities. One other map addition list noted by COBB is from the Map Room, Bodleian Library, Oxford University but this is a legal deposit library and map library of international importance, containing over 2,000,000 maps and is of different status. British university and public libraries in general do not normally exchange additions lists. If they did they would not provide any aid for map acquisition to compare with the major lists to be noted below but would serve another useful purpose. All libraries have different strengths in their coverage of maps, in universities this usually reflects major teaching interests, in public libraries local and other interests, and these strengths, the emphasis on acquisition, should be made known. The distribution of additions lists would help in doing that and also bringing to one librarian's attention a map series, or a specialist atlas that another map librarian expects to be useful in a similar library.

It might be expected that the most widely available map library additions lists are those which are for sale. Royal Geographical Society, *New geographical literature and maps*, 2 per annum, London, and, American Geographical Society, *Current geographical publications, additions to the research catalogue*, 10 per annum. Both these works are concerned with listing all types of material added to the society's collections, books, periodicals and selected periodical articles, as well as maps and atlases. Until 1950 the additions to the holdings of the

Royal Geographical Society were printed in the pages of the *Geographical journal* as a guide to members of the society. The publication of a separate list allows a larger selection to be recorded and to make the resultant bibliography more easily accessible.

New geographical literature and maps is published twice a year covering March to September and September to March, each issue appearing several months after the closing date for additions to that issue. Accessions to the Map Room, appear in part two of each issue, and cover atlases and gazetteers as well as maps. Entries are grouped according to extraterrestrial, world, British Isles and then each continent, and finally a section on oceans. Within each continent the maps are listed under countries, the country heading being followed where necessary by a regional name and then subject, eg Japan—Tokyo—Tectonics. The section oceans is mainly one for charts from the (British) Admiralty and other countries. *New geographical literature and maps* is particularly valuable as an accessible current bibliography which identifies individual sheets, by sheet reference number and/or title, apparently in all the series recorded of scales 1:25,000 or smaller and this is not common for a general list. Prices are not normally noted but do appear for some commercial publications.

It is the declared policy of the society that all important new books, atlases and current maps are included. Maps published in the *Geographical journal* are included if they contain useful information. The Royal Geographical Society's Map Library complements the Map Library of the British Library which, as a legal deposit library, receives all British cartographic publications. The Royal Geographical Society whilst obtaining all important maps does not attempt to be fully comprehensive for British maps but to concentrate on strengthening further the foreign map collections. Similarly, in pursuing a policy reflecting the aims of the society, street plans of towns are not obtained, although road maps in profusion can be found in *New geographical literature and maps*.

Current geographical publications is published ten times per annum by the American Geographical Society, being monthly except for July and August. Like the Royal Geographical Society's list of additions it covers all publications not maps alone and includes references for periodical articles. The additions list is in three main sections; General, Regional and Maps. The Maps and Regional Sections are arranged according to the outline of the Regional Classification used by the Society in the Research Catalogue.

Bodleian Library, Map Section, *Selected map and book accessions* is a monthly listing, the issue for December, 1974 was numbered 289. It is a simple typescript, a few sheets stapled together with no cover, but it

51

is a most valuable publication, from a library which adds over 20,000 sheets per annum. The number of entries varies from month to month, No 280 (March 1974) has 140 map entries, many entries referring to a number of sheets in a series, whilst No 289 (December 1974) had 45 map entries. No attempt is made to list sheets published in the Ordnance Survey topographic series and the US Geological Survey topographic series, instead the accessions list records the latest *Ordnance Survey publication report* number, with the number of new sheets recorded in it and the *USGS topographical quadrangles distribution* numbers with total sheets issued.

Map entries are grouped and universe forms the first section, and other sections are world, Europe, Asia, Africa, North America, Central America, South America, Australasia, Pacific Ocean, India Ocean, Antarctic Region, etc with individual countries as subdivisions. The selection provided reflects a very catholic choice and the list must give many users and other libraries the knowledge of many interesting single sheet maps in particular. Sheets from all official surveys are listed, except those of Great Britain and the USA as mentioned above for which for example, the *Ordnance Survey publication report* has to be used, but that is widely and freely distributed in the British Isles. Additionally one notes commercial maps of all kinds, motoring maps being particularly numerous, street plans, air navigation charts, charts for coastal navigators, and facsimiles. If a large number of sheets have been received for a map series with a scale of 1:50,000 or larger then only the number of sheets is stated, but in other cases the sheet numbers and/or titles are given. A typical entry is as follows:

Bartholomew Post Office Postcode Map. Great Britain and N Ireland. 1:126,720. Edinburgh and London; J Bartholomew and Son Ltd and Post Office, 1974. Sheets 1–63 [With] Key Map at 1:1,250,000, Glasgow area at 1:25,340, Central London at c 1:17,000.

The variety of local maps produced in Great Britain that are listed is a result of the Bodleian Library being a legal deposit library for British publications, and in this the Map Section's *Selected map and book accessions* might be compared with the similar variety of local maps listed in the Library of Congress, *Catalogue of copyright entries, third series, Pt 6, maps and atlases*. The Bodleian list is not however a national bibliography and so one can find an apparently good listing of commercial maps from all over the world. Examples selected from the last few issues of 1974 included: Tourist map of South Korea. 1:500,000. Seoul: Chungang Map and Chart Service 1973; Stadtplan Mainz. 1:12,500. Wiesbaden: H Grosse-Lohmann [1974]; Gdańsk–Sopot–Gdynia. Guide de la Triville. Warsaw: Sport i

Turystyka 1973; A chart showing part of the coast of N W America. c 1:1,400,000 etc Facsimile. Reprinted from the 1st ed of Vancouver's Voyages 1798 for Woodward Stores of Canada by Olwen Caradoc Evans, Conwy and the Cotswold Collotype Co Ltd, 1974. 2 sheets. University and public libraries everywhere, but particularly in Great Britain, should find this select list of additions of major assistance in their selection of current acquisitions. No doubt Oxford University has to limit the number of copies which are freely distributed but it would be well worth the support of all libraries with developing map collections if it could be obtained on a subscription basis.

The British Library, *Catalogue of printed maps. Accessions* is prepared by The Map Library, Reference Division, British Library supplementing the *Catalogue of printed maps*. Unlike the Bodleian Library listing brief identifying entries quickly produced, the British Library, Map Library, accessions list contains the complete catalogue entries as they will be added to the catalogue, and therefore some considerable time may have elapsed between the publication of the map and the appearance of the catalogue entry in this published form. Nor is this a publication to show the receipt of individual sheets of a map; a series is catalogued as a set, or as a set in progress from the cataloguing of the first published sheets. Similarly a map which has been published in a variety of editions using the same base, will receive one entry with a description of the various editions. The British Library map accessions lists shares with *New geographical literature and maps*, which also reproduces catalogue entries, a close attention to the provision of descriptive notes, for map sheet contents which are not discernible from the map title or entry heading. This most commonly is a note on inset maps, information printed on the reverse of the sheet, a map index included and so on, but also, where relevant, phrases such as 'Produced for market research purposes' (of two experimental sheets of OS 1:50,000 prepared in 1970). This accessions list naturally follows the arrangement of The British Library *Catalogue of printed maps* and the headings, alphabetically arranged, are of specific place-names, countries, regions, geographical areas etc, followed by a general or thematic subdivision and the date. When known the date of survey is given, one is pleased to note, preceding the date of publication. Sample headings from Accessions, Part CVIII, 1974 are: CUMBRIA: Administrative maps. 1973; DELHI: CITY. General plans. 1959:1969. Atlases, map catalogues, books of cartography are all included in the accessions list which presumably catalogues all additions to the Map Library, Reference Division, British Library. The accessions lists covering material added to the end of 1973 will be replaced when a ten year supplement to the *Catalogue of printed maps* is published.

The additions list is also of necessity produced for circulation to a strictly selected number of institutions, including some public libraries, but it may be that in future years, different techniques of catalogue preparation may allow the list to be produced in a different format with wider circulation, a possibility which parallels a similar aim of the Library of Congress.

Australian maps Quarterly, publication by National Library of Australia. A national bibliography of maps, it is compiled from the material received in the National Library and full catalogue entries, with classification, are provided following BOGGS and LEWIS. From 1961 to 1967 Australian maps were included, with atlases, in *Australian national bibliography*, and *Australian maps* commenced January 1968. A cumulation *Australian maps, 1961–73* is expected to be published late 1974.

The Library of New South Wales *Maps received in the Mitchell Library* quarterly (1959–   ) is a full map additions list. The content naturally reflects a strong Australian interest, and, as well as listing, in BOGGS and LEWIS classified order, maps of Australia and New Zealand, maps of Pacific Ocean countries, eg Philippines, South East Asia and Antarctica are prominent. Imprint information, size and if coloured is given for each map and the various sheets of a multi-sheet map are clearly listed. A valuable feature of this additions list is that an index to authors and publishers is printed in each issue giving names and addresses, a useful buying aid for other libraries. Directorate of Military Survey, Ministry of Defence, *Selected accessions list of the Map Library*, is a fortnightly publication, restricted circulation, of a very extensive map library. The listing, arranged according to PARSONS classification, has the information noted in columns. This is a system of lay-out of information which finds favour with many librarians of universities who have accessions lists or printed catalogues for internal circulation and it lends itself to the common form of computer print-out. The headings for this *Selected accessions list . . .* are Library Reference; Area (as a subordinate heading within the column) and title, scale, series no, sheet no, or name, edition, date, publisher and/ or printer, remarks (type of map).

Reviewing sources

Almost any geographical journal and many library journals may on occasion mention a new map which has just been produced and sometimes provide a review or even a review-article. Some journals, usually more specialised with cartographical interest provide a regular listing of new maps and sometimes reviews. Any listing in journals of this nature, unlike the bibliographies and some additions lists, will be of a selective nature, for example sheets of a national survey will not be noted unless they are the first sheets of a new map of interest. Selection for inclusion in the list does imply that the maps are of some quality, or thought to be of interest because of their particular content. As with library additions lists, notes in journals are of particular importance in bringing to the attention of the map curator single sheet maps from sources which are not known to the curator. Some of the journals in the following list are included because they note articles etc on cartography rather than notes on new maps.

The American cartographer, American Congress on Surveying and Mapping, 1974– , Q. 'Cartographic news', 'Recent literature', reviews of books, atlases etc, general articles on all aspects of cartography and carto-bibliography.

Bulletin Special Libraries Assoc, Geography and Map Division (USA) 1947– , Q '. . . a medium of exchange of information, news and research in the field of geographic and cartographic bibliography, literature and libraries. Original articles on research problems, technical services and other aspects of cartographic and geographic literature, libraries and collections . . .' Regularly lists new books, new maps, new atlases—with United States emphasis, and there is a regular 'Recent Canadian maps and atlases'. 'Catalogues received' and other valuable listings occur at intervals. A journal of importance to map librarians/curators everywhere for the articles of professional interest.

Bulletin Society of University Cartographers (UK) 1966– 2 pa. Contains extensive reviews of maps, c 26–30 pp; reviews of books, map calendars, etc. The articles are divided between the practice of cartography, with particular interest to cartographic draughtsmen, and articles on maps, not the reviews, usually of interest for cartographic techniques. The emphasis on maps and reviews of maps makes this an important journal for the map librarian.

The Canadian cartographer Bernard V Gutsell, Department of Geography, York University, Toronto. 1964– 2 pa. A separate, quite extensive, section on recent maps; recent cartographic literature; a few reviews of books on cartography etc. Supplements, *Cartographica* 3 pa from 1971, include a number of bibliographical interest, and one on map librarianship, Joan Winearls *editor*, is announced.

The Canadian geographer Canadian Association of Geographers. 1951–3 pa. Reviews on atlases in book review section.

Cartinform Institute of Surveying, Geocartographic Research Department, Budapest. (Languages used—English, German, French, Spanish) 1971– 6 pa. Publishers 'self reviews' of new atlases, maps and books, collected by the Hungarian National Office of Lands and Mapping. Items in the three separate categories are arranged under countries, some have quite extensive and informative notes, others give little more than the necessary particulars which identify the map. The international nature of the publication, including many entries from East European countries, makes it an informative source.

Cartographic journal The British Cartographic Society. 1964– 2 pa. Articles on cartography, emphasising the compilation and preparation of maps for publication, with a strong minor interest in historical cartography. The Society has had a *Map curators' group* since 1966 and news of the activities of the Group is published in the . . . *Journal.* A few long reviews, including maps and atlases. 'Recent literature' lists articles in current cartographic journals. 'Recent maps and atlases' by Miss Betty Fathers, Superintendent of the Map Section, Bodleian Library, University of Oxford, lists with short notes, selected new maps and includes new sheets of series. Notes catalogues received.

Die Erde Gesellschaft für Erdkunde zu Berlin. 1870– 4 pa. Includes atlases in book reviews.

Erdkunde F Dümmlers Verlag, Bonn. 1947– 4 pa. Includes atlases in book reviews.

Geo abstracts Geo Abstracts Ltd, University of East Anglia, Norwich. 1966– Published in seven separate parts, each part is issued 6 pa. Section G, Remote sensing; and cartography. A major, full international abstracts service. As the service has developed from four to seven parts, cartography, whilst always covered, has appeared in different parts and has been in Section G only from 1974. The headings within the cartography section are: Cartography, general; Survey; Photogrammetry; Photo-maps; Map projections; Computerised cartography; Maps and atlases. The latter contains abstracts of articles about maps and atlases, national surveys, historical cartography etc occasionally noting a review of an atlas, catalogue, etc c25 items per issue. 6th issue for each year of each part contains an author and regional index, with a separate subject and author index annually; five year cumulative (Kwic) index.

Geographical journal Royal Geographical Society, London. 1893– (current form) 3 pa. A major geographical journal, the papers presented cover cartography, eg G A Hardy 'The Ordnance Survey 1:50,000 Map Series' *Geographical J* 140 (2) 1974, 275–283, among other subjects of interest. Reviews of atlases, notes on maps were always presented but since 1960 a section 'Cartographical survey' has formed a place for all review articles, reviews of atlases and maps, with notes and news of cartographical interest from all over the world. The three 'Cartographical surveys' for each year are sold as a separate.

56

Geographical review American Geographical Society 1910– 4 pa. A major geographical journal of general geographical interest. A regular section in 'Geographical record' has news and notes concerning cartography at intervals, and there are reviews of atlases in the reviews section, but information about selected maps received by the society is included in the separately published *Current geographical publications*.

Imago Mundi Harry Margary, Lympne Castle, Kent. 1935– Annual. A journal devoted to the history of cartography in all its aspects. Regular features include reviews, and an annual bibliography of books and articles regarding early maps and the history of cartography. This is an essential journal for every library which contains early maps. *Imago mundi* has articles on eg the techniques of using local maps, as well as maps of international importance.

Information bulletin Western Association of Map Libraries, University Library, University of California, Santa Cruz. 1970– 3 pa. Commencing as a *Newsletter* for a regional group of map librarians, and still appearing in stapled typescript format, this professional journal has quickly proved to have a value and influence far beyond its planned parish. Whilst naturally having a regional emphasis there is nothing parochial about its coverage and the professional papers are relevant for discussion and consideration in map libraries everywhere. The *Information bulletin* does not compete with the map listing of SLA Geography and Map Division, *Bulletin* but has relevant bibliographical coverage eg 6 (1) 1974, 'New mapping of Western N America' including sources of free maps. A journal of importance for map librarians/curators.

Irish geography Geographical Society of Ireland. Annual. Reviews atlases etc and notes literature about maps relating to Ireland.

Map collectors' series Map Collectors' Circle, Durrant House, Chiswell Street, London. 1963– . Publishes a series of monographs each year on early printed maps and atlases; cartographers, map publishers etc. The Editor-in-Chief is R V Tooley and writers of the importance of R A Skelton, Coolie Verner and many others have produced bibliographical work in this series which makes it an essential tool in the study of carto-bibliography by scholars, as well as by collectors; if they are different.

New Zealand journal of geography New Zealand Geographical Society. 1946– 2 pa. Particularly of interest for information on New Zealand maps, newly issued maps from the Department of Lands and Survey are listed, but the journal includes others of value to its readers, such as notes on selected Australian maps.

Petermanns geographische mitteilungen Geographischen Gesellschaft der Deutschen Demokratischen Republik, Beuftragtes Kollegium, Gotha. 1856– 4 pa. Cartography bibliography in each issue, dealing with books, maps and articles on cartography. A separate section gives contents lists of current cartographic journals of an international nature. The book reviews section includes atlases.

The professional geographer Association of American Geographers. 1949– 4 pa. Notes on new atlases and a very few maps.

Scottish geographical magazine Royal Scottish Geographical Society. 1885– 3 pa. The . . . *magazine* has two annual bibliographical features of specific cartographical interest, and articles on Scottish maps may appear in the journal as of general interest. The annual features are 'Recent geographical literature relating to Scotland' which includes cartography, and 'Books received in (year)' which includes maps.

Further journals around the world publish regular features or bibliographical lists of cartographic interest. A useful guide to these, even though now out-of-date in some respects is J A Wolter 'The current bibliography of cartography, an annotated selection of serials,' SLA Geography and Map Division *Bulletin* No 58 (Dec) 1964, 9–13, which among others includes the following journals:

Australia *Cartography* Australian Institute of Cartographers. 1954– 2 pa.

Canada *Bibliographical series* Department of Mines and Technical Surveys, Geographical Branch. 1950– Irreg. *Geographical bulletin* Department of Mines and Technical Surveys, Geographical Branch 1951– 2 pa.

France *Memoires et documents* CNRS, Centre de documentation cartographique et geographique.

Germany *Berichte zur deutschen Landeskunde* Institut für Landeskunde. 1941– 2 pa. *Bibliotheca cartographica* Institut für Landeskunde und Deutsche Gesellschaft für Kartographie. 1957– 2 pa. *Geographisches Taschenbach* Zentralverband der deutschen Geographen und Bundesanstalt für Landeskunde und Raumforschung. 1949– Biennial. *Kartographische nachrichten* Deutsche Gesellschaft für Kartographie. 1951– 4 pa. *Nachrichten aus dem Karten—und vermessungwesen*. Institut für Angewändte Geodasie. 1951– Irreg.

Italy *Universo* Istituto geografico militare. 1920– 6 pa.

Netherlands *Tijdschrift* Nederlandsch aardrijkskundig genootschap. 1876– 4 pa.

Sweden *Globen* Generalstabens litografiska anstalt. 1922– 4 pa.

USA *The Military engineer* Society of American Military Engineers. 1920– 6 pa. *Surveying and mapping* American Congress on Surveying and Mapping. 1941– 4 pa.

Chapter references:
AVICENNE; BDT; CANADA; CNRS; COBB; DRAZNIOWSKY;
HAGEN 1971; HARRIS; LAWRENCE; LOCK; STEPHENSON;
TAYLOR; USGS; WINCH.

3

Bibliographical notes on selected official mapping services

Knowledge of the publications of an official survey can be gained from the dealers' catalogues and bibliographies already mentioned, but for a true understanding and up-to-date knowledge of the full programme of an official survey it is necessary, and easier, to examine more specific material, usually the sales publications and annual reports, published by the official surveys themselves. A library acquiring many maps from a survey would ensure that those other publications of the mapping service are received, but at other times information will be needed about other surveys.

LOCK is a good starting point, providing for each country, in a narrative form, the names of the official surveys and major commercial map publishers with a brief outline of their programme, and concentrating on a description of major maps, or important series produced, usually with some note on geological and other thematic maps. The content of Dr Lock's book is however based on information up to November, 1968.

The International Cartographic Association held its Fourth Technical Conference in New Delhi in December, 1968, and the reports and proceedings of the conference were published in *International yearbook of cartography* volumes 9 and 10. IYC 9 contains fifteen reports by national organisations on cartographic activities in their countries. The reports, written in English, French and German, vary in length, but the detailed information on topographic and thematic cartographic organisations official and commercial, and their publications, provided by the reports for—Belgium, France, German Federal Republic, Japan, Netherlands, Sweden and the United Kingdom of Great Britain, is quite comprehensive. Valuable but less detailed information is provided in the reports of the publications of—Czechoslovakia, Hungary, India, Poland, South Africa and the USSR.

The *International yearbook of cartography*, although having a primary interest in the technical aspects of cartography, does include some articles on individual maps and atlases of direct interest to map curators and librarians.

World cartography X. New York, UN, 1970 contains a ninety one page review of the status of topographic mapping throughout the world. It is in two parts, the first providing a statistical statement of the percentage of area of each country covered by scales of 1:250,000 or larger, and the second part is an inventory of world topographic mapping, for most countries the information is as at December 1968. The inventory includes a useful list of names and addresses of national cartographic agencies in 112 centres. Under every country the map series are tabulated to show for each, scale; map series designation or title; sheet size; number of sheets required for complete coverage; number of sheets produced, at that date; relief; style; projection; ellipsoid. The inventory is not produced as a regular feature of *World cartography* which usually contains technical papers.

An excellent 'Select regional list of geological maps and map series' throughout the world with entries under individual countries has been published by E L MARTIN in D N Wood *ed, Use of earth sciences literature* London, Butterworth, 1973, who writes that 'a very useful list of national and international maps prepared by the Commission for the Geological Map of the World (CGMW) was published in the *Geological newsletter of the International Union of Geological Sciences* No 3 (1969); it contains a list of the addresses of publishing bodies and prices of maps are shown in most cases. Since 1963 the commission has also published a *Bulletin* which gives details of new maps and (published) bibliographies.'

The bibliographies are published as a series 'Inventory of available geological maps' in the issues of International Union of Geological Sciences *Geological newsletter*. In the *Geological newsletter* issue 2, June 1974, the inventory of available geological maps was for Brazil, but it also lists all the previous inventories published in the *Geological newsletter* eg Canada, 1972/2, p 147.

Selected official mapping centres

AUSTRALIA
Department of Minerals and Energy, Division of National Mapping, PO Box 667, Canberra City 2601, ACT. Map Sales Section, Department of Minerals and Energy, PO Box 5, Canberra 2600, ACT.

A brochure *Maps of Australia* is published in January and July each year to show the current availability of topographic and resources maps produced by the Australian Government, and the areas covered by air photographs or photomaps. The brochure has index maps for:

1:250,000, 1:100,000, 1:50,000 scale sheets; 1:1 million (1MW) Australian sheets; Small scale topographic maps; Resources map series; Orthophotomaps, at 1:100,000; Guide to the purchase of photomaps and air photographs.

State mapping agencies are responsible for the large scale plans of their own territories. The addresses given are those of sales offices.

NSW: Information Bureau, Department of Lands, GPO Box 39, Bridge Street, Sydney. New South Wales, Central Mapping Authority. *Catalogue of New South Wales maps* has index maps or details of: 1:25,000, 1:10,000 topographic. Rural cadastral maps. 1:4,000, 1:2,000 metropolitan maps. Urban cadastral maps. Aerial photographs and photomosaics (Enquiries to Air Photo Librarian, above address). List of tourist maps.

Qld. Surveyor General, Survey Office, PO Box 234, Brisbane North Quay, Q, 4000. Surveyor General, Queensland, *Descriptions, lists and diagrams of published maps and air photos.* Index maps of: 1:25,000 cadastral, 1:25,000 and 1:31,680 topographic. Lists variety of small scale special purpose maps eg local government boundaries, stock routes. Lists special maps—cities, tourist areas etc, and approximately 750 town maps.

SA: Central Plan Office, Department of Lands, 144 King William Street, Adelaide, SA 5000. South Australian Department of Lands, *Index to cadastral, topographic and orthophoto maps, aerial photography and mosaics.* Booklet containing index maps: 1:31,680, topographic maps (discontinued). 1:10,000 and 1:2500 topographic/cadastral and orthophoto maps. Extent of aerial photography and mosaics programme. Separate leaflet of small state maps, general and pastoral; county and town plans; irrigation maps.

Tas. TASMAP, Lands Department, Box 44 A, GPO, Hobart 7001, Tasmania. Surveyor General, Lands Department, Tasmania. *Tasmap sales brochure.* Index maps: 1:500,000, 1:250,000, geographical maps. 1:31,680, 1:63,360 topographical. Photomaps, towns, national parks. Notes on administrative, town, tourist maps. Atlas.

The NSW, Qld, SA and Tas catalogues all provide indexes for sheets of National Mapping series 1:100,000 and 1:50,000, relevant to the state.

Vic: Surveyor-General's Office, Department of Crown Lands and Survey, State Public Offices, 2 Treasury Place, Melbourne, Victoria 3002. Surveyor-General, Victoria. *Catalogue of maps and index of series.* Out of print. Second edition in preparation, late 1974.

NT: Surveyor General of the Nothern Territory, Department of Services and Property, Darwin 5790.

WA: Surveyor General, Lands and Surveys Department, Cathedral

Avenue, Perth, WA 6000. Surveyor General, Western Australia. *Published maps*. A typescript listing of series, with prices.

Geological; 'Official mapping is carried out by the geological surveys of the various states, supplemented in recent years by the Bureau of Mineral Resources, Geology and Geophysics (BMR). Mapping by the BMR is largely confined to undeveloped areas of northern and central Australia and . . . Papua and New Guinea', MARTIN. The standard scales used are 1:63,360 and 1:250,000. The official surveys are: Department of Mines, New South Wales, Sydney. Queensland Geological Survey, Brisbane. Geological Survey of South Australia, Adelaide. Tasmania Geological Survey, Hobart. Victoria Geological Survey, Melbourne. Geological Survey of Western Australia, Perth.

International Union of Geological Sciences, *Geological newsletter*: 1967/1, 67 Inventory of available geological maps, Australia exclusive of Western Australia. 1970/3, 305. Western Australia.

CANADA

Department of Energy, Mines and Resources, Surveys and Mapping Branch, Ottawa. Canada Map Office, 615 Booth Street, Ottawa, K1A 0E9.

Catalogue of published maps 1974 $2.00 362 p listing (bilingual) of topographical sheets, aeronautical charts, photomaps, and a wide variety of thematic maps excluding geological maps, atlases and gazetteers. National Topographic System and other topographic maps, and aeronautical base charts, listed by computer, providing NTS or ICAO number, sheet name, province or county, style (eg provisional, photomap etc). Sections of a sample sheet of each national topographical map scale, 1:25,000 to 1:1M, are included.

A monthly *New and converted maps* lists each new issue, under the different scales, giving sheet number, title, province, edition, price. Although the number of sheets involved, some 15,000, is much less than the total for some other countries, the publications of the official survey of Canada must be among the most publicised and documented in the world. All public libraries can request one free copy of all topographic maps within thirty miles of the library. The libraries are obliged to provide special map storage and make the maps available for lending to the public. Maps are deposited, in various categories, in some 150 Canadian and foreign collections, including government departments etc, but mainly in the geography departments of universities and colleges.

Useful leaflets issued for public information by the Canada Map Office, Surveys and Mapping Branch include: *How to order a topographic map; Everyone should be able to use a map; Canadian map makers; How to order aerial photographs*, from the National Air Photo Library, at the same address, *Maps and charts*, a substantial folder, which lists all indexes available, individual small scale maps, magnetic maps, national park maps, and a guide to the topographic conventional symbols used.

Index maps available: 1:250,000. All Canada covered (918 sheets); 1:50,000. 18 separate regional indexes but sheets are not available for whole country. Index maps distinguish availability only as photomaps or at 1:63,360; 1:25,000. Five regional indexes cover urban areas only; 1:1,000,000; 1:500,000; 1:125,000; Other miscellaneous indexes include, glacier and alpine, sheets covering Algonquin and La Verendrye provincial parks, electoral maps, reproductions of historic maps; 1:500,000 and 1:1M (WAC) aeronautical charts.

Surveys and Mapping Branch also produces a variety of publications in different series, including gazetteers and, from 1969, technical reports. The latter series, whilst being essentially concerned with techniques of surveying and cartography, has several publications of more general interest, eg Brig L J Harris *Mapping the land of Canada, obligation to an inheritance* Technical Report, 72–2; L M Sebert *The history of the 1:250,000 map of Canada* Reprint 31; E A Fleming *Photomaps at 1:50,000 for Northern Canada* Reprint 39; *National atlas of Canada* 126 sheets, 4th ed. In progress.

Land capability maps; prepared by Lands Directorate, Environmental Management Service, Department of Environment Ottawa, K1A 0H3. Lands Directorate *Index, environmental Canada.* 1:250,000 Soil capability for agriculture, land capability for forestry, recreation, wild-life, and land capability analysis.

Lake, inland waterway and coastal charts; prepared by The Canadian Hydrographic Service. Hydrographic Chart Distribution Office, Marine Sciences Directorate, Department of Environment, Ottawa, K1A 0E6. *Catalogue of nautical charts and related publications.* A series of eleven information bulletins containing index maps and a list of charts giving number, title, scale and price, eg *Information bulletin 1, Great Lakes and adjacent waterways.*

The Canadian Hydrographic Service, Department of the Environment, Ottawa also publishes bathymetric and surficial geology maps, and fisheries charts and natural resource maps for which index maps are available. Published sheets of the latter are 1:250,000, concentrated on the Gulf of St Lawrence and its approaches and the mouth of the MacKenzie River.

Geological: Geological Survey of Canada, Department of Energy, Mines and Resources, 601 Booth Street, Ottawa, K1A 0E8. *List of general geological reports and maps of Canada.* Rev 1974. Lists a variety of geological and mineral maps, and seven sheets of the new 1:5,000,000 series, each topical sheet covering the whole country.

A complete catalogue of the publications of the Geological Survey to date is available in two retrospective volumes, covering 1845–1958 and 1959–1969, and annual *Index of publications of the geological survey of Canada*.

Geological maps published by the Geological Survey of Canada: Index sheet No 1. . . Ottawa, 1960. About seventy regional index maps are issued showing published geological maps on a variety of scales, and seventeen indexes show positions of published aero-magnetic maps 1″ to 1 mile scale and 1:250,000. Geological Survey of Canada, *Monthly information circular* is a listing of all new publications of the survey including map sheets, new map indexes, etc but excluding the Geophysical Series (Aeromagnetic) maps which are issued in batches at specified dates and times in Ottawa and appropriate branch offices and these are publicised by 'announcement cards'.

International Union of Geological Sciences, *Geological newsletter*, 1972/2, 147. Inventory of available geological maps, N America, Canada.

FRANCE

L'Institut Géographique National, 136 bis rue de Grenelle, Paris 7.

IGN, Service de Vente des Cartes, 107 rue la Boétie, 75008 Paris.

Cartes de France publiée par l'Institut Géographique National. A brochure containing index maps, regularly issued, of series covering Metropolitan France, including Corsica. Topographical and military editions: 1:250,000; 1:100,000; 1:50,000, in 5 colours. The sheet lines are geographical coordinates identified by Roman and Arabic numerals. This 'Edition militaire' is replacing edition M 'Carte en hachures, edition en noir'; 1:25,000, in 4 colours. Sheet identification follows the system for 1:50,000 with numerical sub-division of one-eighths, but the sheets are issued as double sheets. 'Edition militaire', replacing 1:20,000 series.

Tourist editions: 1:250,000; in 8 colours. 'Serie rouge'; 1:100,000; in 7 colours. 'Serie verte'; Available as flat sheets or folded. Sheets identified by sheet number and a name. Larger scale tourist maps of major tourist areas are listed.

Large scale plans: 1:5,000 Paris and region, Alpes-Maritimes, Nice.

Cartes générales, a brochure containing index maps of large scale maps prepared by IGN. 1:1,000,000 (IMW) France, Malagasy, Mauritius, Polynesia, African States with French associations. 1:5,000,000 Continents. Sky and moon maps.

Cartes aéronautiques Indexes for ICAO sheets of France and overseas territories associated with France. 1:500,000 and 1:1,000,000. A variety of editions are noted some, eg radionavigation charts, being published by and available only by post, from Service de l'Information Aéronautique, rue Champagne, 91205 Athis-Mons.

Price lists provide a useful checklist for many individual maps eg road map of the Congo, administrative map of Niger. *Liste des prix de vente des cartes et ouvrages. Liste des prix de vente des cartes des départements et territoires d'Outre Mer, d'Afrique et de Madagascar.*

Air photographs are available from: Photothèque Nationale, 2 avenue Pasteur, 94160 Saint-Mande.

IGN publishes *Bulletin d'information de l'IGN*, quarterly.

Geological: Bureau de Recherches Géologiques et Minières, Service Géologique National, Ministère du Développement Industrial et Scientifique. BRGM, Service géologique national, Services des Ventes, BP 6009, 45018 Orléans Cedex. *Catalogue des publications* 1974. Lists, with other publications, geological map sheets of France issued 1971, 1972 and 1973 and provides full general notes for the various scales and series of geological maps of France, slides, etc. Small scale maps and sheets for countries other than France, eg Algeria, West African states, Central African states, Martinique etc, are listed.

Six regional catalogues are published which gather together all books, maps and other publications relevant to the natural geological regions of France.

BRGM Carte géologique de la France. A brochure containing index maps, 'tableaux d'assemblage', of the geological maps of France, 1:50,000, 1:80,000 and 1:320,000 and the geological maps of the area along the coastline of France, 1:100,000 and 1:250,000.

The 1:50,000 series, incomplete, is to replace the 1:80,000 scale and it is hoped to issue about 35 new sheets per year. The 1:320,000 series has ceased publication and from 1975 will be replaced by sheets in a new 1:250,000 series, the first sheet to be for Marseille.

FEDERAL REPUBLIC OF GERMANY

Institut für Angewandte Geodäsie, 6000 Frankfurt am Main 70, Kennedyallee 151. The Institut is the federal mapping agency for small scale series but land surveying for official map series is the concern of each province (Land) in the republic. In each Land there is a survey office publishing maps in the national series to a common style and standard, and also large scale plans and specialist maps reflecting their own publishing programme. The individual official surveys are: Baden-Württemberg: Landesvermessungsamt Baden-Württemberg, 7 Stuttgart N, Büchsenstrasse 54; Bayern:

Bayerisches Landesvermessungsamt, 8 München 22, Alexandra-strasse 4; Hessen: Hessisches Landesvermessungsamt, 62 Wiesbaden, Schaperstrasse 16, Postfach 109; Niedersachsen: Niedersächsisches Landesverwaltungsamt-Landesvermessung, 3 Hannover, Warm-büchenkamp 2; Nordrhein-Westfalen: Landesvermessungsamt Nordrhein-Westfalen, 53 Bonn-Bad Godesburg, Muffendorfer Str. 19–21; Rheinland-Pfalz: Landesvermessungsamt Rheinland-Pfalz, 54 Koblenz, Hochhaus, IV Stock; Saarland: Landesvermes-sungsamt des Saarlandes, 66 Saarbrücken 3, Neugrabenweg 2; Schleswig-Holstein: Landesvermessungsamt Schleswig-Holstein, 23 Kiel-Wik, Mercatorstrasse 1–3; Hamburg: Vermessungsamt der Freien und Hansestadt Hamburg, 2 Hamburg 36, Wexstrasse 7; Berlin-West: Senator für Bau- und Wohnungswesen, Abt V—Vermessung, 1 Berlin 31, Mansfelder Strasse 16.

The Institut and each Land survey office produce a map catalogue (Kartenverzeichnis) and usually separate index maps, although most series are also shown on small index maps in the map catalogue. Each catalogue is descriptive of the scales published, and notes the different editions available for some scales. A common feature is the provision of sample map sections (Kartenausschnitte) to illustrate the style of different scales and editions, these may be printed with the description of the appropriate scale or grouped together in a fold-in plate or separate leaflet.

Only large scale plans of Hamburg are published by the Vermessungsamt . . . Hamburg, the national topographic scales are available from Landesvermessungsamt Schleswig-Holstein.

The following general notes referring to the main national scales can be understood to refer to each Land, with variations of detail, and they are available from the appropriate Landesvermessungsamt. Topographical maps:

1:25,000 (TK 25) Editions usually identified by letters. All surveys produce (N) Normal Ausgabe, in 3 colours, but the following are not all produced by all surveys. (NW) as normal edition, with woodlands green. (W) paths marked. (OH) Orohydrographische Ausgabe. No boundaries, roads or buildings, only waterways and contour lines with hill shading. (A) or (EA) Combined edition—base map. Contours, waterways, boundaries as in (N) edition, but all printed black. (Z) all information printed black, with water blue.

1:50,000 (TK 50) Varied editions as above and (Sch) Schummerungsausgabe—as (N) with hill shading, and sometimes roads red. (Str) as (N) with roads red. (W) as (Sch) in 7 colours with footpaths red.

1:100,000 (TK 100)

1:200,000 Topographischer Übersichtskarte TÜK (200)

There are many variations on the basic types of map listed above. Katasterkarten are produced on scales between 1:1000 and 1:5000, the latter scale as Deutsche Grundkarte seemingly produced in each Land. District maps, outside the normal sheet lines, and state park maps, walking and skiing maps are prepared as different editions of the normal scales. Facsimiles of early maps, including reprints of 19th century official maps are in process of publication.

Institut für Angewandte Geodäsie is the source for maps of the area of pre-war Germany outside the Federal Republic, on the scales of: 1:25,000; 1:100,000 Karte des Deutschen Reiches; 1:200,000 Topographische Übersichtekarte des Deutschen Reichs, and has district maps, eg Breslau, and 'environs' sheets eg Leipzig at 1:100,000 for the same area which includes DDR and part of Poland.

The Institut publishes *Nachrichten aus den Karten-und Vermessungwesen*, irreg, which lists maps in one section.

Geological map publishing:

Baden-Württemberg. Geologischen Landesamt, 78 Freiburg i br, Albertstrasse 5.

Bayern. Geologischen Landesamt, 8 München 22, Prinzregent-strasse 28.

Hessen. Hessisches Landesamt für Bodenforschung, 62 Wiesbaden, Leberberg 9–11.

Niedersachsen. Landesamt für Bodenforschung, 3 Hannover-Buchholz, Alfred-Bentz-Haus, Stilleweg 2.

Nordrhein-Westfalen. Geologischen Landesamt, 415 Krefeld, de-Greiff-Str 195.

Rheinland-Pfalz. Geologischen Landesamt, 6500 Mainz, Flachsmarktstrasse 9.

Saarland. Geologischen Landesamt, 66 Saarbrücken 1, Am Tummelplatz 7.

Schleswig-Holstein. Geologischen Landesamt, 23 Kiel 21, Mercatorstr 7.

Hamburg. Geologischen Landesamt, 2 Hamburg 13, Oberstr 88.

Map series at 1:25,000, 1:50,000, 1:100,000 and 1:200,000 not complete. 1:25,000 pre-1940 series are bought from Geocenter.

Soil maps at 1:25,000, 1:50,000 and 1:100,000 available for some areas, and hydrogeological maps 1:100,000.

GREAT BRITAIN AND NORTHERN IRELAND

Great Britain

Ordnance Survey, Romsey Road, Maybush, Southampton SO9

4DH. Distribution: Ordnance Survey, Dept 32, above address.

British libraries, schools and other educational establishments, who receive a discount, should use official order forms, available on request.

Ordnance Survey, *Map catalogue* Annual, free distribution. Substantial booklet, c50 pages, providing a general description of all series published. Topographical maps; 1:250,000; 1:50,000; 1:25,000, 1:1M (IMW), with index maps for each scale, and lists of sheet numbers and names. Large scale plans, 1:10,000; 1:2,500; 1:1,250. Administrative areas maps on scale 1:100,000, and 1:250,000 for Wales and Scotland, and 1:25,000 for Greater London. Tourist and special maps, mainly 1:63,360; outdoor leisure series (1:25,000), archaeological and historical maps, all sheets described and listed. Other selected official map publications, Ordnance Survey services, general information.

Ordnance Survey *Publication report* Monthly. Complete list of all sheets published in the month, new sheets, revised, reprinted with major changes, etc. The . . . *report* for Dec 1974 listed some 860 sheets. Technical and publishing news of general interest is also printed on occasion in the *Publication report*. The OS also circulates freely in Great Britain for the trade and schools, *Map news and review*, irregular, in which the Publication Division provides advance information on new popular publications.

Leaflets produced by the Ordnance Survey are often of general interest, as: *Ordnance Survey digital maps; Levelling; High and low water marks;* and some distributed leaflets are in a numbered series: No 8 Parcel numbers and areas on 1:2500 scale plans; No 9 Large scale plans; No 20 Metrication of Ordnance Survey maps; No 27 Ordnance Survey services; No 50 Ordnance Survey 1:50,000 map series of Great Britain.

Professional papers are designed for the cartographer and surveyor and will be required in appropriate libraries eg No 23 Col RC Gardiner-Hill, *The development of digital maps*. J B Harley *Ordnance Survey maps: a descriptive manual*, 1975 is the main work for a complete appreciation of this official survey.

Index maps. Indexes on base maps of Great Britain at 1:1,250,000 are available: *Index to the 1:50,000 scale map, and to the one inch Seventh series map, Index to the 1:25,000 First and Second series,* [Index to] *1:10,000—1:10,560 National Grid Series. Index to published large scale National Grid plans* is produced quarterly in loose-leaf book form for 1:1,250 and 1:2,500 scale plans. The book or individual sheets can be supplied on a subscription basis.

Librarians must ensure that they are aware of the current publication programme of the Ordnance Survey in respect of maps in non-conventional media, the developments foreshadowed in this field will require some radical changes in the practice of map librarianship. The needs of the majority of users of large scale plans will naturally affect the publication programme of the Ordnance Survey, as will economy of production methods.

The largest scale used to cover the whole of Great Britain is 1:10,000, the 1:2,500 scale covers the country except for mountain and moorland areas, and the 1:1,250 scale is for towns and urban areas with a population of over 20,000. Copies of the 1:2,500 scale and 1:1,250 scale plans can, since 1970, be supplied on 35 mm microfilm, mounted in aperture cards and, to quote the Ordnance Survey, 'For users requiring maps solely for reference purposes it may now be more convenient to . . . use the map in this form', by using a microfilm viewer and reducing storage costs. Specially licensed users, such as local authorities, may make print-outs, general libraries may buy print-outs and trade agencies in different parts of the country have equipment to make print-outs on demand. In February 1975 the cost of a 1:1,250 sheet in traditional paper form was £2.75, and the cost of the same sheet as a print-out was £0.95.

Digital mapping. In April 1973 the Ordnance Survey published a 1:2,500 scale map, SO 5052–5152 (Leominster and Wigmore RD) and the entry for it in *Publication report* No 4/1973 was marked 'dm', which represents digital map, the first to be published, and maps so designated can be bought in conventional paper form, or a purchaser may buy a magnetic tape containing digital topographic data for the area to be used, probably with a users additional information, for production of further maps. The Ordnance Survey uses digital mapping for its own purposes in drawing maps and retaining master records.

Aeronautical charts are produced by the Civil Aviation Authority, 129 Kingsway, London, WC2. Topographical air chart of the United Kingdom, 1:250,000. Sheets of ICAO World, 1:1,000,000, ICAO Europe, 1:500,000.

The Directorate of Military Survey, Ministry of Defence, produces charts available from Stanford's International Map Centre, 12–14 Long Acre, London WC2E 9LP: Operational Navigation Charts 1:1,000,000, Index sheets; Tactical Pilotage Charts 1:500,000, Index sheets

Inland and coastal waters
British Waterways Board, Willow Grange, Church Road, Watford WD1 3QA. *Waterways Guides* series containing maps and descriptions of general features. Charts of Caledonian Canal, and others.

Stanford's Maritime Ltd, 12–14 Long Acre, London, WC2 *Stanford's Coloured Charts for coastal navigators* various scales c. 1:200,000–1:400,000, eg No 12. English Channel—Needles to Start Point; No 18. West coast of Scotland—Stranraer to Ardnamurcham.

Admiralty charts. Hydrographic Dept, Ministry of Defence (Navy), Taunton, Somerset. Obtainable from agents throughout the world as: J D Potter Ltd, 145 Minories, London EC3N 1NH.

Geological maps etc

Geological survey maps are published by the Ordnance Survey for the Natural Environment Research Council, Institute of Geological Sciences, and the series and published sheets are listed in the annual Ordnance Survey *Map catalogue*. Newly published sheets and Sheet Memoirs are listed quarterly in *Geological report,* which.is distributed with the OS *Publication report*. HMSO, *Government publications, Sectional list no 45* Institute of Geological Sciences, list 'Memoirs' appropriate to one-inch sheets, and 'Explanations' of 1:25,000 geological sheets, but not maps themselves.

OS *Map catalogue* lists, small scale sheets, and 1:250,000 maps of England and Wales; 1:63,360 and 1:50,000 England and Wales, Index map, and similarly, with separate index maps, for Scotland and Northern Ireland. Some sheets 1:25,000 are published and listed.

1:10,560 geological maps. A booklet for Scotland listing all sheets, with index map is available for sale from Institute of Geological Sciences, Museum bookshop, Exhibition Road, SW7 2DE, no similar booklet is available for England and Wales. 1:10,560 sheets have been published for certain areas and these are available from local Ordnance Survey agents and from Cook, Hammond and Kell Ltd, 22–24 Caxton Street, London SW1, manuscript index maps of the series are available in The Library at the Institute of Geological Sciences. Photographic copies of unpublished and out of print maps can be ordered from the Photographic Department of the Institute of Geological Sciences, who publish a tariff leaflet.

Aeromagnetic maps and hydrogeological maps are available from the Institute of Geological Sciences.

Soil Survey maps are published and sold by the Ordnance Survey for the Soil Survey of England and Wales, Rothamsted Experimental Station, Harpenden, Herts, and Soil Survey of Scotland, Macaulay Institute for Soil Research, Craigiebuckler, Aberdeen, AB9 2QJ. 1:63,360 for Scotland, and 1:63,360 and 1:25,000 for England and Wales; index maps being published in the annual report of the Macaulay Institute for Soil Research and the Rothamsted Experimental Station. Index maps for both Soil Surveys are in Winch *International maps and atlases in print.*

Ministry of Agriculture, Fisheries and Food (Publications), Tolcarne Drive, Pinner, Middlesex HA5 2DT, publishes and sells *Agricultural land classification maps of England and Wales*, scale 1:63,360, which are listed in the Ministry's *Departmental publications—maps* price list. An *Explanatory note* on the Agricultural land classification map is produced by the Ministry's Agricultural Land Service. The ministry also publishes *Type of farming maps* prepared by the Agricultural Development and Advisory Service, scale 1:250,000. Soil Survey of Scotland issues *Land use capability maps*, 1:63,360.

Land use maps, publications of the *Second land utilisation survey of Britain*, scale 1:25,000, Director Miss A M Coleman, King's College, London, are available from Stanford's International Map Centre, 12–14 Long Acre, London WC2E 9LP and an index map is in *International maps and atlases in print.*

NORTHERN IRELAND

Government of Northern Ireland, Department of Finance, Ordnance Survey, 83 Ladas Drive, Belfast BT6 9FJ. Distribution: Chief Survey Officer, Ordnance Survey of Northern Ireland, Map Sales Office, above address, and through booksellers.

Map catalogue, a new edition to be published 1975.

Map publication report, quarterly, listing all new issues.

Index maps issued separately: *Half-inch map (Second Series)* four sheets; *Index to the One-inch map* Third series nine sheets; *Index showing Ordnance Maps of Antrim on the six inch and twenty-five inch scales.* County series large scale maps, there is a similar index for each of the six counties, ie Antrim, Armagh, Down, Fermanagh, Londonderry, Tyrone. The County Series maps are in process of replacement, to be completed by 1980, by maps of the Irish Grid Series.

Index to the Irish Grid 1:10,000 sheets and 1:2,500 sheets, which comprises four sheets, named NW, NE, SW and SE, and are maps, scale quarter inch to one mile, on which are drawn the sheet lines for the two scales in accordance with the Irish Grid coordinates. Irish Grid coordinate figures are given on the maps but sheet identification is by an arithmetical numbering system not by reference to grid numbers. The indexes identify areas which are only covered at 1:10,000 scale. A regularly produced *Availability index showing state of publication of large scale Irish Grid series maps, as at . . .* complements the index to the grid to show sheets published on 1:10,000, 1:2,500 and 1:1,250 scales.

Administrative maps include Northern Ireland Local Government areas (1:250,000), Local Government District Maps (1:63,360), and for Belfast, 1:25,000.

Geological Survey maps and Land Utilisation maps, scales
1:63,360 are sold by the Ordnance Survey of Northern Ireland.

ISLE OF MAN

Isle of Man Local Government Board, Department of Architecture
and Planning, Government Buildings, Tromode, Douglas. Distribution: from the above address, price list available.

Ordnance Survey maps of the Isle of Man, scales: 1:63,360;
1:25,000 (reduced from 1:10,560, or enlarged from 1:63,360);
1:10,560. Large scale: 1:2,500 a) full coverage. 1869 edition. b) partial
coverage, for towns except Douglas, National Grid, 1968 ed. 1:1,250
Douglas and Onchan only. National Grid, 1965–66 ed.

CHANNEL ISLANDS

Jersey
Authorised by States of Jersey, produced by Hunting Surveys Ltd, 6
Elstree Way, Boreham Wood, Hertfordshire, WD6 1SB, England.
Distribution: Hunting Surveys Ltd, Sales Dept (above address).

1:25,000 Full colour, 25[1] contours. Popular folding edition is also
available from Lexicon Book Shop, King Street, St Helier, Jersey.
1:15,840, 1:5,000; 1:2,500—all uncoloured.

BKS Surveys Ltd, Cleeve Road, Leatherhead, Surrey, England in
1970 produced maps of Jersey on scales of 2" to 1 mile, and 4" to 1
mile, printed by George Phillip Ltd, compiled from Ordnance Survey
maps and revised by aerial photography. A review by G B Lewis of
these maps and other BKS maps noted below is in *Bulletin of the Society
of University Cartographers* 5 (1) December 1970, 107–108.

Guernsey
BKS Surveys Ltd 1:21,120 [see above]

Sark
BKS Surveys Ltd 1:10,560. By aerial photography

Herm
BKS Surveys Ltd 1:5,280. By aerial photography

Alderney
Quail Map Co, Exeter. Map (1:10,500) and guide.

J Bartholomew and Sons Ltd publish touring maps of the Channel
Islands on various scales (c 1:35,000 etc), and *International maps and
atlases in print* notes Ministry of Defence maps, 1:10,000 for Sark,

Alderney, Herm and Jethou.

IRELAND

Ordnance Survey Office, Phoenix Park, Dublin. Distribution: Assistant Director, Ordnance Survey Office, as above, and many agents, bookshops in Ireland, and Messrs Sifton Praed and Co Ltd, 67 St James's Street, London SW1, England.

Price list available and three index maps: *Index to the one inch scale maps; Index to the half inch scale maps; Index to the quarter inch scale maps.*

The 1:63,360 sheets are uncoloured, but coloured district maps on the same scale are available for Cork, Dublin, Killarney and Wicklow. 1:126,720 is an up-to-date, detailed, touring map. Other scales published, 1:250,000 (five sheets); *General map of Ireland* 1:575,000 in English or Irish editions; town plans with street indexes for Dublin (1:18,000), Cork City (1:15,000).

Geological maps: produced by Department of Industry and Commerce, Geological Survey of Ireland, 14 Hume St, Dublin 2. Distributed as Ordnance Survey maps noted above.

List of memoirs, maps, sections etc published by the Geological Survey to February 1962 is updated by a 'List of recent publications . . .'

Geological map of Ireland 1:750,000

1:63,360 (reduced from 6″ to 1 mile) survey, sheet numbers and titles given in '*List of memoirs, maps* . . .' with an index map.

1:10,560, sheets for some areas of economic importance. Unpublished sheets of this scale are available for reference at the Survey Office, Dublin.

ITALY

Istituto Geografico Militare, 50100 Firenze, Via C Battisti 10. Distribution: Istituto Geografico Militare, Sezione vendite, 50100 Firenze, Viale Filippo Strozzi, 14.

Catalogo delle Pubblicazioni 1974–75. Contains map sections to illustrate style of each edition of every scale; a list of map series and other publications; index maps for every scale including some maps of Libya, Eritrea and Somalia. Separate *Listino prezzi* (price list) for maps and books published by IGM. Current issues are noted in *Aggiunte e varianti al Catalogo delle Pubblicazioni*, published at intervals giving numbering and titles of sheets.

Carta regionale d'Italia 1:250,000

Carta d'Italia 1:200,000 (excluding Sardinia); 1:100,000—three editions, contoured, contoured and hill shading, administrative boundaries; 1:50,000; 1:25,000—three editions, black and white, three colours, five colours.

Aeronautical charts prepared by the Stato Maggiore Aeronautica are published and sold by Istituto Geografico Militare; scales 1:500,000, eleven sheets covering Yugoslavia, Corsica, Sardinia also; 1:1,000,000 World aeronautical charts, Italian sheets and *Carta aeronautica del Mediterraneo* 1:2,000,000 and *Carta aeronautica di navigazione* (for Europe) 1:2,000,000

Geological maps are published by Servizio Geologico d'Italia, Largo S Susanna N 13–00187, Roma.

NEW ZEALAND

Surveyor-General, Department of Lands and Survey, PO Box 8003, Wellington. Distribution as above or any Map Sale Branch. Agency: New Zealand Book Shop, Royal Opera Arcade, Westminster, London, SW1.

Department of Lands and Survey, *Maps* fifth ed 1971. A booklet listing all topographic series, individual maps with index maps.

Topographical maps: 1:500,000, seven sheets, seven colours and layer tints; 1:250,000, relief shading; 1:63,360, six colours; 1:25,000, five colours; Antarctic Topographical Series, 1:250,000, five colours relief by hill shading, and Provisional Series, two colours, no relief shading.

Tourist maps, national park maps, of relevant regions, various scales.

Street maps of all major towns.

Maps should be ordered by series code number and sheet number.

Air Photographs. Available for whole country on scales 1:15,840–1:80,000, from Department of Lands and Survey.

Geological: 'Map series at scales of 1:250,000, 1:63,360 and 1:25,000 are . . . published' MARTIN. NZ Geological Survey, Department of Scientific and Industrial Research, Wellington.

International Union of Geological Sciences, *Geological newsletter* 1970/3, 305 Inventory of available geological maps, New Zealand.

NIGERIA

Federal Ministry of Works and Housing, Lands and Surveys Division, Lagos. Map depot, above address.

Catalogue of maps (June, 1971). A complete catalogue of 109 pages published by the Survey Division, Lagos but including, as well as all the map series produced by the Lands and Surveys Division, the map series published by the Survey Departments of Northern, Mid-Western, Eastern and Western States, and by the Department of Geological Surveys.

Catalogue is regularly up-dated by 'Additions lists'. The catalogue has index maps and accompanying lists of sheets giving sheet number, title, edition, year, for every series.

Topographical maps: 1:500,000; 1:250,000, some sheets contoured; 1:100,000; 1:50,000, sheets either 'Planimetric' or 'Contoured'.

Township maps: Scales 1:2,400 to 1:4,800, with additional scales for Ibadan at 1:12,500, and at 1:1,200 and 1:1,250 for Benin, Lagos and Ibadan. Indexes and lists for fifty four townships.

Miscellaneous maps; scale mostly smaller than 1:250,000. Administrative, Roads, Rest houses, Province and thematic maps.

Aerial photographs. Listed in *Catalogue of maps:* Index map, 1:40,000 aerial photography showing dates of photographic coverage. Lists of large and medium scale photographs by State, showing name of area, scale, province, total number of photographs, date.

Geological: Listed in *Catalogue of Maps (1971).* 1:250,000 Index map and listing of twenty sheets, to be completed in eighty five sheets. Individual wall maps, 1:2M Geological (1957) and 1:5M Geological and mineral (1957)

UNITED STATES OF AMERICA

Department of the Interior, Geological Survey, (Topographic Division), National Center, Reston, Virginia 22092. Distribution offices: Maps of areas east of the Mississippi River: US Geological Survey, Washington Distribution Branch, 1200 South Eads Street, Arlington, Virginia 22202. Maps of areas west of the Mississippi River: US Geological Survey, Denver Distribution Branch, Federal Center, Denver, Colorado 80225.

Overseas customers, except in Canada and Mexico, are required to pay an additional twenty five per cent on the net cost to cover postage for surface mail. Maps will be sent air mail if the full cost is included in the remittance.

Publications of the Geological Survey, 1879–1961. Publications of the Geological Survey, 1962–1970. Washington, US Government Printing Office, 1972. Annual supplements. Pages 345–358; National Atlas and topographic maps, General notes on National Topographic Map Series, Antarctica Reconnaissance Series, Air photographs, and a listing of small scale maps (1:1M or less), State maps, Metropolitan area maps, special topographic maps—commonly national parks maps.

Annual supplements, list new or revised small scale sheets, as Antarctica 1:250,000, River surveys, State maps, special topographic maps.

New publications of the Geological Survey Monthly, from US Geological Survey, Reston. Lists issued topographic maps by state and titles (arranged alphabetically), giving latitude and longitude of SE corner of sheet, scale, contour interval. Date of map after map title. The monthly list covers maps which are new, resurveyed, revised, ortho-photo maps and orthophotoquads. Lists new State Topographic Indexes.

Useful pamphlets issued for sale by the US Geological Survey, available from Superintendant of Documents, US Government Printing Office, Washington, DC 20244, include: *Topographic maps; The United States Geological Survey; Information sources and services; US Geological Survey Library; Geological Survey Photographic Library; Aerial photographic reproductions; Select bibliography on maps and mapping.*

Index maps. Indexes, supplemented by the monthly *New publications of the Geological Survey* for up-dating, provide full coverage. Each state index provides sheet identification for the National Topographic Map Series on scales of 1:240,000 and 1:62,500. Sheets (quadrangles) cover $7\frac{1}{2}$ minutes of latitude and longitude on the larger scale and 15 minutes on the smaller scale. State indexes also list special maps and sheets, identify the sheets covering national monuments and his-toric sites, list small scale general maps of the United States, give names and addresses of libraries in the state which are depositories for maps, and note addresses of local map dealers.

1:24,000, 1:62,500; three colours, contour lines are brown and intervals differ according to the relief of the country. Sheets are ordered by name, series, and state. Order forms are available listing all sheet names for the state.

1.250,000, National Topographic Maps, Index. 473 sheets. Alaska, on a separate index, 153 sheets. Sheets identified by name; date of survey, and revision if any, given for each sheet on index map as on state index map for larger scales.

1:1,000,000 in progress. First edition, IMW sheets; Second edition, Army Map Service

State indexes to aerial mosaics, air photographs.

Official maps are produced by twenty five government agencies other than the Geological Survey. As well as aeronautical, geological, hydrographic and soil maps there are many other thematic maps published. A leaflet produced by the Geological Survey *Types of maps published by government agencies*, available for sale from US Government Printing Office, lists types of maps, the publishing agency, and the distribution agency.

US Geological Survey *National atlas of the United States* 1970, pp 295–328, 'Mapping and charting', index maps, samples of maps and charts and text describing the work of major federal mapping agen-cies.

Lake and inland waterway charts, and indexes showing charts for coverage of a geographical area are obtained from a number of agencies on a regional basis:

US Department of Commerce, National Ocean Survey, Lake Survey Center, 630 Federal Bldg, Detroit, Michigan, 48226. (For Great Lakes and NE region)

National Ocean Survey, Washington Science Center, Rockville, Maryland 20852

Corps of Engineers: 315 Main Street, PO Box 1159, Cincinnati, Ohio 45201; 536 South Clark Street, Chicago, Illinois 60605; PO Box 60, Vicksburg, Mississippi 39181; PO Box 1216, Downtown Station, Omaha, Nebraska 68101; PO Box 1229, Galveston, Texas 77550; St Louis District, St Louis, Missouri

Tennessee Valley Authority, 311 Broad Street, Chattanooga, Tennessee 37401

Nautical charts of coastal waters: National Ocean Survey, Rockville, Maryland.

Aeronautical charts are also published by the National Ocean Survey, Department of Commerce, these, and the aeronautical charts available from the Defence Mapping Agency Aerospace Centre, are supplied by National Ocean Survey Distribution Division (C44), Riverdale, Maryland 20840. *Catalog of aeronautical charts and related publications* which includes indexes of aeronautical charts for mainland USA and Alaska and world indexes for World Aeronautical Charts (WAC), Global Navigation Charts 1:5M (GNC) and Jet Navigation Charts 1:2M (JNC).

Geological: US Geological Survey, Geologic Division. Distribution as for topographic sheets. Maps are supplied folded unless ordered flat.

Publications of the Geological Survey, 1879–1961; Publications of the Geological Survey, 1962–1970 Washington, US Government Printing Office, 1972. Annual supplements. pp 196–344; Geological, geophysical, mineral resources, water resources maps and charts listed.

Selected special or general interest publications of the Geological Survey, January 1974. Geological maps listed are mainly general maps, 1:5M, of the USA and maps in the Miscellaneous Investigations Series, 1:1M, with geological maps of moon landing sites on larger scales.

New publications of the Geological Survey Monthly. Lists all new publications, including geological maps.

Index maps to geological mapping of the United States are issued for each state by the US Geological Survey and include maps published by the Geological Survey, state and commercial organisations, universities and professional societies. Some indexes are up to twenty

78

years old but those published since 1968 are compiled on topographic index-map bases and identify maps at a scale of 1:250,000 or larger, outlining in colour the areas for which geological maps have been published. For some states a supplementary index is produced for maps published in recent years. Example: L Boardman *Geologic map index of Colorado* 1954. Areas for which geological maps have been published are marked with coloured outline, and mining maps which show local geology are identified. The areas are numbered for reference to text in margin where each map is cited. W L McIntosh and M F Eister, *Geologic map index of Colorado, Part B, 1953–1969,* 1972.

Lists of *Geologic and water supply reports and maps* are available for sale for individual states. The listing covers all Geological Survey Professional Papers and Bulletins, Water Supply Papers as well as maps, charts and atlases of geology and mineral resources including Geologic Quadrangle maps and Geophysical Investigation maps.

International Union of Geological Sciences, *Geological newsletter* 1970/3, 309 Inventory of available geological maps, USA (general map)

UNESCO
Unesco. *Scientific maps and atlases and other related publications. Catalogue 1971–1972.* Updating sheets are issued. Distribution: Through national agencies, in Great Britain these are the Government Bookshops of HM Stationery Office.

Geological, geomorphological, mineral, hydrogeological, climatic, soil, vegetation and oceanographic maps on scales between 1:1,500,000 and 1:10,000,000 but mostly of 1:5,000,000, of the world, but primarily for Europe, Mediterranean area, Africa, South America. *Geological world atlas*, 1:10,000,000, is scheduled to commence publication in 1975.

DIRECTORATE OF OVERSEAS SURVEYS
Directorate of Overseas Surveys, Kingston Road, Tolworth, Surbiton, Surrey. Since 1946 (then Directorate of Colonial Survey) has mapped many countries of Africa, West Indies, Pacific islands and British Antarctic territory, [see LOCK (1969) pp 70–71 etc] for general and geological surveys.

Directorate of Overseas Surveys: Mapping is a sales catalogue produced in 1971 by Edward Stanford Ltd, London, in the absence of an official DOS catalogue since 1960. The Stanford sale catalogue incorporates all the DOS *Map additions lists* up to and including number 130, May 1971.

In many countries the DOS maps are being superseded or added to, by national surveying departments and for the latest publication information for these countries the national survey catalogue, if any, should also be obtained, or checks made with K Winch *International maps and atlases in print*.

Chapter references:
ADMIN; BKS; HARLEY 1975; IUGS; IYC; LOCK; MARTIN; PANGBORN.

4

Guide-lines for current map purchases in British general libraries

This section should be considered in conjunction with the latter part of the chapter 'Content of the map collection—current maps', where views on many maps have been discussed as part of the comments on LA, RSI Section *Standards* . . . and also the entries under 'Great Britain and Northern Ireland' and 'Ireland' within the chapter 'Selected official mapping services'.

World maps
International map of the world 1:1,000,000, prepared by the cooperating national surveys of the world; or *International map of the world* 1:1,000,000, Series 1301, published by the Directorate of Military Survey.
    Tactical pilotage charts 1:500,000 Directorate of Military Survey, Ministry of Defence. Sheets as published.

Europe, and any countries with which the library has a specialist connection. The need for maps of European countries, to which should be added countries of the Middle East and North Africa, is for geographical and commercial purposes, and for tourism which includes road maps, walking and climbing maps. The maps of national surveys or of commercial companies may satisfy one or both needs. Scales of the order of 1:200,000 would probably be bought for countries of western Europe and at this scale consideration might be given to buying all sheets of the official survey. For Italy, *Carte stradale d'Italia* this would require sixty seven sheets, whilst Austria would occupy twenty three sheets. Except in special cases (Leeds Metropolitan District has a mountaineering collection for example) there would not seem to be any need for a public library to buy official surveys on a larger scale, but through the ready availability of map bibliographies and publishers' catalogues readers should be given every encouragement to identify large scale walking and climbing maps they would buy for a holiday. Again with Austria as an example, the

81

official survey produces a number of general maps for Vienna and other tourist areas on various scales between 1:25,000 and 1:50,000. University libraries will have a need for larger scale official survey maps of selected areas in relation to the regional emphasis in teaching in the geography and other departments. The provision of larger scale foreign maps within the libraries of a region would seem to be a suitable subject for cooperation in acquisition.

Commercial publishing will be the prime source of maps which are to be available for tourist purposes, particularly for road maps. Scales of 1:200,000 or 250,000 are quite large for road maps and whilst such scales are desirable for western Europe, other countries where population and roads are more sparse might be quite adequately represented by scales of half the size. It is not sufficient to select one well-known map publisher and buy that firm's maps for the whole of Europe or whatever coverage is available. There is every reason to suppose that the recognised map publishers in each country are more probably accurate, up-to-date and comprehensive in the mapping of tourist information for their own country than any foreign publisher is likely to be. Unless there appears a very good reason to do otherwise, buy Spanish tourist maps for Spain, Norwegian maps for Norway and so on.

Austria: Hölzel. Strassenkarte 1:200,000; Freytag-Berndt. Wanderkarten 1:100,000

Belgium, Netherlands, Luxembourg: Michelin 1:200,000

France: IGN Carte de France 1:250,000; Michelin Carte routière 1:200,000; IGN Carte pour le tourisme (Serie verte) 1:100,000

Germany: Mair (Bartholomew) Deutsche generalkarte. 1:200,000

Great Britain: Bartholomew National map series 1:100,000 [commenced publication 1975 to replace 'Half-inch series']

Greece, Yugoslavia: Touring Club Italiano. Carta stradale d'Europe. 1:500,000; Corfu: Fairey Surveys. Fairey leisure map. 1:100,000

Ireland: Bartholomew. Ireland travel maps. 1:250,000

Italy: Touring Club Italiano. Carta automobilistica d'Italia. 1:200,000; Dolomites: Kompass. Wanderkarten. 1:50,000

Norway: Cappelen. Bil- og turiskart. 1:325,000; Norges Geografiske Oppmaling. Topografiske Kart 1:100,000

Spain and Portugal: Firestone Hispania. Mapas turisticas. 1:200,000

Sweden: Generalstabens Litografiska Anstalt. Svenska turist Kartan. 1:300,000

Switzerland: Michelin. 1:200,000; Service Topographique Federal. Landeskarte der Schweiz. 1:50,000

Hallwag. Europa auto atlas.
Kummerley and Frey. Auto Europa atlas.

Town plans are not a great deal of use if they are printed in an alphabet not normally read by an English speaking user, but otherwise they too should be sought from local publishers as much as possible. It would hardly be acceptable to buy a French or German town plan of Edinburgh, when Geographia Ltd can offer *Street atlas of Edinburgh*, or town plans of Edinburgh Central, and Edinburgh and environs. Geographia Ltd are the main publishers of town plans for the British Isles, having well over 100 town plans in print. Falk-Verlag of Hamburg, the British agents are Geographia Ltd, currently produce sixty two plans of German towns, and nearly forty for towns in other countries, eg Rio de Janeiro, Leningrad, Peking, Tokyo. Plan Guide Blay of Paris produce plans of 123 French towns. These latter offer a folded sheet plan incorporated within a small book which provides a variety of information on such things as bus routes, places to visit, principal hotels as well as a street index for the map. The arrangement of *International maps and atlases in print* with each country arrangement having a subdivision B—'town plans', readily provides a guide to availability. The individual entries for the plans are then usefully given in one alphabetical sequence of towns with only a general bibliographical description at the beginning of the subdivision. In countries such as the German Federal Republic where there are a number of significant town plan publishers, their combined output is given in this one sequence of towns, the individual plans being noted by scale, publisher and price. In other countries the subdivision B has an entry which concerns the dominant town plan publisher, and any additional plans by another, possibly foreign, publisher are also included in the list but with an individual publisher note. There is therefore no difficulty in selecting town plans produced in the same country. More than one British city library has assembled a substantial collection of foreign town plans by diligently checking through the whole of *International maps . . .* and the dealer's catalogue which can be looked upon as its predecessor, Edward Stanford Ltd *Stanford's Reference Catalogue* and making a generous selection from the reference librarian's estimate of the potential interest in the various cities and towns of the world.

Town plans, road maps and schematic maps of tourist areas can be obtained in quantity from donating sources. Such maps cannot normally be compared with the maps noted above but they are often good and add a new dimension to the library's holdings of maps. Letters to all foreign official tourist offices within the country will produce some very useful material, but one can develop this and write abroad to the various regional tourist offices within a foreign country and even towns. Towns, through city councils, chambers of commerce, banks etc may produce suitably interesting material of reference value, and material which is regularly revised. In North America particularly, petrol companies provide free folding maps; Special Libraries Association, Geography and Map Division *Bulletin* No 92 (1973) 16–21, 34 has a source list for highway and tourist office maps and petrol company maps in North America. A similar list can soon be developed for other countries of the world by a little imaginative search for appropriate addresses in reference books, but the tourist office is the main point for commencement.

Ordnance Survey maps will be purchased in public libraries for reference and lending collections, only maps for reference purposes are noted here but it might be said that lending library collections of maps could be extended with advantage beyond the normal 1:50,000 OS maps of Great Britain.

1:250,000 17 sheets in a loose leaf atlas, with a gazetteer. Standing order for later issues of the individual sheets.

1:50,000 and 1:63,360 (One-inch series) For the whole country 198 sheets, with standing order for 1:50,000 Second Series sheets. One-inch maps of the Ordnance Survey of Northern Ireland, and of the Ordnance Survey, Ireland, should also be obtained, and for the other islands of the British Isles.

1:25,000 Second Series, or First Series. Standing order for Second Series sheets as issued, publication began in 1965 and only 160 sheets were available early 1974, but 61 sheets were issued in 1974. At current prices a set of 1:25,000 to cover the country would cost c £700, but as, at the present rate of production, the series will not be complete before the next century this total cost hardly matters. Currently, First Series sheets should be bought for a wide area relevant to the library, not just on a regional basis but to cover areas of interest to walkers such as English Lakes, as 'Outdoor leisure maps' series.

1:10,000 and 1:10,560 (Six-inch series) For the library's geographical region, minimum 150 sheets. Major libraries have an extensive collection of 1:10,000 sheets, sometimes to cover, if an English city, the whole of England and Wales. Standing order for 1:10,000 first publications, and reprints with major revisions within the identified National Grid area.

1:2,500 For the natural geographical area, including whole of the local authority area, if a public library.

1:1,250 As available for urban areas within the local authority area.

Administrative areas maps. Sheets for whole of country.

Archaeological and historical maps. All maps.

Geological Survey maps are, beyond the varied needs within a local area, of primary interest to students, major professional interests would require their own and make their own surveys. In a university, student interests will vary with courses and research, which is of course the prime factor in selection. In public libraries minor professional interests, eg a house building firm will sometimes require local geological information, and there is a wider study interest.

1:50,000 and 1:63,360 sheets. Whole country, all editions.

1:10,560 map. Sheets covering natural geographical area including the local authority area, for sheets published if available, and otherwise photocopies of unpublished sheets.

Land use etc maps, see details in section in chapter, 'Selected official map services', Great Britain.

Second Land Utilisation Survey Standing order, all sheets.

Ministry of Agriculture . . . *Type of farming* . . . *maps* All sheets.

Agricultural land classification maps of England and Wales or Soil Survey of Scotland *Land use capability maps*.

Soil survey 1:63,360 All sheets as published.

Inland and coastal waters maps are for recreational interest, but a library in a coastal area will require Admiralty charts of the coastal waters and harbour plans, as part of its regional interests, and other libraries for estuaries.

British Waterways Board *Waterways guides*.

Stanfords Maritime Ltd *Stanfords coloured charts for coastal navigators* The whole coastline.

Hoseasons Boat Hire Holidays *Inland cruising map of England for larger craft*.

Bartholomew. *Maps of the Norfolk Broads*.

Other maps, not part of a regular series, will be observed from time to time, in map additions lists or in reviews in cartographic journals, which map data of a form not previously represented in the library. The addition of such maps probably represents the best area for future useful growth in a general library and is a valuable extension to the information service of the library rather than any specific geographical interest. Properly exploited such maps will form useful additions to the general interests of the library. *Cartactual*, a map service, issued bi-monthly by Cartographia at Cartactual H-1367 Budapest, POB 76, Hungary, is a fine example of this point, as a service not a single map. Each issue is a folder of maps (26 × 37 cm plates) illustrating matters of topical interest. *Cartactual* No 49, 10 (5) 1974, contains fourteen sheets, most with two or more maps, for example Czechoslovakia, railway network; Leningrad, underground railway lines; England and Wales, motorway system; France, international goods traffic of maritime ports; Sulphur industry of Scandinavia and Belgium, Netherlands, FDR. The key to library use of this service is subject indexing.

Department of the Environment *Maps of administrative areas* 1:63,360, showing the boundaries of county and municipal boroughs, urban and rural district councils, parishes and wards as they existed on the day of the 1971 census. They provide the necessary knowledge for the use of census statistics.

Other materials The map collection, where appropriate, will not be kept as one unit because of the form of the material but maps will be filed in different departments adjacent to the books and other materials of that department, so that geological maps will be found with geological books, early local maps with the department of local studies, etc. No watertight groups of use can be made however and consideration should be given to the provision of a map catalogue which includes all maps. Similarly in a map library which might be said to represent the geography nucleus of the map collection some books should be present, atlases of course, but perhaps also bibliographies and catalogues of maps, books and journals concerned with cartography, current guide books, and gazetteers. Of great importance in this latter group are the publications of:

Permanent committee on geographical names for British official use, and the United States, Board on geographic names.

Chapter references:
HIGHWAY; LOCK.

5

Content of the map collection: early maps and their acquisition.

The collecting of early maps is one of the functions of those specialist map libraries which are concerned with the history of cartography and they are usually connected with national libraries, important geographical societies and some older universities. A list of these libraries is given in—E Meynen *ed., Orbis geographicus 1964/66* Vol 1 Wiesbaden, Franz Steiner Verlag, 1964, in a section 'Important map collections'.

Whilst the acquisition of early maps will probably emphasise the national interests of the library concerned these libraries do have collections of world and national atlases, early maps, charts and plans which provide the necessary sources for basic research for students of many branches of interest in the field of cartography. These collections often reached a significant size in an era before the collecting of early maps was seen as a means of private investment. It is interesting to see the quality of collections in the Netherlands and to appreciate that the outstanding historical importance of cartographers from that part of Europe is now reflected in the substantial numbers of atlases and early maps which are preserved and studied in that country. Ir C Koeman *Collections of maps and atlases in the Netherlands, their history and present state* Imago mundi, supp III, Leiden, E J Brill, 1961 is a history of the growth of commercial map publishing in the Netherlands and the collecting of maps in libraries, from the evidence of old catalogues and inventories. Dr Koeman also provides a list of the map and atlas collections with notes on their holdings and provenance. These number 151, with an additional list of thirty five small collections. Many of these collections are however concerned with early local maps, in the same way as a department of local studies in a British public library system collects early local maps, and every other kind of document, for its own region. For early printed maps the greatest collection in the Netherlands is that at Leiden University (founded 1575) and this position was achieved as a result of the bequest in 1872 of a collection formed by an antiquarian bookseller, J T Bodel Nijenhuis. One window upon the riches of these map collections was afforded by an exhibition at the Amsterdams Historisch Museum on the occasion of the 3rd International Conference on Cartography meeting in Amsterdam 1967, and the catalogue of this exhibition *The world on paper* prepared by Y M de Vrij, is a permanent record of the temporary exhibition and of value to later students of the subject, as all such catalogues should aim to be. The journal, founded by Leo Bagrow, devoted to the study of early cartography is *Imago mundi* 1935–, the current editor being Professor Eila M J Campbell. An examination of the *British union catalogue of periodicals* shows that, up to 1960, only eighteen libraries in England, one in Scotland, and one in Wales had a file of *Imago mundi*. Probably this number has been increased during the intervening years, but it is significant that only two public libraries then appeared in the list and they, two provincial city libraries, only had incomplete files and were not apparently current subscribers. The remaining library subscribers include those institutions containing internationally famous map collections, but others are of less obvious importance as map libraries but their presence on the list mirrors the known interest in the history of cartography by geography departments.

The study of the history of cartography is a field which has developed enormously during this century. The publication of *Imago mundi*, the recent organisation of conferences on the history of cartography, the development of societies devoted to cartography (not exclusively in the historical aspects) all indicate the growing professional interest among geographers, map curators, bibliographers and others. The publication of many manuals on information for collectors of early maps and the growth in the number of dealers specialising in maps, and the good support given to almost any exhibition concerned with or including old maps, shows a similar interest among the population generally. Because of this one imagines there is justification for more library collections, university and public, to provide not only selected publications on cartography but a collection of atlases and maps which will allow the student or interested layman to make his own appreciation, for example, of the style of a famous cartographer.

Collections of early maps furnish the means to study cartography in two broad aspects, history of cartography *per se* and cartography as an adjunct of geographical and historical sciences. An essential element for any study is that extant early maps are located, identified, described and the knowledge of them disseminated; this is the basic task of an early map collection and of cartobibliography. No one with any interest in early maps should fail to read R A Skelton *Maps, a historical survey of their study and collecting* Chicago and London, University of Chicago Press, 1972, and there will be found ten tasks that Skelton suggested were important matters for attention. Skelton's second listed task is the recording of map resources with locations, and he continues to itemise the types of record which seem desirable and some, at least, are well within the professional competence of the map librarian. Once the materials are recorded the scholar can commence study of a variety of aspects of the history of cartography and surveying, and, for printed maps, the specialist bibliographical aspects of map publishing. The study of the history of cartography will involve research on the development of surveying as a technique, of study of projections, of use of meridians, the establishment of the degree of accuracy in early maps, knowledge of the life and work of the surveyors who made them, the draughtsmen who drew them, the progress in the use and style of graphic representation, of conventional signs. The bibliographer will use early printed maps as evidence for part of the history of publishing, the history of printing and the growth of the bookselling trade, whilst to other specialists the maps reveal knowledge on the development of engraving, on calligraphy, and as a minor graphic art. The committed private collector is, of course, equally interested in all these aspects of cartographic history and he forms a significant proportion of the users of early maps in libraries.

The historical geographer, the historian, and others will value the knowledge of what early maps exist and where they are stored, so that they can follow research interest in other appropriate fields. The evidence of a map, manuscript or printed, may confirm suspect evidence in other documents of record, or, because of the cartographer's potential ability even in an early map to show on his plate more information and more effectively than could be described in a written descriptive account, the map may show possible facts which indicate fresh lines of research. A map drawn centuries ago can be used to appreciate the contemporary knowledge of the region displayed, and thus with others, illustrate the development of geographical knowledge, the changing ideas of mankind towards his world and the general conception of that world. A comparative study of early maps gives data on land measurement, place-names, land tenure, settlement, house types, routes, and many other social and economic facts, sometimes from recorded information only incidental to the cartographer's main purpose.

Most of this research is able to proceed because of the existence of the major map collections of the world, and indeed the curators and staffs administering the collections are numbered among the expert, particularly in the studies which are more obviously cartobibliographical. The late R A Skelton, a prolific writer on the history of cartography, was superintendent of the Map Room, now Map Library, British Library. A bibliography of his work compiled by Robert W Karrow, jr is included in the posthumously published *Maps, a historical survey* . . . His work covered many facets of the subject but histories of cartography and of cartographic publishing, guides on the examination of early maps, and bibliographical works, are particularly numerous and of enormous value to the map librarian or curator. Walter W Ristow, Chief of the Geography and Map Division, Library of Congress, and previously Chief of the Map Division, New York Public Library, is equally well known for his writings on cartography, for early and more recent maps with a natural interest on those of America, but not exclusively so, and this writer produces many periodical articles which are often a survey of developments in the field of map librarianship generally and which provide the map librarian or curator with one means of discovering some of the references or events he has previously missed.

The major specialist collections still add to their resources and the more completely representative their collections are, the more scholarship generally and the study of cartography in particular will be stimulated and rewarded. However it should be obvious that the support of smaller map collections, providing a range of maps and atlases which are characteristic examples of the landmarks in the development of cartography, is desirable. An increased number of collections which can produce early maps offer the possibility of some requirements of the student being met locally and this will stimulate the use of early maps generally. In all libraries the provision of books and other materials in depth on a subject, attracts an interested clientele who were not catered for before and who therefore had to forgo their interest or study, or travel to another library which did cater for that interest. An increase in the number of collections of early maps is also beneficial for the major collections because it will have the effect of reducing the use of some copies of maps or atlases. Maps are drawn on a media which has to be carefully preserved, and all handling and use is a step towards their deterioration.

Until recent years it was not often possible for the general library to participate in the acquisition of early atlases or maps, except where there was local or regional interest involved. Donors of major collections would tend to present maps to the national map collections, and the maps appearing for sale were thought too expensive. The attraction of the collector to the buying of maps has now shown however that maps were very cheap in earlier decades. There has been a major change as a result of the growth of facsimile publication, which for maps and atlases is far from new, but it has not made a great impact until comparatively recently because the range of facsimiles was not wide. Now a general library in a public sector has the means to accumulate very good facsimiles of famous early foreign maps and world atlases which, together with original maps in the collection, can offer a conspectus of cartographic history. The university library can have the means to provide examples useful in a course in the history of cartography and many other studies in disciplines where the map can carry useful topical and contemporary information. Skelton (1972), pp 101–102, in reflecting on the pervasiveness of maps because the data depicted on them may be drawn from many subject fields, shows the range of articles about maps which were listed in the bibliography in the first issue of *Imago mundi*. 'Some were published . . . in the journals of geography, history, local history, geodesy and survey, hydrography and,navigation, the history of science. But articles on early maps appeared in many other less obvious quarters—periodicals devoted to physical science, biology, agriculture, magnetism, economics, political science, art history, oriental studies, the classics, archaeology, printing history, bibliography and library science, archives'. Students in all these fields have a right to expect that their occasional use of early maps can, to a reasonable degree, be satisfied by their local map collection.

Acquisition of early and local maps.
Broadly speaking there are three ways in which a map librarian adds fresh material to the holdings of both early maps in general and local maps. These are the purchase, or gift, of original maps; the purchase of facsimile publications, and the purchase, or probably commissioning, of photocopies and for some purposes, slides.

Photocopies of maps are limited in their use, they can only partially satisfy the needs of a cartobibliographer for example, but they do provide guidance as to the content of a map and for some map users this could be sufficient for their purpose. Even when a user cannot be satisfied for a piece of research work until the original map is examined by him, the photocopy both identifies a map which is housed in a distant library and, in detail, shows a research worker whether he need visit that library or not. All that is a bonus for the map user, because the library normally has no alternative to providing a photocopy, except nothing at all, the photocopy usually being obtained for a unique map in which the library has a particular interest. An example of the type of occasion where a photocopy would be useful would be for maps with local interest, stored in the national archives collection, to be made available locally. The map librarian who wishes to create as comprehensive a local, or any other specialist, collection as possible should be aware, basically through the medium of printed catalogues, of the relevant contents of national map libraries, archival collections, etc. There are many maps which could be useful in this way and it would be advisable to set a sum of money aside each year and to systematically build up the collection with the aid of photocopies as finances allow.

For some purposes photocopies are unsatisfactory, they do not show the richness of colours in early maps for example. Many major map collections have colour slides for sale and, particularly for educational purposes and viewing by an audience, these can be most worthwhile. The British Museum prepares slides of maps for sale and issues a catalogue from which the following three examples have been chosen?

K 7144 China, from Fra Mauro's world map, 1459.

K 7006 North Atlantic, from an Italian Portolan atlas of 1508, attributed to Vesconte Maggiolo of Genoa, showing the discoveries of John Cabot.

K 7043 New York as it was in 1661, drawn in 1664 after its capture from the Dutch.

Similarly the Bodleian Library, Oxford, sells mounted slides and film strips of which a particularly fine example is: Roll 136 B, Map of Laxton, 1635, 9 frames showing the unenclosed manor.

Facsimile publications offer a more satisfactory means of gaining an understanding of the facts, style etc concerning an early or local map but the initial selection is here made by the reprint publisher, who will obviously choose to publish maps which are expected to have as wide a sale as possible. The atlases and maps are therefore usually of outstanding importance, not necessarily from a world view but at least from a national viewpoint. Map librarians should not be parochial in their search for worthwhile and varied facsimiles because they are published throughout the world and foreign facsimile publishers will provide a width to the range of possibilities which might include maps which would make better selections for the local library. World atlases in facsimile are well publicised, are often very good and therefore rather expensive, whereas single map facsimiles are less easily observed if they are produced by a foreign publisher.

One of the tasks which needs to be done as suggested by R A Skelton in *Maps: a historical survey of their study and collecting* cited above, is '. . . to prepare an index of published facsimiles'. This remains to be done, even a check-list, regularly brought up-to-date, of facsimile publishers would be helpful and is something a map curator might compile. W W Ristow has prepared a number of editions *Facsimiles of rare historical maps: a list of reproductions by various publishers and distributors* which is published by Library of Congress, but new names appear all the time in advertisements and reviews of new facsimiles in cartographic journals, and some are noted in the published map additions lists of libraries with legal deposit rights, and similar publications. The following brief survey from a British viewpoint is designed merely to show the range of publishers to be considered.

Possibly the greatest facsimile publication programme is that of the firm Theatrum Orbis Terrarum Publishing Co Ltd, Amsterdam, Netherlands. They have published about forty facsimile editions of old and rare atlases, and pilot books, in a continuing series, each being accompanied by an introduction and bibliographical notes written by a major scholar. One publication in the series is Blaeu *Le grand atlas* 12 vols. Most map and atlas facsimiles are made by commercial publishers who often exhibit a national bias in the emphasis of the maps they produce, which is why it is so worthwhile to know the productions of foreign publishers of facsimiles. The Sahab Geographic and Drafting Institute of Tehran, Iran, for example, produce a series of facsimiles of decorative early maps of Iran by European cartographers, including the Englishmen Emanuel Bowen and John Speed. Similarly Cartographia of Budapest have produced reproductions of early maps of Hungary which are in the National Széchényi Library in Budapest.

Bulletin of the Society of University Cartographers 7 (2) March 1973, has a dozen pages of learned reviews of a number of facsimiles of English maps which are among the publications of Harry Margary, Lympne Castle, Kent in conjunction with Phillimore and Co Ltd, Chichester, which are mostly in a series of large scale 18th century maps of English counties being reproduced. Any librarian with little experience of buying facsimiles would find the reviews in this issue of SUC *Bulletin* very illuminating as a guide to the points to be checked when selecting the good facsimile from unsatisfactory work which might be produced by a non-specialist printer. The Harry Margary facsimiles include: Van den Keere *Atlas of the British Isles* c 1605; John Rocque *An exact survey of the City's of London, Westminster ye Borough of Southwark and the country near 10 miles round London* 16 sheets, scale $5\frac{1}{2}''$ to 1 mile. 1746.

John Bartholomew and Son Ltd, Edinburgh, have a series of facsimile maps, with an emphasis on Scotland, but not entirely so, eg: John Ogilby *Jamaica* 1671; Timothy Pont *Lothian and Linlitquo* c 1632. From Mercator's *Atlas* by Henricus Hondius.

David and Charles Ltd, Newton Abbot, Devon have reproduced maps and atlases: E Bowen and Thomas Kitchin *Royal English Atlas*

93

1762, but their major work of reproduction has been the series of the 97 sheets covering England and Wales, each with a bibliographical history of: *First edition of the one inch Ordnance Survey*. The sheets of the Old Series (or first edition) one inch to one mile Ordnance Survey maps are also proposed for publication in 10 bound volumes by Harry Margary.

Other commercial publishers of early map facsimiles in Britain include the following but this cannot be a complete list: George Philip and Son, London; SR Publishers, Wakefield; Brian Stevens, Monmouth [County maps by Thomas Moule]; J M Dent and Sons, Ltd, London; Kelly's Directories, Ltd, Kingston-on-Thames, Surrey; Scotia Maps, Edinburgh; Frank Graham Ltd, Newcastle-upon-Tyne; Osprey Publications Ltd, Reading.

Many British facsimiles are of county maps which are usually decorative, but Brian Stevens of Monmouth has reproduced: G Cole and J Roper *21 plans of English towns*, which were prepared for *British Atlas* 1810. An American firm, Historic Urban Plans of Ithaca, New York has a wonderful collection of reproductions of 'historic city plans and views', some 300 examples from towns throughout the world, eg: J B Homann *St Petersburg* 1718; Nicholas Bellin *New Orleans* 1764. Numerous other publishers of early maps in the USA include Rand McNally and Co Chicago, who have a reproduction of *The Vinland map* and Penn Prints, New York.

The national surveys, official map publishers have also entered the field of early map facsimiles, examples are: Canada. Surveys and Mapping Branch,—reproductions of early maps of Canada, eg J Arrowsmith *British North America* 1834; France. L'Institut Géographique National—cartes anciennes, eg Carte géometrique de la France *Carte de Cassini* 154 sheets. 1798–1812.

Societies, both geographical and local history, and other institutions, appear frequently as publishers of early maps. Local history societies have a limited regional interest but their maps are usually fine productions with good introductions or texts. The Royal Geographical Society was a pioneer publisher of good facsimiles with a production programme covering early manuscript maps, maps of Britain, of counties, and of explorers' maps. The British Library has a number of reproductions of which the Saxton county maps are particularly popular. The Bodleian Library, Oxford University has reproduced one of its treasures *The Gough map* with booklet, and explanatory overlays. University of Exeter published the manuscript maps of Cornwall by John Nordern which had been almost ignored in Trinity College, Cambridge for nearly three centuries. Among societies with local interest, the London Topographical Society has a large selection of plans of London, but more commonly a local society will produce two or three of the more significant maps of the county as Andrews and Drury *Map of Wiltshire* 1775 published by the Wiltshire Archaeological and Natural History Society. In America, John Carter Brown Library has reproduced a number of important maps of America and states.

National map libraries finding sales for maps it is not surprising that local map collections have also gone into the market, perhaps at first in some cases rather tentatively, but it has usually been found that what they have produced of reproductions of maps and plans in their own collection have been sold quicker than the proverbial hot cakes. Two major publishers are archives or record offices, those of the Greater London Council and Essex County Council who have substantial programmes. Greater London Council Archives reproductions includes: Braun and Hogenberg. London, in *Civitates Orbis Terrarum* 1572; Essex Record Office. John Norden, *Essex* 1594.

In recent years however these publishers have been overtaken in output by the maps produced by other local authorities, usually by the public library. Northampton, Birmingham, Hull, Derby and many other public libraries have found this work one which has been welcomed by the citizens and others interested in maps generally. The appetite for reproductions of local maps and local views is there, all map collections should have suitable copies of important local maps to be able to have them facsimile printed and reproduced. A commercial publisher Harry Margary of Lympne Castle, Kent has written a very interesting introductory article on the publishing of facsimiles, Harry Margary, 'The facsimile reproduction of early engraved maps' *Bulletin of the Society of University Cartographers* 7 (2) Mar 1973, 1–7, which any librarian thinking of beginning a publishing programme for the reproduction of maps for sale, should find most helpful.

Purchasing early maps.
Although the facility to buy facsimiles is of great value for map collections and their users, there should be an attempt to own originals in order that the full flavour of an early map can be appreciated in all its detail. According to the available finances a collection with some theme of greater or lesser extent should be aimed at. In public libraries it will at least be to collect copies of all local maps and this should be extended to mean all editions, or issues of local maps. Gifts to university and public library map libraries are usually the superseded copies of modern maps no longer required by a central government or military map library, but other gifts, and of early maps, may be made.

The map collection will only attract gifts of early or local maps if it is a good library, practising good methods of storage and preservation for the maps, exploiting the collection by using the maps for worthwhile displays and occasional public exhibitions, by promoting the sensible use of early maps by the publication of bibliographical lists and catalogues. In a few words, by being a map library which cares, and is seen to care, and where a donor would be pleased to leave his cherished collection or one rare map.

For most libraries, for most of the time, early maps have to be bought. Although occasions will arise for private purchase, buying will usually be from map sellers or specialising dealers. Maps and atlases, both early printed maps and manuscript plans, are sold at auctions of course, although individual maps, such as English county maps, are usually grouped in lots, unless they are individually of substantial value. A map librarian in a general library will follow the library's policy on major auction sales which will usually be to commission an agent to act on behalf of the library. Dealers in maps are basically of two types, the true specialist map dealer and the bookseller who sells maps as well as books, probably being a specialist in topographical works. Almost any bookseller may have a map for sale so a map librarian must be constantly aware of the catalogues of antiquarian booksellers who have a regular interest in maps, and encourage librarian colleagues in other departments to alert the map library if apparently significant maps appear for sale in other, less obvious, catalogues. Only British dealers can be dealt with in this work but the pattern of the trade is expected to be rather similar elsewhere.

Specialist map dealers are comparatively few, but small businesses do appear at regular intervals even if they do not seem to last more than a few years. Specialist map dealers are probably more directly concerned with the collector buyer, but are naturally keen to serve libraries or any buyer. Unfortunately these days libraries are competing for maps which are sometimes priced as a very desirable type of wedding present, not only in competition with the serious personal collector. The following list of booksellers and dealers is in no way exhaustive. 'Maps' signifies a map dealer solely, whilst the booksellers include maps among their books in appropriate catalogues, usually 'British topography'.

Maps: Baynton-Williams Gallery, 70 Old Brompton Road, London, SW7.

Clevedon Fine Arts Ltd, The Gallery, Cinema Buildings, Old Church Road, Clevedon, Avon BS21 6NN.

Francis Edwards Ltd, 83 Marylebone High St, London WIM 4AL—Bookseller, map specialist.

Olwen Caradoc Evans, Perllan Caradoc, Conway, N Wales.

Folio Fine Art Ltd, 6 Stratford Place, London WIN)BH—Maps, rare books and objets d'art.

Mapsellers Ltd, 37 Southampton Street, London WC2E 7HE.

P J Radford, (CA) Sheffield Park, Uckfield, Sussex.

John E Rawnsley, 'Warde Croft', Renton Ave, Guiseley, Leeds.

Regent Gallery, 14 Regent St, Cheltenham.

Weinreb and Douwma Ltd, 93 Great Russell St, London WC1.

Some booksellers: Beeleigh Abbey Books, Beeleigh Abbey, Maldon, Essex.

A J Coombes, 25 Tynedale Road, Strood Green, Betchworth, Surrey, RH3 7JD. Specialist in British topography and local history.

E M Lawson and Co, Kingsholm, East Hagbourne, Berkshire OX11 9LN.

Thomas Thorp, 170 High St, Guildford, Surrey GU1 3HP.

G W Walford, 186 Upper St, London N1 1RH.

Although many map dealers have a long and distinguished history in the trade others seem to appear and disappear quite regularly. It could be a useful duty for any map curator to follow the example of the Map Department in Birmingham Central Public Library where an attempt is made to keep a listing of dealers in early maps, on cards filed in a catalogue drawer.

Chapter references:
BM CAT; DE VRIJ; HARLEY 1963; HARLEY 1968–1; KOEMAN 1961; MARGARY; RISTOW; SKELTON 1970; TATE.

6

Content of the map collection:
local maps

Public libraries have always accepted the responsibility for maintaining a research collection of materials relevant to the study of any aspect of the history of their locality. Historically the urban public libraries have been most prominent in this service but more recently the county libraries developed notable collections. The reorganisation of local government in the United Kingdom has created a great change in the development of Local Studies departments in British libraries by producing new library authorities administering a service for areas which previously were served by a number of library authorities—perhaps a county library and several urban libraries. The Department of Education and Science, Libraries Division *The public library service; reorganisation and after* 1973, (p 11) recommends that 'two considerations—the need of local historians for comprehensive collections, and the need of residents for conveniently accessible local collections—should determine the deployment of local history material within each new authority.' The result might be expected to be a concentration of the materials of local interest which are of research value and of an archival nature, with the dispersal among the many home-reading libraries of the library authority of at least the duplicate copies of the secondary materials.

Maps and plans are related to some part of the earth's surface and because of this they are of value to anyone studying a locality. Maps have therefore always been an important part of any local studies collection and many libraries have acquired over the years large and important collections. The amalgamation of map collections from groups of libraries which in England and Wales were independent prior to 1974 has created many more collections of size and in many cases this will show the necessity, as well as provide the opportunity, for a reappraisal of the policy for the acquisition of maps and the exploitation and preservation of the collection. Although in Britain the study of local history is invariably connected with the specialist department in public libraries and county records offices, both of which include printed and manuscript early maps of a county, region, town, village or estate, these types of maps are also present in lesser degree in university libraries. Early maps are often found to be within the accepted province of the main university library when modern maps are only held in the map collection of the department of geography of the university. Even if one omits the map libraries of Cambridge University Library and of the Bodleian Library at Oxford University, considering them to be more appropriately classified as specialist map libraries, the remaining collections of early maps in British university libraries vary considerably in coverage and importance. In some cases the few early maps available may be of individual value but cannot be said to form a collection which would stimulate their use and provide the means for useful work based upon them. In these cases the maps seem to have been acquired almost accidentally with no sense of a planned development. Elsewhere there are good collections of early maps of Britain and of atlases, one at least owing a great deal to a benefactor, the Harold Whitaker collection at the University of Leeds. Archival collections whether in university libraries, city archives or county record offices have many maps and more particular manuscript plans which have arrived as an integral part of a deposit collection, and are usually concerned with property ownership of land, mines, etc, together with enclosure award maps and tithe maps, and others which were required to be deposited with the clerk of the council, but printed maps in variety are present in significant numbers too. The Lancashire Record Office has an important collection, for example.

Maps in local studies collections are frequently the main source of information for an enquirer but are more frequently an ancillary source of information. For the student of local history, whether a professional historian, a post-graduate research student, or an interested amateur, maps and plans have many possible uses, and may even contain information which, when appreciated by the student, stimulates fresh lines of research. Every librarian or map curator should be aware of the historical information that is displayed in old maps, or can be deduced to be confirmed with the help of other records. There is no better guide than Maurice Beresford *History on the ground* rev ed London, Methuen, 1971 for examples of research over a number of years using maps within several broad categories, typical of the types of maps which should be found in most collections.

As well as the university lecturer making an academic study the same maps may well be used by the ladies of a Women's Institute embarking on the compilation of the record of the history of their village, usually with the guidance of the map curator or local history

99

librarian. The student of the development of road, canal and rail routes finds an enormous amount of material to interest him in ordinary topographical maps as well as those designed to illustrate communications or those legally required for planning approval as in canal building, accompanying bills promoting railways, or tramways. Comment will be made elsewhere on the accuracy of early maps but it should be noted here that railway information on nineteenth century local and regional maps is particularly prone to inaccuracy and so can lead the unwary reader into inaccuracy. Local maps and plans may well provide evidence in disputes of ownership or rights over land. Members of the Ramblers' Association and other interested persons made good use of appropriate maps in tracing and checking rights-of-way which were to be documented under the Town and Country Planning Act and which, when confirmed, are now finding their way on to Ordnance Survey sheets. The individual householder opposing a levy of road charges for the making up of a road may prove his case with the certified copy of an old map in the keeping of his public library. This is an area of use where maps or plans containing information added by their owners before the old map came to the library can be of great, possibly unique, value. The large town plans produced by the Ordnance Survey during the nineteenth century on the scales of 1 : 1056 (five feet to one mile), 1 : 528 (ten feet to one mile) and 1 : 500 were designed for the benefit of municipal authorities and copies exist in libraries which were originally used by other departments of the local authority at a period when the area was growing rapidly and the basis of the modern town was being planned. The nineteenth century planners may have drawn on these sheets their sewage system and street drainage, road improvements etc. An example of this is recorded in KG Bonser and H Nichols *Printed maps and plans of Leeds, 1711–1900* Leeds, The Thoresby Society, 1960.

The information included on any particular map varies but it is in the nature of maps to identify locations as a norm. Old maps are therefore one of the basic sources in the study of the distribution of place names, and, by the changed spelling of place names in different maps and other documents, sometimes reflecting local pronunciation of the past, clues as to the origin of the name may be offered. An examination of the sources used for a county volume of the English Place-name Society, eg Kenneth Cameron *The place-names of Derbyshire* 3v, 1959 soon reveals the importance of local maps both manuscript and printed, and incidentally may introduce the librarian to maps not known to him; see K Cameron 'Maps in the study of place-names' *Bulletin of the Society of University Cartographers* 4 (2) 1970, 1–9. Maps have a regular use in the world of education, from the primary school child to the post-graduate. The post-graduate may require old maps of a town to provide a series of topographical bases for the graphic display of the distribution of data illustrating his geographical or historical thesis.

Many schoolchildren have pored over maps in the department of local studies or archives department in public libraries or record offices since W E Tate, as the young headmaster of a village school in Nottinghamshire introduced his pupils to the enclosure plans of their village. Their work was eventually published by the county historical society; TATE (1931).

The invaluable book by J B Harley *Maps for the local historian, a guide to the British sources* London, National Council of Social Service, 1972, should be available with every collection of local history maps, in Britain. Dr Harley describes, in six major categories, all the types of map likely to be met in such a collection and gives a selective bibliography of the subject up to 1971.

The collection of local historical maps and plans cannot be fully developed by ordinary commercial purchases alone. Buying from map dealers will take place whenever relevant maps become available but unfortunately that is not as frequent as one might wish. County maps and old Ordnance Survey sheets are the types most commonly available from dealers, but for the remainder the map curator has usually to exercise two of the typical virtues of the local history librarian, an awareness of possible sources of useful material and a watchfulness over these sources, together with the exercise of the necessary diplomacy which seeks to ensure that maps or plans about to be dispersed or sold by some institution or from private ownership, are found a safe haven in the library's map collection whether being bought or donated. This means that the map curator must take every opportunity to make known his wish to collect local maps and plans. When it is opportune notes should be written in the local press about the collection and its holdings or even about an individual map which can be of interest because, perhaps, of a connection with contemporary events. The map curator should also give talks to interested groups outside the library. Maps are normally a popular subject, local maps even more so, particularly if the speaker is armed with good slides in addition to whatever original maps can be taken along for examination. If as a result of a talk a member of the audience offers a collection of manuscript estate plans, along with other documents kept in a number of metal trunks in the roof-space of a house, then it will not be the first time it has happened.

In many areas of Britain the curators of map collections are competing for these scarce local maps to build up the resources of a university library, public library, county record office, and with regular forays from the many schools, colleges of education, museums, local history societies and others. The position has been somewhat improved by the amalgamation of public library authorities in metropolitan districts and in counties and it might be hoped that eventually the department of local studies within the public library and the county record office for the same area, might join forces to produce a county local studies centre whose value will be much greater than the sum of their two collections. Such a centre, efficiently administered with a proper care for the preservation of the holdings, might also prove an attraction for a greater number of gifts and bequests of series and collections of maps from institutions and private individuals. It is still not unknown for useful collections to be thrown away because the owner, or the responsible person, was unaware of the need to preserve local studies materials, an example being the disposal of large scale plans relevant to tramways after the tramway system was discontinued.

Although many of the local early maps which are acquired will be unknown to the map librarian until they fortuitously present themselves, an essential process in establishing a comprehensive collection of local maps is to make a search in the many cartographical publications, in order to compile a skeletal carto-bibliography. The area or region for which the library intends to collect maps comprehensively should be defined. In the case of the public library, this will be the same area established for all materials by the department of local studies and will often cover a whole county. In a county record office there will be a similar county interest although maps and plans directly relevant to other areas may be found there as they form part of an archival group which should not be broken up. Other libraries should seek to establish a definition of their area of interest rather than haphazardly collect items which seem relevant at the time they become available. These latter libraries should also establish a policy concerned with the types of map to be collected because, unlike the public library's department of local studies, they have no self-imposed obligation to seek comprehensiveness, and should therefore give consideration to their known and potential requirements for local maps. From this it may be found that only a few maps are required in some categories as examples, perhaps for teaching purposes, whilst for other categories the need is to be as comprehensive as possible in order to satisfy the varied and detailed demands of a known research programme.

The compilation of the skeletal cartobibliography can be most easily commenced by concentrating first on county maps. For some counties a published bibliography of county maps is available and will be a useful guide to the local map librarian. Fine examples of county map bibliographies are P D A Harvey and Harry Thorpe *The printed maps of Warwickshire, 1576–1900* Warwick, Warwickshire County Council 1959, and D Hodson *The printed maps of Hertfordshire 1577–1900* published 1969–1972 in *Map collectors' circle* publications numbers 53, 59, 65, 75, 83. These works offer a remarkable amount of information about the maps they include, particularly on publication history, and even a cursory examination of them is sufficient to show how complex this might be. Other county map bibliographies are published, some being highly selective and probably published in the transactions of the regional historical society, whilst others attempt to be comprehensive but might be less complete in detail and less accurate than the works cited above, usually because they are earlier pioneering works. Any published bibliography of the maps of the county should be available in the department of local studies in the public library but, if necessary, a check for a county cartobibliography can be made in the text of J B Harley *Maps for the local historian* . . . 1972, and in the 'Bibliographical postscript' section of the same work. An older shorter compilation, which however appears to include some entries for items listing county maps which are not in Harley, is J West 'Printed editions of county maps' pp 70–72 in his *Village records* London, MacMillan, 1962.

It will be found that county maps were often published with similar maps of other counties, produced by the same cartographer or publisher to form an atlas volume. Copies of these atlases still exist but many have been broken down and the individual map plates dispersed. Guides to these atlases of county maps are available in: T Chubb *The printed maps in the atlases of Great Britain and Ireland, 1579–1870* reprint ed, London, Dawsons, 1966, and; R A Skelton *County atlases of the British Isles, 1579–1850* vol 1 (1579–1703) London, Carta Press, 1970.

Skelton's work was first published in five parts, each a publication of the Map Collectors' Circle, between 1964 and 1970. With the aid of these bibliographies, which are described in the chapter 'Cataloguing: early and local maps', it is possible to compile the nucleus of a basic checklist of the maps covering one county by identifying them from the details of maps provided in each entry in the cartobibliography. But other county maps were truly individual sheets and never appeared within the covers of an atlas. There is no comparable general bibliography of the county maps published individually but other works can be helpful, notably: British Museum *Catalogue of printed maps, charts and plans* 15v London, British Museum. 1967.

E M Rodger *The large scale county maps of the British Isles, 1596–1850—a union list* 2nd ed Oxford, Bodleian Library 1972, is a much smaller but specialised checklist of these important maps, mostly of the latter half of the eighteenth century, based on original surveys, using scales greater than 1″ to 3 miles and mostly of 1″ to 1 mile scale. These works are an important aspect of English cartography prior to the national survey and two works by J B Harley are illustrative 'The Society of Arts and the survey of English counties' *J of Royal Society of Arts* 112 (1963) and 'The re-mapping of England 1750–1800' *Imago mundi* 19 (1965), 56–67.

Town maps and plans are less well catered for by bibliographies than other types of map, but a first check can be made in the British Museum *Catalogue . . .* (1967). The maps are listed by direct entry under the names of counties, towns, parishes, making it necessary to check under every possible place name in the area of interest to ensure that nothing is missed. Naturally local libraries normally will form the largest repository of local town plans and most gaps in the holdings of plans will probably not be identified readily within any other library. Bonser and Nichols *Printed maps and plans of Leeds . . .* will provide examples of the range of maps that can be expected to exist for an English city or town, whilst the rather special case of London has a cartobibliography complete in two works: I Darlington and J L Howgego *Printed maps of London, circa 1553–1850* London, G Philip, 1964, and Ralph Hyde *Printed maps of Victorian London, 1851–1900* Folkestone, Wm Dawson and Sons, 1975.

Since the first half of the nineteenth century the sheets of the Ordnance Survey covering the area are the backbone of the map collection for local studies, and this, of course, applies to the villages and countryside as well as urban areas. Too often the Ordnance Survey element of a local maps collection has 'just growed' over the years of this last century, by the addition of sheets which were bought when they were current, and earlier sheets that have been presented by a national government or local authority department which was clearing out of date or duplicate material, and a hodge-podge of single sheets presented or purchased from individuals. The sheets in the latter category, probably having begun life in the ownership of a victorian rambler, are often dissected, mounted and folded, and because of this format often seem to cause the librarian embarrassment in how to file them. The map curator has useful assistance in identifying at least the outline of his potential collection of old Ordnance Survey sheets. The guide in this field is: J B Harley and C W Phillips *The historian's guide to Ordnance Survey maps* London, National Council of Social Service, 1964. Reprinted from articles in *The amateur historian* [now *Local historian*] from 1962 to 1963, it offers a wealth of information on the OS series in the various scales, including sheet index diagrams for the old series of one inch, six inch and twenty five inch maps for England, Wales and Scotland, together with similar diagrams for town plans on the obsolete scales of 1 : 500, 1 : 528 and 1 : 1056. In this work Professor Harley cites further sources which would be used for the detailed study of local sheets, in particular *Catalogue of the six inch and twenty five inch county maps and town plans of England and Wales and Isle of Man of the Ordnance Survey of the United Kingdom*, 1914 and the equivalent catalogue for Scotland.

Old Ordnance Survey sheets do appear in second-hand booksellers' catalogues and are frequently available for sale from small private libraries but the map curator would be well advised to obtain the sheets required systematically as photocopies from the British Library, Map Library, or some other holding library. The great value of the Ordnance Survey map for historians is in the information provided by the cartographers, even the first edition one inch sheets give a dimension of topographic detail which is vastly superior to the general run of earlier county maps, although in certain cases individual county maps may include a distribution of particular data which does not appear on OS sheets. Only in exceptional cases of advanced study in cartographic history will the reader find it essential to consult the original published sheet, for all other purposes of local studies the photocopy is adequate. It will be replaced by an original copy if one appears on the market. The photocopy is not quite as satisfactory for county maps, town plans by early land surveyors and most manuscript plans. Although of course it is highly desirable that a photocopy is available of, say, an eighteenth century plan of a village and surrounding closes, rather than nothing at all, the loss of quality and of the colour and the absence of something intangible about the texture of the original is a matter of regret. In some cases, where an original is a little damaged, or deteriorated, or where the parchment or vellum original will not properly flatten, it is very difficult to get a good copy and a great deal of detail can be lost. Nevertheless the copy is a most welcome substitute if the original cannot be obtained.

There are other categories of old maps where a photocopy is a most adequate substitute, although often the maps or plans are accompanied by an associated text which might also be photocopied or microfilmed. This group is all the great variety of plans prepared by the promoters of parliamentary bills for public projects such as railways, tramways; plans presented to local authorities in connection with what the victorians named town improvements; estate plans prepared for the sale of landed property, and many more. A few of these for any particular area may be traced in British Museum *Catalogue* . . . but the vast majority are not listed there and most will only be acquired over the years by the continuous watchfulness of the map curator. For these printed maps reprography offers the opportunity to make copies wherever maps are traced and therefore a map curator seeking to improve his local collection should make searches for maps and plans in those libraries which have maps of possible local relevance. National archives for transport maps are an obvious possibility but museums, public libraries, local historical societies, registries of deeds, local authority departments, churches, etc may all contribute to the total. Others, published to accompany reports, to contain statistical information, etc, may show land or townships in the process of change and illustrate more effectively than the text the distribution of the data contained in the report, but because they are contained within a volume they are concealed and it is not always easy to trace them. In the second half of the nineteenth century for example it was common practice in Great Britain for the local medical officer of health to include maps in his annual report to his local board of health provided by the powers contained in the first Public Health Act, 1848. These maps commonly showed the distribution of cases of notifiable diseases, and deaths, in the locality and are a reminder of the importance of medical geography and the pioneering work of Robert Baker *Cholera plan of Leeds* contained in the 1833 Report of the Leeds Board of Health, a voluntary body.

Alexander McGechaen and Coolie Verner *Maps in the parliamentary papers by the Arrowsmiths* (Map Collectors' Circle Publications. Nos 88, 89) London, Map Collectors' Circle, 1973, provides a fine example of using another source which will be very fruitful for many localities in Britain and the whole of the Commonwealth. They observe in the introduction to these publications that 'The nineteenth century . . . illustrated government reports'. Their own research concerns the cartographic work of the members of the Arrowsmith family between 1790 and 1873 and they identify the maps prepared for and included in parliamentary papers by searching the British *Sessional papers*. The same task could be undertaken hopefully to produce a listing of maps concerned with a locality or region, or a category of map. Using the bibliography made by McGechaen and Verner it can be seen that the series of Parliamentary Papers includes: A *Chart of the Boyne River* . . . 1834; a plan of *The District of Adelaide South Australia; As divided into County Sections, from the Trigonometrical Surveys of Colonel Light, Late Survr. Genl* . . . 1839; *Plan of the Town of Auckland in the Island of New Ulster or Northern Island of New Zealand by Felton Mathew* . . . 1841 *Map of Part of the Valley of Red River North of the 49th parallel to accompany a report on the*

Canadian Red River Exploring Expedition by H Y Hind.

Although the Arrowsmiths may have been among the most prolific parliamentary paper cartographers during this period, some idea of the amount of cartographic material concealed within the series of *Sessional papers* can be assumed from the listing of 462 Arrowsmith items alone.

Every possible guide should be used and no published library catalogue left unexamined, sometimes unexpected sources produce results. British Museum (Natural History) *Catalogue of the books, manuscripts, maps and drawings in the British Museum (Natural History)* 8 vols Trustees of the British Museum, 1903–1940. Reprinted Codicote, Herts, Wheldon and Wesley Ltd, and Verlag J Cramer, 1964, includes the following for example: *Map shewing route of exploring party under command of Col P E Warburton from the centre of the continent to Roebourne, Western Australia etc* [Scale 1″ = 17.1/4m. about] 2 sh Adelaide, 1874, and *Kenya-Tanganyika Territory boundary:—Anglo-German boundary survey* 1903–4. Motor roads in red and other detail by C H B Grant etc Scale 1 : 300,000.

Conducting a search by these methods will soon bring to light copies of maps or plans in other institutions which will be found to be manuscripts. These are probably unique although not necessarily so because many land surveyors made more than one manuscript copy of a plan, if only a rough draft and a finished plan taken from the draft. The Fairbank Collection in the Department of Archives and Local History at Sheffield City Library includes 4650 plans which were the property of a firm of surveyors active from 1739 to 1850. Some of these plans are mirrored in plans held elsewhere, plans which were originally in the possession of the clients for whom the surveys were made.

In any one area the largest collection of manuscript plans will be in the county or city record office, although there may be substantial numbers elsewhere as in the department of manuscripts of a university library. There is no good reason why the map librarian in the public library should undertake a programme of copying the maps in the local record office, but there are excellent reasons why the record office and the local history department of the public library should amalgamate. This consideration should not however prevent the map librarian obtaining photocopies of selected plans in the record office which would be used frequently in the map library as well as copies of manuscript maps found elsewhere, if permission can be obtained to have them copied. The first step in this direction might be taken by examining: Public Record Office *Maps and plans in the Public Record Office 1. British Isles, c 1410–1860* London, PRO, 1967. In this catalogue maps are entered under the parish or town, and the parishes etc are arranged alphabetically within their counties. The counties are grouped regionally, eg The Midlands. Many more maps are preserved in the Public Record Office than are listed in the British Isles volume and a map curator elsewhere may find it useful to trace maps referring to areas outside the British Isles. Similar catalogues exist of course in other countries, US National Archives *Guide to cartographic records in the National Archives* Washington, Government Printing Office, 1971 being one published example.

Other sources of manuscript plans of a local area abound, in private hands, in solicitors' office archives, in long-established surveying firms, at the National Coal Board, river boards, British Waterways Board, diocesan registry offices, etc. J B Harley's *Maps for the local historian . . .* provides information on the types of manuscript map which are met in any British region. Where there is an obvious source for copies of a particular category of map, such as tithe plans which are to be found in the Public Record Office where the Tithe Commissioners copies were deposited, then Harley will state this and his very extensive literature guide will mention any descriptive lists. Other possible aids are the catalogues of major map exhibitions where the maps displayed have been lent by a number of owners, the variety offering clues as to the possible source of maps within any comparable area. Two examples of published exhibition catalogues of this type are Royal Institution of Chartered Surveyors (Surrey Branch) *The story of Surrey in maps, catalogue of an exhibition* Esher, RICS, 1956; and RICS (Yorkshire Branch) and Leeds City Libraries *Surveyors and map makers; catalogue of an exhibition* Leeds, Leeds City Libraries, 1955.

The county or city archivist is equally desirous of locating local manuscript plans not represented in the record office, primarily to seek the deposit of the plans but also to record their interest. The map curator, having the same aims should cooperate fully with the archivist and with the local studies librarian, and the combined knowledge, experience and personal contacts of each will build up a picture of the majority of the possible sources that can be expected to be fruitful. Which repository can claim the deposit of an original manuscript, or indeed printed plan, depends largely on who saw it first and emphasises the need for some amalgamation of effort in most authority areas. The archivist, at least, will be aware that the National Register of Archives retains a file of reports locating documents, including maps and plans, reported to the NRA by individual record offices. A local record office should receive copies of the reports or documents which are in one record office but have topographical relevance to another city archival or local record office.

F Hull *ed Catalogue of estate maps, 1590–1840, in the Kent County Archives*

Office Maidstone, Kent County Council 1973, includes an appendix of some seventy two maps which depict estates in fourteen counties outside Kent. This catalogue also provides an example of the disappointment that a map curator may sometimes experience when having succeeded in tracing a local map. John Garfield *Croxall Manor 1687* is a map of a Derbyshire estate which on enquiry is discovered to be in a deteriorated condition not suitable for photocopying.

It must not be overlooked that archival collections are not the prerogative of county record offices, they are also to be found for cities. The Greater London Record Office can offer the seeker of Derbyshire maps *A Description of the Mannor of Tibshelfe . . . Taken in May 1628* by A Bowen, because the manor once belonged to St Thomas's Hospital whose archives have been deposited with the Greater London Record Office. There are other types of archival collections of course, such as those of Oxford and Cambridge colleges, which have owned land in various parts of the country. There are also collections in a wide range of major libraries, the Bodleian Library, Oxford; Lambeth Palace, London; Chetham's Library, Manchester which for Derbyshire can contribute *A Survey of the Mannor of Sutton on the Hill . . . 1671*. Many of these collections have to be checked at the library or record office but in some cases the record office has produced a catalogue or a handlist which may include out-county materials. Similarly holdings of some manuscript maps and plans in the British Library, Reference Division are in the Department of Manuscripts, not all are in the Map Library. There are many, for example, which came to the library as parts of private collections of documents, and some are bound in volumes along with other documents in the same collection. A Derbyshire example in such a volume is *A survey of a sheepwalk on Darley Moor . . . [c 1700]*, BM Add Mss 6687, ff 162-3. Some catalogues are printed for the earliest collection: *Catalogue of the manuscript maps, charts and plans, and of the topographical drawings in the British Museum* 3v 1844–[1861] Reprinted, 3v London, British Museum, 1962–3. This catalogue includes maps and plans held in all departments at that date. Guidance on the various catalogues of the Department of Manuscripts is provided in: British Museum *The catalogues of the manuscript collections in the British Museum* London, Trustees of the British Museum 1962 Revised ed, and T C Skeat 'The catalogues of the manuscript collections in the British Museum' *Journal of documentation* 7 (1951), 18–60.

In the Map Library of the British Library, Reference Division there is an *Extract from the indexes to the Catalogues of additions to the manuscripts in the British Museum* which attempts to cover manuscript maps added from 1845 to 1935. This however, as indicated in the title, is compiled from the 'indexes' and not from the actual materials added, and the indexes in the Department of Manuscripts should be searched for all periods to complete a fully comprehensive checking as required for the period, and after 1935, by using the Department of Manuscripts' *Handlists of additional MSS*. Often it may be thought necessary to examine the collections themselves to appreciate fully the coverage of entries such as 'Maps and plans of estates in England and Ireland, 17–19th century. Eg 3021 A-BB', or 'Miscellaneous estate plans etc, 17th–19th cent, 43737 A-EE'.

To undertake a programme to compile a comprehensive list of all the maps or plans that can be traced which are relevant to the locality, requires a great deal of time and some money, but it is an eminently useful exercise for the appropriate library and important for the users and students of maps of that locality. It should be done by all public library authorities, the 107 in England, for example, each accepting responsibility for collecting the materials of research for the study of their area which will be basically either a metropolitan district, a non-metropolitan county or a London borough. Other libraries will only collect such materials selectively according to their estimated and their potential requirements. If the public library has traced the material comprehensively, and has, or is in the process of making, copies of the plans that cannot be obtained, then that library can act as a guide to the other libraries in this particular class of maps. There would also be obvious value in developing the skeletal cartobibliography, as suggested earlier in this chapter, into a full bibliography for publication. It can be justifiably spoken of as a bibliography because the material included will be all that can be traced using a variety of collections, but it should be in the form of a union catalogue incorporating the location of the maps even if the compiling library has photographic copies of each map or plan. A regional bibliography whilst of outstanding importance to the student of the region has also national importance and contributes significantly to the history of cartography in general. If confirmation of the value of this work is needed one need look no further than the writings of R A SKELTON (1972) who suggested a number of tasks for cartographic historians, and on p 105 described one task as 'the recording of map resources, with locations' one division of this being compiling a 'union catalogue or checklist of maps or atlases of a particular type held in a country or region'. And this, for maps of a region, is a task quite suitable for the attention of the curator of a collection of local maps in a general public library. The librarian or curator in a general library does not have the wealth of facilities and cartographic resources to undertake research in many fields compared with the curator and cartographic historian in the great specialist map libraries, but this field is mainly his own and waiting to be cultivated.

The heights to which one can aspire are probably best represented by the fine work by James Clements Wheat and Christian F Brun *Maps and charts published in America before 1800, a bibliography* New Haven and London, Yale UP, 1969. 915 maps are enumerated with many descriptions noting the rather tortuous story of the various states of printing in which copies are now found, a story presented with a clarity which belies the hard work which must have taken place to achieve this knowledge. Harold Nichols *Local maps of Derbyshire to 1770, an inventory and introduction* Unpublished thesis, Leicester University, 1973, includes a bibliography of all Derbyshire maps, covering areas smaller than the whole county, most being manuscript, up to the period of the first large-scale printed county map by Burdett, newly surveyed in 1767. The inventory contains notes on 429 maps and records their location in libraries, archives and private hands. This is the type of bibliography which ought to be prepared for all regions.

Chapter references:
BERESFORD; BM CAT-MSS; BM MSS; BM NAT-HIST; BONSER; CAMERON; CHUBB; DARLINGTON/HOWGEGO; DES; HARLEY 1965; HARLEY 1972; HARLEY/PHILLIPS; HARVEY/THORPE; HODSON; HULL; HYDE; McGE-CHAEN/VERNER; PRO; RICS 1955; RICS 1956; RODGER; SKEAT; SKELTON 1970; SKELTON 1972; TATE; US-NAT. ARCH.; WEST; WHEAT/BRUN.

7

Storage

Tradition suggests that librarians through the ages have rather shunned maps because of their physical format, a format which in recent times has led to maps being included in the general term 'non-book materials'. Maps have however an antiquity not shared by the modern audio-visual materials and should be considered as a species of document which, because of the number which exist and their variety, demands its own requirements for handling, storage and preservation. Depending on the number in a collection, librarians have often turned them as near as possible into codex form, by cutting or more usually folding so that they will fit standard boxes for shelving or by mounting and folding particular large ones so that they will fit a slip case, a leather bound slip case fashioned to look like a book as it stands on the shelf. Others, perhaps more decorative, have been framed for hanging as pictures, a natural method of treating a map which is in almost permanent use, or mounted on rollers for wall hanging. The bulk were probably always kept in rolled form tied with tape.

Only in recent times has special storage furniture been available for maps, firstly in large drawers in cabinets and later this century in a variety of vertical filing systems. Librarians owe the multiplicity of manufactured containers for maps largely to the much bigger market for drawing office draughtsmens' files, and architects' and planners' plan files, and the map curator has to consider the storage of his maps in relation to the availability of equipment primarily designed for these allied plans and drawings, rather than with the earlier inhibiting effect of book storage methods. With this freedom to consider storage equipment designed for maps and plans the map curator must not however forget that the maps she has to file are far more varied in age, format, purpose and use than materials which are in engineers' drawing offices for example. The book librarian (in a well founded general library) does not merely use shelves for storing books but, because of the similarly wide variety of book materials, he uses shelves of

112

different sizes, some designed for horizontal storage, some glazed and locked, and some in strong rooms, whilst the books themselves are bound or bound and slip-cased, or unbound and boxed with others, etc. There is no one correct way of filing books in a large library and there is no one correct way of storing all the maps in a large map collection.

This truth is not always obvious when seeing the storage furniture in a map collection. Not many libraries have had the opportunity of completely equipping an established collection with planned furniture and so storage has been added when the stock has grown. This usually provides diversity in the storage equipment available but it is a diversity owing more to the availability of makers' equipment at the time of purchase than planning for a particular type of map. On the other hand, some map collections rehoused in a new building exhibit a uniformity of storage which seems to be the result of architectural requirements rather than the needs of different sets of maps. Of course, it is desirable to achieve an acceptable visual appeal with the equipment used, the maps when filed are not visible like books, so the appearance of a map room is largely that of the map containers. However, one feels that in newly housed collections just as a book librarian would estimate the amount of shelving needed for octavo, quarto, folio sized volumes, for fine and rare books needing special protection etc, the map curator should make similar estimates to define the quantity or type of storage needed for different purposes. To a great extent, in Great Britain at least, general libraries do not appear to have fully appreciated this necessity because the collections are usually quite small, and largely consist of maps in series. As the collections grow, as indeed they will and should, the development will mean the much greater introduction of maps in single or very few sheets, and of parts only of official surveys etc from all over the world, and this must mean a wider variety of size, frequency of use etc, and a greater attention to the early map. The use of the term map collection here should be understood to mean all the maps in a library, these however will not necessarily be brought together in one 'map department', in some cases it might be thought more appropriate to disperse them according to use. In a public library early maps of the locality are probably better filed in the local studies department, and modern geological maps stored perhaps in the science department.

But wherever the collection, whether the maps are collected together for economy in storage or dispersed according to their use in various departments, the equipment used and the method of storage should reflect the storage requirements involved. There are of

113

course differing opinions amongst map curators about the virtues or otherwise of different types of storage but some fundamental qualities or requirements can be isolated, differences of opinion tend to relate to the equipment made by different manufacturers for a particular purpose. The least difficult type of map to store is that which is ephemeral, or rather will be treated as such in a library, remembering that some maps of an ephemeral nature will be permanently preserved in a local studies department because they concern the locality. Ephemeral maps are usually those which a library only expects to keep for a very short time and then be replaced, and for which the minimum of indexing is done, if any. Typically they would be a file of town plans from all over the world, some bought and usually of the folded to pocket-size type, many acquired freely from tourist offices, extracted from town guides, presented by commercial concerns. Currently they are a feature of the public reference library rather than of a university library since they have little or no value to the study of geography, but if provided in a university main library they could be as well used as in the public library. The keynote of their use is that of public awareness of their availability by ready access to them. Ready access is obviously possible because they are expected to be replaced in a short period of time, some annually. They are of very different formats, some substantial folders, others small single sheets unfolded, and so filing must allow space for this lack of uniformity. They are commonly kept in ordinary steel cabinets designed for office letter filing where a number of suspended folders, supported by rods on either side of the deep drawer, can hold a number of such sheets each and the folders have projecting guide labels at the top. These files offer no support for the map, merely a means of protecting them from dust etc when the drawers are closed and a means of guiding their arrangement. Any flimsy sheet of paper should be put into an ordinary large envelope to prevent it being torn by the handling of other maps kept in the same folder. Similarly, lateral filing cabinets might be used containing either suspended lateral pockets or filing containers. Tabs on the front edge of the files provide a means of guiding to the contents of the files, and projecting labels are available for pockets. Cabinets of this nature are usually 18″ deep but as with the filing cabinets previously mentioned larger sizes are available if required, although this would not be normal for maps of the type suggested. Large lateral files which have a 1″ capacity are available from one manufacturer and these are suspended in cabinets up to 36″ deep, or for an A1 sheet size a rail height of 37″ combined with cabinet depth of 30″.

Some collections of town plans are made accessible to the reader by filing them in open racks as in a map shop, the cover title facing the reader. This does not however protect them from dust and this can make them unpleasant to handle, racking being difficult to have cleaned properly as a daily chore, but mainly it implies that only the substantial folder type of plan is available; small single sheet plans could not be accommodated in this way. It does not seem desirable to have to limit the collection to a certain type of format because the storage equipment demands it, some interesting and useful plans would be lost.

Folded town plans with paper covers and motoring maps of similar format, usually have a title, and sheet number if in a series, on the 'spine' of the cover. This allows such maps to be filed on prepared book shelves with the 'spine' projecting to the front of the shelf so it can be read. This of course gives reader accessibility and is useful where appropriate, usually in the lending department of a public library or college library for motoring and walking maps, and in a university geography department for walking maps probably used in field studies but they will be used by students for any walking needs. In public libraries where these maps are very well used the sheets are commonly prepared by a library binding firm and they have been specially mounted on a substantial base material and the publishers paper cover replaced by a board cover. To file these folders on ordinary library shelving would give them no support and the shelving is prepared possibly by the addition of many partitions so that the 'pigeon holes' created hold a few copies and preserve the arrangement in a tidy manner. Cut-away library file boxes might also be used, with the opening facing the user, and these would allow the map file to be easily removed to other shelving if this was required at a later date.

Where, with material which is not to be preserved indefinitely, accessibility and the preservation of an acceptable arrangement are the main qualities to be considered, there are no doubt many possibilities for filing maps according to the needs and the geography of a library. Such maps, folded, might be interfiled with appropriate books, particularly in a lending library. The maps, in a cut-away box container, possibly colour coded for a country, being adjacent to guide books, gazetteers, camping directories etc of that country, in the travel section of the library.

Arrangement according to storage needs
Much more thought must be given to the storage system used when the map has to be preserved in good condition for use over many years or even permanently, some maps being added as current sheets, others many years old. The storage system must not only provide a means of ready access to an individual sheet among the thousands in

stock, and provide a means of guiding so that a planned arrangement can be followed, but also assist in the physical preservation of the sheet. The medium on which the map is printed or drawn is usually paper, although on early manuscript maps it is commonly vellum or parchment. The paper for a modern map may be new and strong but an early map added to the collection may have paper which has become fragile through age, mishandling or inadequate storage. Storage equipment itself may be insufficient protection for the full protection of certain sheets and other methods have to be used in addition, but this would only be for selected maps or sets of maps. It would be quite unnecessary, as well as uneconomical, to treat an Ordnance Survey 1:10,000 sheet covering an English village in the same way as a contemporary manuscript plan of the same village as a manorial estate in the 16th century. If such maps are not kept in different departments but housed in a centralised map collection then any basic arrangement or classification used should have a pre-arrangement which would put the elizabethan plan in a category requiring particular arrangements for preservation. Even among modern maps it would seem advisable to have a pre-arrangement sizing as in a book library of size. Map collections, so often ignoring individual maps, and thinking small to boot, have not done this. This has led to the development of interior fittings in large cabinets to accommodate small sheet series in large plan cabinets. As the library map collection increases, particularly with maps of one or few sheets, this could lead to a great wasting of space if one sequence of classification or other arrangement was maintained. This is a matter for thought by each individual library but it seems a very appropriate action for a general map collection as opposed to one which is primarily geographical. The development of manufacturers' fittings for accommodating small size maps in large files would still be useful in order to fit the library with one manufacturer's type of equipment if this was thought desirable, but the sizes for storage would be in blocks which would greatly help house keeping and it could lead to the buying of different sizes of the same range of storage equipment.

Horizontal filing
Elizabeth M Nokes, in 'The provisions for the storage of maps in libraries' submitted for the degree of MA, Loughborough University 1970, unpublished thesis, Loughborough University of Technology 1970, has provided an extensive comparison of the value of different storage methods and equipment and I am indebted to the work of Miss Nokes in this chapter, particularly the section on horizontal storage. Miss. Nokes writes 'The ideal of storage is to preserve the face

of the map and eliminate factors tending to cause strain, fracture and decay'.

There are many manufacturers of map storage furniture, and a list is given at the end of this chapter of manufacturers or agents who market map storage equipment in Great Britain. This is only for guidance and to explain details of equipment described. Anyone wishing to buy equipment should realise not only that other manufacturers exist and come into existence, but that mergers of commercial firms create newly named firms which may however be still supplying a type of equipment previously sold by a constituency firm. In checking directories for the name and addresses of manufacturers, the term 'Drawing office equipment manufacturer' or 'supplier' will probably be the most fruitful.

The earliest type of special storage equipment used by map librarians was map cabinets for filing sheet maps flat in large drawers, and this probably remains the best method of storage for preservation as long as good equipment is used. However horizontal filing creates problems in handling the sheets which means that if the maps are in regular use they can suffer more from handling than in other methods of filing. Map curators introduce other equipment or stationery to be used within drawers to obviate the possibility of damage caused by withdrawing or inserting a sheet into the file.

Horizontal map cabinets are made of either metal or wood and there are advantages in both materials. Many librarians prefer the appearance of wood although this might be because of the dull colouring normally associated with metal furniture rather than the appearance of the woods commonly used, and this is no longer always true. Also, librarians along with others tend to forget that wood needs to be cleaned at intervals, not just regularly dusted and polished. Wood furniture in public places does not develop a patina, it becomes filthy. A major advantage of wood cabinets is that they can be tailor-made to fit spaces in a particular library and incorporate reasonable adaptations required by the local map librarian. This tends to appeal to architects who can have, for example, melamine surface on the working top of a cabinet which is uniform with similar surfaces on reading tables. Wood, however, needs greater care in maintenance and careful use, dryness and large temperature changes can make drawers stick or warp. Wood drawers have to be bigger than is required, usually 3" deep, in order to obtain the necessary strength over quite a large area. Such a drawer depth is much too big to fill with maps, they could not be effectively or carefully handled and the drawer would be too heavy. The drawer should not be more than two thirds filled and this large number of sheets further divided by the introduction of folders. Wood

117

drawers seem to require a slightly larger clearance which increases with age between drawer and carcase than metal cabinets and so there is a greater avenue for dust to enter the cabinet.

Metal cabinets can be expected to keep in better condition than wood for a longer period, although attention to maintenance is required. They are much lighter in construction yet the material is stronger, so drawers can be made much shallower than wooden ones. This implies a more economical use of the volume occupied by the cabinet. Light metal can however become out of true if pressures are applied unevenly to it. A drawer full of maps, fully withdrawn and not properly supported could be twisted. The cabinet itself could be put out of true if it were lifted and moved without fully emptying it.

Royal Geographical Society *The storage and conservation of maps* 1955, a report of a committee of the society, states, on page 3, that metal cabinets have every advantage. 'They will withstand harder and longer wear, the drawers are less likely to jam and to require force to open and shut, with consequent damage to the maps . . . they are free from the risk of dry rot or worm, and reduce the risk of fire. The only advantage of wooden cabinets is their cost . . .' A British Standards Institute, Draft standard on *Storage of documents* 1969 recommends the use of metal cabinets.

In selecting horizontal filing cabinets certain precautions must be observed; perhaps the main one being, and this applies equally to vertical filing cabinets, that the inside measurements are adequate for the sizes of maps to be filed. It must be remembered that paper sizes have changed and filing cabinets, not necessarily designed primarily for maps, have changed to accommodate the metric sizes. Often the size known as antiquarian can be considered the equal of the DIN A0 size, but with the various manufacturers what this means can differ. RGS REPORT states, 'Standard sizes of drawers are double-elephant (approx 43×31 inches) and antiquarian (54×32 inches). One manufacturer offers an antiquarian size at $48\frac{3}{4}'' \times 34\frac{1}{2}''$. The actual DIN paper size, A0, A1, A2, A3, when used to identify the measurements of a file should be ignored and the actual inside measurements of the filing space or the maximum size of map which can be stored in the space should be noted. It has been suggested that maps should be $2\frac{1}{2}''$ less than the inside drawer measurements to allow for ease and care in removal, and this should be taken into account.

Maximum sheet sizes to be filed in cabinets built by one manufacturer are given as follows:

A0	$53 \times 36\frac{1}{4}$ ins	1345×920 mm
A1	$25\frac{1}{4} \times 36\frac{1}{4}$ ins	640×920 mm
A2	$25\frac{1}{4} \times 20$ ins	640×460 mm

For the A0 size other manufacturers quote maximum sheet sizes down to 1220 mm and down to 800 mm.

The importance of adequate drawer, or vertical file sizes, has recently been dramatically brought to the attention of many librarians who have bought the new Ordnance Survey map, Scale 1:50,000 published only for the southern half of Britain, and found it to be of a new size different from anything they previously filed, with dimensions approaching a square shape. One firm has produced a new size for their horizontal filing cabinet of 41" × 36" to allow for the map size of 88 × 100 cm.

Drawers should not be more than two inches deep, (RGS Report suggests $2\frac{1}{2}$" max) inside measurement, although drawers up to three inches deep are available. At the larger depth the drawer should not be filled as it provides too many unmounted sheet maps to handle conveniently. A one inch or 1 5/6" deep drawer or partially filled two inch drawer is probably the best to use, but it depends on the type of map being stored. Even in shallow drawers with the reduced number of sheets there is a considerable amount of weight, and therefore of friction when maps are withdrawn. If maps are to be filed permanently this must be reduced and it can be done by breaking up the mass in the drawer by the use of thin card folders. The appropriate folder will be fully drawn from the drawer in order to select and remove the required map, a method of handling which leaves the remaining maps in the drawer untouched and greatly reduces the handling even of sheets adjacent to the one required. It might be considered acceptable with the use of folders to have deeper drawers, but one must also consider the weight of the drawer contents, particularly if it is a large paper size, and the consequent difficulty of removing a lower folder. Weight to be handled, difficulties in manipulation, lead a person removing or refiling sheets to attempt short cuts usually with disastrous results. This is usually done by 'scooping', bending up the maps at the front of the drawer to identify them. A drop front drawer would help on this point, LE GEAR mentions 'The unique feature of the Library of Congress built-in map files is the hinged front which swings forward and down as the drawer is opened'. The Ordnance Survey has drop-fronted steel trays but these installations are tailor-made and no manufacturer in Britain appears to supply similar drawers, ready-made, which in the Library of Congress have to be two inches apart to allow for the hinges with consequent loss of space which could be used for filing. Deep drawers, well-filled, and using folder separators, should, if used at all, be reserved for the economical filing of a little used section of the map collection.

Folders used in drawers are particularly helpful if maps can be filed

119

side by side in two halves of the same large drawer, in that they prevent inter-mixing. If filing of this nature were planned to occur then drawers with dividers can be bought, or in some cases self-adhesive uprights can achieve a similar result. Folders do however have another asset. Tied, they should be provided with ties, they hold the sheets firmly, which in itself is of assistance in preservation, and the cover, as well as absorbing friction, prevents a lot of dust reaching the sheets. Drawers and trays do tend to 'leak' dust in a busy library. If the library is carpeted and vacuum cleaned, and has a clean-air system, this might be of no moment, but failing these external measures a dust flap of material over the front portion of the inside drawer is very helpful, but not often seen. Alternatively, and where security is of importance, locked cupboard doors on the front of the cabinet prevent dust entering. 'Ranplan' steel cabinets with one inch deep sliding trays, can be provided with a dust cover door which slides out-of-sight when open. The door should be used in any library system.

Specifications for horizontal systems using drawers or trays, provide for a cover to be over the rear of the drawer and manufacturers appear to supply this as a norm, but in a tailor-made system it should be seen to be supplied. In wooden drawers it is usually a piece of hardboard tacked on the top of the drawer, in metal drawers it is an integral part. The purpose of the hood is to prevent single sheets pushed to the rear, going over the back of the drawer with consequent crumpling and creasing, probable tearing and perhaps being temporarily lost. The RGS REPORT recommends that the hood 'should extend for at least nine inches, and its fore-edge should be visible when the drawer is fully open'. Fully open in this sense means the fullest position to which the drawers can be opened for the handling of maps, a position at which in steel cabinets there may be a check stop, and this might require a hood of at least twelve inches on larger drawers. Similarly at the front of the drawer it is normally recommended that there should be a device for holding the sheets or folders firmly flat. Manufacturers tend to provide hinged metal pieces in metal cabinets but there have been a variety of devices over the years to achieve this aim.

'Harvey' plan cabinets, to quote the manufacturer's catalogue, have 'Hinged flaps and cover plates in each drawer (to) prevent drawing curl and can be used as place markers'. This suggested use as a place marker for the return of the map is probably not feasible in map library use, certainly not with any drawers holding frequently used maps. Several maps may be withdrawn in the one day and they are probably re-filed collectively. Leaving the flap to act as a marker could lead to careless and inaccurate filing if more than one map had been removed.

Metal drawers are expected to run freely, the RGS REPORT notes that 'it is desirable that the metal drawers should have ball-bearing suspension and a device to lock the drawers in the open position', and BSI DRAFT STANDARD suggests that drawers should run on bearers which shall support them to about two-thirds of their extent when open—to prevent canting. Whatever form of drawer slide is provided it should be tested for easy running with a full drawer. Map handling can be tiring work in a busy library and everything should be done to ease the process, both for the sake of the librarian and for the wear and tear which might be caused to the maps if, for example, drawers stick or during their movement have to be lifted slightly because of an imperfection in the slide etc. Whatever support is supplied for the drawer it must work properly with the drawer adequately open. A librarian cannot be expected to hold up the drawer at the same time as attempting to select a required sheet. Cambridge University Library has metal drawer cabinets, no longer made, which have cupboard double door fronts. When the doors are opened they lock in the full open position at right angles to the drawer fronts and the inside of the door contains slides to take the drawers as they are withdrawn. The drawers are thus fully supported when completely open. In the same way importance should be attached to the front of the drawer, the means of pulling the drawer. In wooden drawers and older metal cabinets drawer handles usually project and are quite strong, but weak plastic handles should be avoided.

Currently, metal drawers appear to favour sloping fronts externally which provide a labelling surface at an optimum angle for the eye-view of a standing person and a continuous hand hold underneath the sloping front. The sloping front does not project from the cabinet but is contained within the measurements of the carcase of the cabinet.

A major advantage of horizontal storage cabinets which in different ways appeals to many librarians is the facility of the properly planned cabinet to form a storage module. At its simplest, and with no projections of the top cover, the cabinets can be placed together to form an even working surface of substantial area.

This working surface must be recognised as only of value for standing users. The provision of high stools for readers to use such surfaces is a waste, no one should be expected to sit in a twisted position, the map drawers below preventing knee room beneath the working surface. But such surfaces are valuable for the quick consultation or selection of sheets, and most importantly as a place in which to place a folder or set of maps withdrawn from a drawer, to allow the desired sheet to be located without difficulty. If working surfaces at an acceptable height are not available on horizontal storage cabinets, then

121

tables must be provided adjacent to the cabinets so they can temporarily accommodate weighty folders for example, in the same way.

But the great virtue of the horizontal cabinet as a storage module is that it can be built up vertically. This is very important for the economical storage of large collections which do not receive frequent consultation. It is a category already well represented in university geography departments though perhaps less so in public libraries. As a category it will grow, map librarians find themselves loth to discard recently superseded large scale sheets of official surveys because they will acquire value as an historical record, but the frequency of the use of any one sheet is dramatically reduced once a revision or new edition is published. 5' 6" is the maximum height permitted in the Map Room of the Bodleian Library, Oxford, and, for 'well used maps' RGS REPORT suggests five feet as the maximum height, with the BSI DRAFT REPORT selecting 3' 6" to 4' 6". As the height of the storage equipment increases two factors must be kept in mind, the strength of the flooring on which the cases will stand, and the physical strength required of the librarian, and indeed her safety, when using high drawers. BAHN has published a table of weights of filled map cases which shows that, for example, 6,000 maps occupying thirty, two-inch deep drawers in a flat storage cabinet occupying an area of four feet by three feet and a height of 8' 8" weigh 3593 lbs and exert a pressure of approximately 310 lbs per square foot. Some libraries at the time of writing store up to around eight feet high but such a height should be avoided even if building surveyors give the assurance that the floor can carry the weight. Anyone filing or removing maps from a drawer should have sufficient height above the drawer to be able to do the task efficiently. Even at a drawer height of 5' 6" a girl 5' 4" high would require to stand on a support at least 2' 3" high to handle maps in the top drawer with any comfort, and as it would be more comfortable if a little more height was possible and not all assistants will be even as tall as 5' 4", probably a support of 2' 6" should be available. The support must be of a platform type, not a ladder, with sufficient space to rest a folder of maps temporarily, at say waist height and, whilst capable of mobility, can be effectively made static when in use.

Vertical filing
The simplicity of supporting a single sheet in a horizontal filing system, by the act of lying it flat on the base of the appropriate size drawer, is one reason for many map librarians approving that system. This must not mask the fact however that access to one sheet among 100, 200 or more sheets in a drawer is not easy, and it is the ease of accessibility to a single sheet which makes the suspension type

of vertical filing more acceptable to some map librarians.

On the evidence of statements in manufacturers' catalogues it is reasonable to assume however that vertical filing evolved primarily with the idea of reducing the floor area occupied for the storage of a given number of drawings in a drawing office and in its simplest form might be looked upon as tipping the horizontal filing cabinet on one end with access to the cabinet being provided at the top. This cannot be done unless some means of support is found so that the flat plans will not crumple and concertina into a self-destructive pile at the bottom of the vertical container.

As already noted ordinary office filing cabinets can be used for storing maps which are intended to have only a short life in the map collection. Other special types of office filing cabinets can also be found in use in map collections, cabinets designed to hold special office stationery, medical records, air photographs and similar documents of comparatively small area which have been found to be a suitable size for accommodating a series of sheets which are issued and received folded. These are not necessarily folded maps with covers, such as motoring maps folded to be kept comfortably on a car shelf or in a pocket, but also large sheets which are issued folded, but uncovered, to facilitate distribution. It is inadvisable to keep the latter type of folded sheet in this way, nor should the covered folded maps be left in folds if they are to be retained permanently. With relatively few consultations the folding and unfolding of the paper, even if always done correctly, creates a breaking strain on the paper at the folds and holes soon appear, initially at the intersections of folds at right angles to one another. Correct practice is always to keep a sheet flat even if previously folded. Where it is thought appropriate to keep maps folded they are perhaps best kept in envelopes and in filing cabinet drawers without suspended file pockets but with a compressing plate whose position at the rear of the file can be adjusted to hold the envelopes firmly upright. This might make acceptable storage for folded maps but does not prevent their inevitable damage by ordinary consultation. Cambridge University, Map Library folds modern official topographical maps to a single size and files them vertically in ordinary office filing cabinets with a number of board separators at intervals to hold them. Here however is a national library; no one sheet is regularly required and this type of storage is continued when the map is superseded, by filing old editions in similar sized cardboard boxes.

The various forms of vertical filing available for drawings, plans or maps are differentiated by the devices incorporated to support sheets in the vertical plane, so that gravity will not cause self-destruction. Broadly speaking there are two groups of storage, files which exert

123

friction to keep the sheet in position and suspension files which have a means of allowing the sheet to hang freely.

Vertical compressor filing cabinets employ spring compressed plan pockets. Compressor springs are attached to flexible steel sheets used as separators, and pockets are suspended from bars running on side rollers. Folders to hold groups of maps are placed in the pockets which have flexible canvas bases to hold the folders. The folders project above the pockets to allow them to be gripped to remove, and for ease in identifying the folder. The compression springs press the pockets, folders and map sheets continuously and so the maps are supported. To withdraw a sheet the folder must be withdrawn until it is no longer compressed before a map can be removed. To attempt to pull a map out of the folder would be the same as pulling a map from the middle of a group in a drawer, the leading edge of the map would soon suffer and pieces would be torn off. The action of removing a vertically held folder naturally causes all sheets contained in it to concentrate at the bottom if not to crumple, and because of some maps being smaller than others there is a bulking at the bottom half of the folder. This is common enough in ordinary suspended folder files used for letters, but with a compressor file, springs will be acting on the upper thinner portion of the file, as well as on the lower portion making it additionally more difficult to withdraw. Maps are, however, well kept in this type of file if it is not overloaded. A British manufacturer supplies folders, to fit four standard size cabinets, up to fifty five by thirty four inches but the sheets must be four inches shorter and two inches narrower than the folder used. The same manufacturer supplies half width folders for double banking some sheets and can make to order smaller folders. Rear folders of the fifty five inch width with say fifty maps included, can be very difficult for one person to remove, pulling against springs, reaching over the front of a forty two inch high cabinet towards a rear which is thirty inches deep. This is possibly made worse because it is a system rather more prone to over-filling than others. Introducing additional sheets is little difficulty initially in the withdrawn folder but the folder then has to be pushed into a tight cabinet. These factors have led some librarians not to use the rear folders.

All non-suspension vertical filing systems share the benefit, with horizontal systems, of the maps being filed without the addition of any strips etc. This is obviously a consideration when archival preservation is a factor with some maps, although it is not necessarily deemed essential not to add 'strips' to archival maps by all map librarians, in the National Archives of Canada at Ottawa, for example.

Nevertheless compressor type cabinets, if vertical filing is required, offers the least disturbance to the flat original state of the map. It is significant that an earlier, apparently tailor-made, form of compressor filing has been in use with the excellent and large Fairbanks Collection of eighteenth and nineteenth century surveyor's drawings and maps, at the Department of Local History, Sheffield City Library, since the nineteen thirties. In this case the compression files are mounted in large wooden drawers which have of course to be withdrawn for access, whilst the cabinet currently available is accessible via a top lid, which is the norm with all types of vertical filing. Drawer compression files have ball-bearing roller suspension, the drawers filled are very weighty. Such cabinets should be fastened to the floor or they will tip forward.

Another type of vertical filing which does not need any material to be added to the sheets to be filed, uses wave-like dividers forming pockets in the storage compartment. Paper sheets filed between the gently corrugated rigid sides of the pockets are both held vertically by the resultant increased friction when the corrugated dividers are closed, and given rigidity as they take a similar shape. The familiar experiment of standing a loose cylinder of ordinary paper on one end and applying a weight across the top of the cylinder demonstrates the latter effect. The hinging of the rigid dividers at the bottom of the cabinet requires the front of the cabinet to be hinged to allow the dividers to open but access to the maps is from the lidded top. Flexible separators which allow intermediate division and guiding are available from the manufacturers in full and half widths and wallets can be used to retain smaller sheets. For using the width of the cabinet in two halves a telescopic bar can be obtained which, fastened back and front through the dividers, separates the two half width sets for individual filing. The required map is selected by leafing through the group in the appropriate division. The whole file, on the opening of the front of the cabinet is available for leafing and the compression due to the corrugations is now largely lost and wholly so in the selected division.

Sheets need to be fairly tightly packed to be properly supported even when the divisions are closed, so there is a tendency to use this type of filing, at least within divisions, for sheets within uniform series. There is no apparent curving of maps, which would destroy the possibility of taking accurate measurements from them if it occurred, but archival maps for long period storage would not be thought suitably filed in this type of storage. It is very straight forward in use which suggests its usefulness if public access is to be provided to a particular set. NOKES discovered that the need to have the maps fairly tightly packed has lead some map librarians to put in card sheets to help pressure on the maps. If these are not flexible they will of course significantly reduce the storage space. One library was found by Miss Nokes to have introduced card folders for maps which negates the principle of the wavy dividers. Actually adjustments can be made within the cabinet, there are slots in the base and dividers can be moved to suit the amount of contents, and additionally intermediate dividers can be obtained. The expediences discovered by Miss Nokes may well reflect in some cases, the fairly common inability of librarians to appreciate the need for proper maintenance and the correct use of equipment and machines.

Vertical filing—suspension types
Suspension filing is the most common form used in vertical filing and it exists in several different forms, but only differing in detail. All forms require the addition of a strip of material to be fastened along one edge of the sheet, the strip being punched, or bought ready-punched, with holes which will go over prongs in the cabinet and the map thus supported. The strip may be of strong paper, plastic, plastic and a paper side for writing on, press pahn, fabric-reinforced, and no doubt others, and is usually self-adhesive. The strip, or map holder, can be added by hand, but a simple machine is more economical, to any edge of the sheet for suspension. For sheets in sets, identified within the map boundary by sheet number, or national grid number, etc there is obviously point in making sure this number is visible at the top. For maps not in series the identifying title may be at the southern margin of the sheet and it might be more helpful to file the map with east at the top, not to read the title, but because the size of the map is more suitably accommodated in appropriate equipment that way. The suspension strip can be used to write on or label with the location symbol for that map in the library, and this can include the sheet reference, whether it is visible or not on the face of the sheet as it is filed.

The rods or prongs supporting the maps pass through the map holder strip and are arranged so that when a sheet is to be withdrawn the rods are parted to leave a gap where a sheet can be withdrawn. The sheets must be parted before the rods so that the required map is adjacent to where the gap in the rods will appear. In cases where a large number of small prongs are used there is usually a separator or device to prevent sheets, other than the one required, slipping off when the prongs are opened. Prongs, or in other makes longer and fewer rods, can be in the form of a gentle uniform curve which probably assists in retaining unwanted sheets in situ when the prongs are opened. If sheets do come off they will probably fall to the bottom of the cabinet, perhaps unnoticed. Other makes use straight prongs or

126

rods, the latter being formed in pairs with a hollow cylinder rod fastened to the rear of the cabinet and a solid piston rod fastened to the movable front which when the cabinet is closed moves into the cylinder, preventing the removal of maps. Vertical suspension files using multiple prongs to hold the maps are divided and have the interlocking prongs mounted on a number of movable file bars. The depth of the cabinet, back to front, must allow sufficient space for the chosen file bar to be opened, the other file bars having to be moved away to allow this. In this type of cabinet librarians should ensure that file bars are easily movable and the moving parts made of material which will have a long and efficient life. Cabinets with file bars do not require an opening front, access being entirely from the open lid on top, but it is always useful to have a 'trap door' at the bottom providing access for retrieving dropped maps or cleaning. When cleaning cabinets it is usually necessary to use a vacuum cleaner, lips in the metal edges usually preventing any form of dusting. As a precaution against losing maps from opened file-bars there are a variety of makers' devices which cause a file bar to be opened in two stages. The first action is for the librarian to select the file bar required, this may be done manually by moving other files bars away, or more automatically by pressing an appropriately identified switch or turning a knob. In either case the file bar will initially only be partly opened so that the prongs do not part and thus allow more freedom to leaf through the group of sheets to locate the one required and part the maps at that point. The opening of the file bar will then be completed, by moving a further lever or catch, and the sheet required withdrawn. This type of precaution is not necessary in the larger rod suspension cabinets because, not being divided into sections more space has to be provided, to allow for the selection of the map which could, for example, if the back sheet is wanted, require all the other sheets in the cabinet to be pulled forward before the rods are parted. This can be heavy work, particularly as this type of cabinet tends to be taller than most, one of its virtues being that it takes up less floor space and maps are then suspended from their shortest side.

Suspension files can vary a great deal in their dimensions. Typical dimensions for a two rod model to file A0/antiquarian size sheets is Height 1520 mm (60″), width 900 mm (36″), depth 460 mm (18″). When the front is opened, hinged at the bottom, the top is of the order of thirty six inches deep at sixty inch height, and the map has to be lifted up from the gap in the prongs. The result is that a user frequently draws the map sideways, or pulls it forward, the face being stretched against the point of a prong, neither being a practice to be commended. Yet the simplicity of this type of design makes it

127

popular. If space for storing maps is not extremely scarce every thought should be given to using suspension files which have dimensions which are wider and lower. This will allow the depth, perhaps, to be increased a little but not too much, because in seeking a lower height for suspension one should be looking for easier access and so less physical effort for the handler and consequent protection for the map. In wider and lower cabinets some sheets may have to be suspended from their long side but this is not an impossibility.

Some makes of suspension filing for smaller sheets are opened on the drawer system but most are top entry. When file bars are used either the lid has to be raised or a tambour shutter run to the sides, but this is light work. In the case of rods occupying the depth of the cabinet the front, hinged at the bottom, has to be brought forward to a mechanical stop, after the lid has been raised. This suggests instability for the cabinet, normally unfounded because of counter-weights but this point must be checked and in any case of doubt the cabinet bolted to the floor.

Instability could occur in spite of a manufacturer's built-in precautions, if a floor is uneven. As always the manufacturer's directions should be carefully observed in setting up the equipment and in using it. Techniques can be learned, the correct way to move a file bar, the correct way to insert a map. In this latter case it should be emphasised that it is not necessary to lift a sheet to a height above the suspension cabinet at which the bottom of the sheet is above the gap in the suspension rods. The sheet can be 'fed in' being held a little way above the bottom edge with the height of the sheet in a gentle roll. If the height of the sheet is such that this leaves a lot of paper in front of the handler, the sheet should be held in folds, not creased, to lift it above the file bar.

There is every indication that vertical suspension filing is the most acceptable method of providing easy access to a large number of sheets, and offering less wear and tear to maps so filed than any other system. When a map is withdrawn only that map is handled, some others may have to be moved aside but only their plan holder strips are touched. With well fitting lids they prevent a high proportion of dust in the air from entering. In the wider and lower dimensions and using a file bar in the half open position, they bring a new possibility of browsability among filed maps. The multi-prong file bar types in particular seem to offer the most sophisticated systems, albeit at a price, but in their simplest form they are less expensive than many models of other types of storage. The file bar systems offer the most varied range of sizes, and because of the large numbers of prongs in the width of a file-bar, narrower maps can be filed side by side without any special

128

additional equipment. Similarly small maps which would not occupy an economic part of the depth of a cabinet can be filed in a train of plastic pockets hanging from the same map holder strip. A similar use of plastic pockets to which the map holder strip is attached allows an archival type to be filed if desired without any strip addition to its surface.

Care should be taken with the quality of the tape which is to be used for map holding and its adhesive. In earlier types of suspension filing thick paper strips caused difficulty in photocopying, where this was permissible. Newer tapes can be very thin which also increases the capacity of the storage system. Thought should also be given to the tape being of the appropriate type if it will be necessary to write on it. The application of the holding tape to the map is a very simple and quick process if a tape applicator, like an edge-binding machine, is used.

In general terms the more sophisticated the equipment the more costly it is, as an initial expense, and expensive equipment suitable for quick and careful access would never be obtained for the storage of large seldom-used parts of a map collection. This category would probably be relegated to a stack area in any large library with lower standards of circulation space, greater height of storage and so on. Vertical suspension files with top access cannot be mounted one on top of the other. The librarian must always establish the principles of storage to be observed for each identifiable category in the collection and equip appropriately for each part. Too often however map librarians or curators seem to pay exaggerated attention to manufacturers' and representatives' claims, which will be true in general terms but can often be irrelevant to the needs of the group of maps requiring storage. Representatives will demonstrate their equipment and how to use it properly but it is a good idea to see a variety of storage in use, if at all possible, before making a selection. Again, do not take a colleague's opinion of a type of storage without some critical thought of your own. If she does not like it, it could be because someone else was instrumental in selecting it. If she does like it, find out what storage was used before, it may have been so inadequate that anything new is an improvement.

Roll maps

Roll maps may well seem to be a cartographic invention to defy the curator. Because of this they are also frequently the most ill-kept and dirty of any maps in libraries and record offices in the country. Without doubt if they can be stored flat in the equipment available this should be done. Unfortunately some, mounted maps, have been stored for so long in a roll that unrolling would only cause the map to crack at intervals and provide not a flat sheet but one in a series of curves. In all cases where actually flattening the map would cause damage to it, or where the flat sheet would be too big, the roll has to be retained, even in some extreme cases to be filed in a very long wooden container built to size. Large early maps were commonly mounted on rollers for wall display. The maps might be found to be tacked on to the wooden rollers in which case the tacks have probably become rusty and are destroying the adjacent paper, they should be removed and the map attached in a less destructive manner. Usually, rolls can be stored in special tough card tubes with a removable lid at one end. The lid may be one of a variety of types, a plastic cap or a springy metal snap closure. The map should be tied with tape in a roll rather less in diameter than the tube to allow it to be removed easily. If this is not done the sheet or sheets will unroll in the tube to press against the interior of the tube and make removal difficult. Where this does occur take hold of the innermost edge of the map and rewind it on the inside with as small a diameter as possible and reduce the pressure against the tube wall in this way before attempting to withdraw the roll map.

Too often tubes are not used for roll maps, which are merely wrapped in brown paper, tucked in at the ends to keep the dust out, and tied with tape. If this has to be done there should at least be a former in the centre around which the map can be tightly wrapped. Tubes used for posting maps might be collected for this purpose. In map collections where maps are only wrapped in brown paper it is probable that they are also merely laid one on top of another in cupboards or deep shelving. In this case the former will provide the protection of physical strength.

Soon the problem arises, what to do with the tubes? Ingenious solutions have been devised in the past, usually depending on the furniture and geography of a library—store them along the length of otherwise dead space under a catalogue cabinet by building pigeon hole shelves with cupboard doors at either end, lay them on top of shelving, some have fixed back-sloping pegs to the walls and laid the rolls across them. Roll maps are long but of many different lengths, ordinary shelving is not really adequate to hold them because of the uprights. The Department of Local Studies at Birmingham City Reference Library has a wall of cantilevered shelving with no vertical divisions between the lengths of shelves and so the roll maps can be layed lengthwise for whatever length is required. To prevent maps rolling off, and increase storing capacity, small metal uprights have been attached to the front edge of the shelves at intervals. In addition, the 'pigeon hole' type of shelving described above is now commercially available for rolls. 'Planstore' cabinets are in a variety of sizes,

130

the largest providing storage for rolls up to $71\frac{1}{2}''$ long. The 'Planstore' is a metal cabinet of pigeon holes, each square being capped by plastic seal which projects to form a handy 'pull' and a sloping base for labelling. 'Rolafile' units are cupboards containing tubes each open ended but the units have doors. 'Rolafile' tubes cover DIN paper size storage. In most cases maps of these sizes will, in libraries, be stored flat, but there may be many accessions of surveyors' drawings for example which have always been rolled at the surveyor's office and may be best retained in that shape. A vertical file housed in a cupboard will probably house five foot long rolls, but it would be a rather expensive piece of equipment for the capacity available, its use would depend on the quality of the maps or rolls to be stored.

Display storage
There are probably several maps in any library which should not be stored in any manner which hides the map from public sight. The potential use of such maps demands that they are visible, not only because of the frequency with which they are requested but by being on show additional people will see and consult them. A town plan and similar maps of the area, a map showing local ecclesiastical boundaries, and a globe, come into this category. Wall display is as good as any but often there is insufficient wall space free.

Several firms make plan holders, primarily for use in drawing offices, in which the plan is held by a metal arm and several can be supported at one end in a wall mounted unit which allows the plan holders to be moved so a reader can consult the one required. If the holders are fixed to the wall only one person at a time could consult the unit, so it might be possible to allow the user to unhook the map and examine it at a table as he might use a periodical. If space is available a tailor-made unit could be made for holding a number of such maps mounted on spring loaded rollers which are housed parallel to each other in a box above the viewing area. In both examples the maps should be numbered and a key to the numbers provided, so that the right map is quickly selected.

Makers, or suppliers, of storage equipment mentioned
Addressograph—Multigraph Ltd, (Admel Division), Brooklands Road, Weybridge, Surrey.
Vertical filing, suspension on multiprong file bars, selector. 'Monarch'.
Angula Engineering Co Ltd, Windmill Road, Sunbury on Thames, Middlesex TW16 7HR.
ADM Business and drawing office systems: Vertical filing,

suspension rods. 'Metalfile'; 'EV plan'. Horizontal plan chests.

Art Metal, Dominant House, 85 Queen Victoria Street, London EC4V 4HS.

Office filing cabinets; lateral filing cabinets; vertical filing with compressors, 'Plan file'.

Elite Manufacturing Co Ltd, Elite Works, Station Road, Manningtree, Essex CO11 1DZ.

Vertical filing, suspension on multiprong file bars. Cabinet and drawer types.

Frank Wilson (Filing) Ltd, Railex Works, PO Box 19, Manor Road, Southport.

Lateral filing cabinets, with large sizes for plans. 'Railex'.

Harvey Office Furniture Ltd, Woolwich Road, London SE7 7RJ.

Office filing cabinets; lateral filing cabinets, horizontal plan chests.

J Hodsman and Son Ltd, 82–84 Eldon Street, York YO3 7NE.

Plan display units, 'Vistaplan'.

Metal Shelving (Industrial) Ltd, Paddington Green Works, London W2 1LD.

Horizontal plan chests, with door. 'Ranplan'. Roll map filing, 'Planstore'.

Nig Banda Ltd, Colchester, Essex CO1 1XU.

Vertical filing, suspension rods, 'Arc-Ao', 'Arclight', 'Economic', 'Vertifile'. Vertical filing, suspension on multiprong file bars, 'Plandale', cabinet with selector, and drawer types; 'Gabs'.

Normidaire Ltd, 8–10 Oxford Road, Gerrards Cross, Buckinghamshire SL9 7AY.

Plan display units, with cabinets.

Office Equipment (John Dale) Ltd, Winchester Wharf, Clink Street, London SE1 9DQ.

Distributors: Vertical filing, suspension on multiprong file bars with selector. 'Plan-o-Class', 'Plandale'. Plan display units, 'Plan-o-Pend'.

Roneo Vickers Ltd, Roneo House, Lansdowne Road, Croydon CR9 2HA.

Vertical filing with 'wavy' dividers. Office filing systems.

Sankey Sheldon-Unistrut, Windsor House, Temple Row, Birmingham B2 5JX.

Office filing cabinets; lateral filing cabinets, 'Euromaster', 'Varimaster'. Vertical filing, suspension rods.

Swallow and Hicks Ltd, Tanners Works, Tanners Hill, London SE8 4QE.

Roll map filing, 'Rolafile', vertical tube file. Distributors; plan display units, 'Plan Hold'.

132

Chapter references:
ALONSO 1973–1; BAHN; GALNEDER; LE GEAR; NOKES;
RGS REPORT.

8

General considerations on the classification and cataloguing of maps

Map librarianship in general libraries is, in the majority of cases, in its infancy and in no aspect of librarianship is this more obvious than in the arrangements made for the retrieval of required maps. A wide variety of systems, part systems, or no system are used and even when the system is working well it is often spoken of with some diffidence by the map curator or librarian, probably because it is felt that there is no corpus of knowledge to which one can appeal. In fact there is an extensive modern literature of quality, but apparently little known, which should be consulted far more than it is. This literature however, if it is written by a map curator, does often seem to omit the down to earth considerations which seem to cause some concern to those responsible for maps in a collection or library, and if it is written by a cataloguer, a knowledge of the special needs of the map curator seems absent. The literature on cataloguing non-book materials does offer points of interest but is more concerned with very small collections of sheet maps as one of several non-print media in a resources centre.

One might imagine in some university geography departments that the collection is being administered satisfactorily in that the curator can produce wanted sheets, but all that would change if that curator were to leave. The reasonably satisfactory current operation owes much to the knowledge of the present curator who knows that such a set is in a particular file because she put them there for a reason, such as they are handy there for the head of the geography department to use, unconnected with any principles of arrangement. This of course is not a professional system of administration, which might be summarised as a system which can be readily appreciated by a succeeding qualified, or professionally trained, curator. This does not mean that the system of classification used, for example, need be the same as an accepted published scheme devised by a national map library for its own purposes, but that it should have a logical foundation which is relevant to the assumed needs of the library, and that this is recorded.

134

Too often in university map collections the knowledge of evolved practice, not only in cataloguing and classification, is not put to the discipline of being written in a manual for present staff and successors, which would both stimulate the suggestions for refinements to the practice and provide a training manual.

In public libraries the maps are invariably classified and catalogued but often in a manner which takes little account of their nature. The work is usually done by the cataloguing department for the whole library system, quite naturally more used to the cataloguing of books, and maps are forced into the 'book-mould'. The operation of the catalogue which includes the map entries is probably in the hands of every reader-services librarian, in the absence of a specific map librarian, and no feed-back to the cataloguer occurs for any inadequacy in map cataloguing. In a department of local studies there is a specialised staff who will observe any inadequacies more readily, and it is significant that in such departments specialist arrangements are frequently made for classifying and cataloguing local maps.

Collections administered in or from university main libraries would appear to have the best chance of being well indexed and arranged, by a curator who is both professionally qualified and has been selected for the post for her cartographic knowledge. These arrangements are not the general rule however. Many university map collections have grown from very small personal collections formed by a head of the geography department some years ago and the original form of indexing and arrangement has been followed which might exhibit idiosyncracies owing more to to personal habit, the pattern of an early syllabus, or the geography of the room which held the collection in its infancy, rather than to the logic of usage. The same might be true of a scheme for maps in the local studies collection of a public library. It is a fallacy to imagine that a collection arranged and indexed according to the wishes of the lecturing staff will therefore be the best system to use. It might be very good. Thomas R Smith, Professor of Geography and Curator of Maps at the University of Kansas has produced an excellent manual for his own department's map collection *The map collection in a general library, a manual for classification and processing procedures* Lawrence, Kansas; University of Kansas, 1961 (typescript), which is unfortunately not readily available in Great Britain, but he has adopted the Library of Congress schedule of area classification. In most cases however a 'lecturing staff scheme' is not as good as one developed and refined by map curators over a period of time.

The main reason why general libraries and university geography departments have so far managed to operate with inadequate classification and indexing systems is that they are, in Great Britain, still small collections. Fifty thousand sheets is a lot of units to be housed but when it is remembered that the majority of these sheets belong to one series or another, the actual number of maps is much smaller. It is, or it should be, the map which is the cataloguing and classifying unit. One would expect much larger collections in general university and public libraries in the USA because of the depository programmes which have existed during the last thirty years but even here very few libraries have more than 100,000 sheets, yet it is said that estimates of world cartographic production range from 60,000 to 100,000 per annum, (CURRENT). Map curators and librarians do not seem to take heed of the fact that the collection will grow and become very much larger within a few decades. This affects classification and indexing. The systems used in university departments are often 'cut-down' versions of an accepted scheme, and these can deal reasonably effectively with comparatively small numbers of sheets, particularly when so many are within series, but problems of access will occur when the collection becomes larger and more single sheet maps are included. History can give guidance for the future and the history of most library institutions, public, university and college, exhibits the arrival of the time when the change had to be made from the first book classification methods used to one more suitable for the larger book collection. All libraries, unless they are home-reading libraries, or similar, which have a withdrawals policy, should always follow processes which are suitable for large collections for surely the library will grow. If this is not the case the decision must be made to change before the process becomes too large to contemplate, a decision which regularly is taken in these circumstances on the appointment of a new librarian.

In changing systems of classification and cataloguing, or amending and adapting current schemes, some general principles must be considered, as well as local conditions. Text books on cataloguing, even of map cataloguing, must deal with problems in a general way for a wide audience and so the discussion of procedures appears to take place in a vacuum rather than against a specific background. The individual librarian must make his own general policy decisions, enlightened by the knowledge gained from the works of cataloguing specialists but constructively developed to reflect local conditions.

The virtues of dispersing library materials to separate collections devoted to subject fields are well known and accepted, and it might be thought that this is a natural concomitant of growth in size. The earlier advocacy of the move of a university map collection from a geography department to the university main library is not necessarily to imply a completely centralised map collection, it is to remove a centralised collection from what might be thought to be an inappropriate centre. The policy on the location of maps should be in accordance with what are thought to be the needs of most users. It would seem therefore that, if there is a library department labelled 'science' and this contains books, investigation reports, etc on geology, then geological maps should be available there also. Maps of the local area should be in the department of local studies in the same way that gramophone records for learning a language should not be in the music library just because most records are of music. This would suggest that, in a large public library for example, there would be three main map collections, topographical maps, geological and similar maps, and local maps, which could be treated differently in the different departments. It must be realised that subject departments can not be equated with the way every reader wishes to use books, readers' needs can only be generalised, the departments cannot have watertight divisions. Continuing the example of a large public library, certainly many hundreds and possibly thousands of sheets of current series will be local and the common practice is to allocate these to the local studies department. These sheets may in fact, in underdeveloped libraries, form such a high proportion of the current British series in the library that even non-local sheets are kept with them as a set, no doubt to the confusion of readers who are equally confused if directed to the local studies department (popularly equated with local history) when requiring a modern map of an area within the local region for a purpose quite divorced from the historical. Only comparatively few sheets would warrant duplication on the amount of use they attracted. A similar 'overlap' occurs between geological maps and the local studies department. There is no one correct way of dealing with this problem which is confusing to a small minority of readers, the majority of readers are obviously directly catered for by the titles of the different departments. It would seem however that more duplication of well-used sheets should take place than is the present case so that most users would find modern maps of the appropriate type, in the geography and travel department, or the earth resources section of the science department whether the areas they covered were local or not, and, in the local studies department would be the superseded local maps from the other departments and modern sheets received on publication because they were expected to be used fairly extensively in local studies or were local but not required by other departments.

Local considerations in any one library might affect this. Map collections do not need open access for readers. Often in a university geography department library, the storage of the maps is in the same room as the provisions for reader consultation of the maps but, except for teaching collections, only the map curator or her staff may handle the maps in the cases. This practice, in a library with a small number of users, is obviously also going to be followed in a university main library with more readers who are less directly concerned with maps, and in public libraries. A new library building may therefore contain a single map storage room with convenient access to the three departments most concerned with maps. With common access to the collection neither duplication nor problems concerning the initial allocation of additions to departments are likely to occur. The maps are kept together in one collection with the economy of administration arising out of the unity of storage, matched by the retention of the benefits to the overwhelming majority of readers by the use of subject departments. The classification can obviously be a uniform and appropriate system.

The general tendency is however towards dispersal. Map collections grow, it is in the nature of libraries of the information type to grow. The simplest way to deal with growth is to provide additional space which gives, say twenty per cent additional storage capacity, rather than build a completely new building which has 120% storage compared with previously, and scrap the old. A twenty per cent addition to a general library can usually be best used by allocating to it an appropriate section of the library, a subject department is created. If maps are appropriate to the newly created department, as it would be if our example were a science library, then geological maps should leave the parent collection and space is also released for the expansion of the topographical and other maps. It should be observed that for many map libraries the division of the collection into physically separate subject collections will show, forcefully and dramatically, the inadequacy of map provision in some categories.

If a previously unified map collection is divided it is probable that the cataloguing in the differing sections may more easily be arranged to differ in detail in response to the needs of the different users of the varied kinds of maps. This can be done and should be done where necessary in a single unit collection. Whenever this is done however, it should only be in relevant details, the cataloguing in all map departments should be compatible. If the maps within a library have originated in different sections of the library it is more likely that different forms of cataloguing and classification have been in being from the outset and that these are not compatible. This is most obvious in the case of the variety of 'home-made' classification schemes used in the departments of local studies in some public libraries, for books as well as maps and other records. This was realised in London several years

138

ago with the creation of new larger London boroughs, and more recently in the rest of Great Britain as municipal and county libraries have been amalgamated in new local government areas, often meeting a great disparity in map classification and cataloguing within the constituent library systems. Even where the maps are in different departments in one building there should be a uniformity of map cataloguing which, even if a union catalogue of maps is not prepared, will allow, for example, local geological maps to be classified and entered in the catalogues of both the science library and the local studies department, the fact that they are filed in one department or another only being relevant for the necessary addition of whatever location symbol is necessary.

Thought should be given to the phrase 'location symbol' or perhaps 'call number'. Confusion between 'classification' and 'location symbol' does exist in the minds of some map curators and map librarians. The librarian often looks upon the classification notation as the location symbol, and the curator and the archivist in the record office often looks upon the location symbols as classification. The two may well be the same on occasion and it is common, and desirable, for the classification notation to be an element within the location information, but the two can be completely different if this will assist in the efficient administration of the map collection. The association of location with classification is at its most valuable when the materials to be arranged are accessible to the library user who can browse among them to make the best selection for his needs. This is unlikely to be the case for maps, as indicated above. Even with books it is only fully applicable in smaller libraries, very soon as the library grows a sizing of the books has to take place and different sequences introduced, not just providing a so-called 'oversize' section, which modifies the value to the reader of the subject classification used on the shelves. The classification order should be retained as much as possible as a locating system, for the benefit of staff handling materials at the point of storage, as a means of subject or area access, but this should not inhibit other considerations and the classification order will normally form a sub-arrangement for the maps. The maps may be primarily located by department, then by size and, with maps requiring special treatment, by specific filing cases, before the classification scheme is brought into use; the appropriate letters and/or numbers specifying these component parts being, as a whole, the location symbol. This may have to be even more detailed by further subdivision by scale and date for example. These further subdivisions might be used in a very small library but would be essential in a large library in order to reduce the number of maps bearing the same location symbol. The

139

catalogue entries, whether on cards or lines in a computer print-out, will however be arranged by the classification scheme alone, with a subdivision by scale or date or whatever other informative characteristic has been used, to obtain the benefits of classification, if a classified catalogue is to be used. Otherwise such benefits are to be found in the sub-arrangements of the actual maps in their filing, and other benefits derived from the different, but not concerned with location, arrangement of the catalogue entries.

To underline the inevitability of growth, the necessity of providing compatible cataloguing and classification for maps within one library but separated by their access, and often their storage, being in different departments, and providing cataloguing descriptions which vary according to the needs of different categories of maps, it is possible reasonably to anticipate a future event. The plans concerning map collections in the newly amalgamated local authorities in Great Britain must be affected by the future of maps in record offices. For many years city libraries have had archives departments existing side by side with the local studies department, often both being administered by the library authority. The city archives department has been concerned with archival records of the region, though not with quite the same attention to the appropriate 'sphere of influence' as the local studies department. There were two departments therefore, each concerned with the same subject, the local region; an example of the common trait of the librarian, to observe administrative convenience rather than reader service. Now, in many authorities, a county record office, at least for non-current records, will be administered under the same administrative umbrella. Surely the local historian in particular has a right to expect that all these departments concerned with the history of his region will amalgamate, at least to a degree which will end the necessity for him to visit these different departments to check on available materials. Some authorities will consider providing a single local studies centre. The use of the printed and manuscript maps and plans in the library's local studies department should be coupled with the use of the manuscript and printed local plans and maps in the archives department and record office. They are the same form of record and should be catalogued similarly, though properly and necessarily differing in the descriptive detail provided, according to the type of map catalogued not according to where the map is located.

The classification scheme used for all of them, should be one thought to be, or created to be, of the greatest value to the student of that locality, bringing together in the classified catalogue those maps most likely to be used together by the average reader, which are maps of a given area. The combined catalogue will then have overcome the difficulty of the maps of the area which the reader is studying being filed in diverse locations. This is a difficulty for the reader without a combined catalogue, although it might, in particular situations be a necessity from the point of view of the archivist or of the librarian. The archivist for example may wish to preserve the physical unity of a particular deposit of documents which includes a map. This example can be mirrored in universities, in a variety of ways, but most obviously where, even when the map collection is said to be wholly administered within the geography department and not by the university library, a manuscript plan or early map often concerned with the local region, is filed and listed or catalogued within a rare book room, local studies department, or department of manuscripts. In most universities a complete census of all the maps available in all the departments of the university would reveal a surprisingly useful addition to the maps available in the one map library.

The arguments concerning the importance of having a combined catalogue of all the maps held in a general library are equally to the benefit of the library user when applied to the amalgamation of the map catalogue with the catalogue of books in a library. It is of immense advantage to have one point of access to all the information resources available to the library user. A handlist of map series available filed near the book catalogue, entries for maps in a separate set of catalogue drawers following the book catalogue, are inadequate substitutes for the amalgamation of entries. This is a normal process in a public library, although somewhat spoiled by the also normal insistence on cataloguing a map as a rather oddly shaped book and with little or no attention being paid to the different nature of the information offered by a map. The amalgamation of map entries with book entries is not normal in a university because of the absence of the main map collection from the university library. The result is that even if the geography department map collection purports to be for the use of the whole university it can not operate fully in that direction. A geographer may, on every occasion when a map may be of use to him, think, 'I must consult a map', but that does not apply to everyone who has a need for information. If a member of staff is to be a visiting lecturer in electrical engineering, at say, Hong Kong, it is probable he will visit the library to see what they have got 'on Hong Kong'. It is not probable that, having looked at the library catalogue under Hong Kong, or the classified entries to which he has been referred by the subject index, that he will then take the added, unguided, step of saying to himself, 'Now if I want a map of Hong Kong I must go to the geography department map library'.

There is no major difficulty in amalgamating map entries into a catalogue primarily of books. BOGGS and LEWIS have written 'To provide card entries for maps in a consolidated catalogue of books and maps, or in a dictionary catalogue primarily of books, the *content* of the map catalogue card may be the same or almost the same, as in a separate catalogue of maps and atlases . . . Adaptations in *headings*, however, will be necessary. In incorporating cards for maps with those for books, two possible arrangements for entries for maps are evident:

a) To form their own section within a catalogue primarily for books. This could be effected by using the word "Maps" as entry word in front of all subject and area headings. Author, title and series entries would be unchanged and would be dispersed alphabetically through the catalogue. This grouping would be effective only where the number of entries for maps is limited.

b) To be dispersed through the consolidated catalogue. The chief problems which arise in this dispersion are: 1 To differentiate for the catalogue-user between the entries for maps and those for books . . . 2 To provide a main entry for maps which does not call for treatment too different from the practice for books. 3 To provide harmony between general subject and area headings used for maps and for books'.

BOGGS and LEWIS are, throughout the above quotation, speaking in terms of a dictionary catalogue. In British libraries a classified catalogue will be more in common use. If maps are in a public library they are almost certainly catalogued for a classified catalogue which is a consolidated catalogue, maps and books. However, it is also correct to say that they are normally inadequately catalogued because, to paraphrase the first sentence quoted from BOGGS and LEWIS above, the content of the catalogue card for maps is not the same as it would be in a separate map catalogue.

Many university departmental map catalogues are neither dictionary catalogues nor classified catalogues in a usual sense but 'shelf lists' expressed in verbal forms, the arrangement is as classified but usually without a notation, and without a subject index. The general remarks about dictionary catalogues apply to such arrangements also.

Entries in a consolidated classified catalogue will naturally be made at the appropriate sections of the classified scheme as designed for maps by the creator of the scheme. The heading will be that of the appropriate notation. To a certain extent this will bring together all the maps in the collection, certainly the topographical ones, as effectively as putting the word 'Maps' as entry word in a dictionary catalogue preceding subject and area headings. However in a classified catalogue access for the reader to this grouping of topographical maps, arranged by their notation, is through the subject index where the headings of countries etc will be used, followed by the word 'Maps', and of course these index references are alphabetically related to other entries for the same country. It must be admitted that observation suggests that there is a paucity of such subject entries in many classified catalogues. Subject index entries will, of course differentiate for the user between subject entries for maps and books because they have to refer to different classification numbers.

A 'main entry' for maps is of little concern but it will be discussed later in cataloguing practice. Suffice to say here that many libraries continue to make an author entry as the main entry for maps, particularly and naturally if the catalogue is primarily that for a book library. It has no relevance when unit cards are used, except as a means of recording tracings, but there would seem to be no reason why the area entry, or the classified entry for area, should not be used for this purpose even in a combined catalogue.

It is perhaps appropriate here to mention the value of alternative access to information in a library, and this can be provided by the catalogue. With maps it is perhaps less obvious than with books that the catalogue can allow an access to documents different from the classification scheme, because maps are not as readily 'browsed' among, as is possible with books. However, browsing is not an impossibility, and is very much easier physically if a suspension type of storage is in use. The point of cataloguing and of classifying is to create ways of finding the record, be it map, book or any kind of record, which contains the information required. Often an enquirer will ask for a map because he has made a preliminary assumption that a map will give the information he requires, and he could be wrong if he asked for an Ordnance Survey map when he wished to locate the entrances to pot holes in the Pennines. Another reader may require general statistical information about farming in a nation, and is quite unconcerned if the information is presented to him graphically as a distribution map or tabulated in a reference work. These types of enquiry become more numerous as the means for satisfying them are collected by a library, success breeds usage. The more diverse the collection, the more diverse the usage made, and the greater the need for gaining access to information. If the catalogue follows the same arrangement as the maps in the storage files, as it does in the classified catalogue, then the quality possessed by the classification scheme for assisting in tracing maps which are potential bearers of the needed information is duplicated, but serves the useful purpose of reducing browsing among older maps. The subject index should present through its terminology and different arrangement an alternative means of access to the information. If, for example, a caving journal has published a map showing the location of the entrances to pots in the Pennines, then if an added entry is given at pot holes or caves, 551.44 in DDC, 18 ed, the subject index should refer to this, as a map. Too often in practice the subject index is inadequate and fails to provide a fully useful alternative. The nature of the dictionary catalogue provides an alternative arrangement, and form of access by terminology, compared with the classified maps in store, but the catalogue can also be inadequate. But even more importantly in university map library collections it is quite common to find that no index at all is prepared. The so called index or catalogue, presented to the user, follows the same pattern as the filing of the maps, but not using a notation, just area headings. This prevents any rearrangement of the headings as an alphabetical index because there is no means of reference to the headings in the classified arrangement, although a notation is provided in the body of the entry to locate the map. Probably all maps of a country are filed together, with a sub-arrangement under the country which includes a heading for geology. This is a reasonable arrangement for maps but the catalogue could be arranged differently to include, say, a heading for geology, subdivided by countries, allowing then an alternative approach by bringing together all the geological maps in the possession of the library.

This common inadequacy in university geography department map collections, matched in public libraries by their unfortunate emphasis on author entries, is alleviated by the high proportion of the maps in stock being in multi-sheet sets or series. This means that so much of the access to the holdings is via index maps, the most important of which are, in university geography departments, prominently and publicly displayed. Invariably there are wall surfaces well used for this purpose. Other methods, at Birmingham University high sliding screens which protect roll map cupboards, show the importance given to the display of index maps, or index diagram, or topographic index, or graphic index, whatever name is used locally. The index maps bearing the name of the official survey or commercial publisher, showing an outline of the country or area concerned, are a readily seen visual shorthand to the maps possessed, but not for single sheet maps or maps in but a few sheets. The importance of index maps does not seem to be fully realised in university or public libraries where the maps are part of the book library. Not every library would have the space for the 'full-face' display of index maps at the point where they can have most effect adjacent to the catalogue and it would often not be desirable aesthetically. Index maps for current sets of sheets should however be at least as prominently available as the national and other frequently used bibliographies and catalogues which should also be within the same area as the catalogue so that they all can be used if necessary, by the reader to identify the record he wants. The index map loses all the value it can have for a map user if it is kept in the map storage cabinet with the set to which it refers. There it can not publicise the fact to the reader that the library possesses this set or part of it, and the reader cannot ask for the sheet he wants except by verbal description to a librarian. The catalogue card is no substitute, and library cataloguers do not seem to appreciate this.

HORNER in his book *Special cataloguing* and the section on maps should be read by everyone who has to catalogue current maps, writes of 'maps,' or 'the individual map in the series', when a sheet of a map is meant. This criticism is not a pedanticism but a means of correcting some errors in thoughts on map cataloguing, if the correct terminology is used. The Ordnance Survey map known as *One-inch seventh series* was a map of Great Britain which for obvious reasons had to be 'cut up' into smaller sheets of which there were 189. These 189 sheets were parts of the map, not individual maps; the fact that for convenience some sheets overlapped and partly duplicated each other does not alter this fact. The catalogue entry for this map should be for the whole 189 sheets, just as the catalogue entry for an encyclopaedia covers all the volumes in which it is published. Access to a particular piece of information in the encyclopaedia is via the index volume and then the appropriate volume numbered on the spine. Access to a topographic representation of an area within a map produced in many sheets is via the index map. The catalogue entry should state the number of sheets on which the map is produced, and if the map is in process of publication and is not yet complete, but the library will obtain all the sheets in due course, then the entry will be 'left open', the date of commencement of publication being noted with a following dash, or the words 'in progress', which will be altered to the date of publication of the last sheet eventually. If as a matter of policy only part of the map is bought by the library then the catalogue entry will note the map as 'incomplete' and the sheets in stock will be identified in broad terms. In such a case the map librarian will have decided to buy the map just to cover the local county, or the coast of Brittany or something similar, and it would seem better to put this type of description as the note of the coverage unless very few sheets are taken which can be readily identified. The area named in the description will also be the heading for the area entry. It is not feasible to provide area entries for every place covered on a map, it must always be assumed that for any given area a smaller scale map covering a larger area, including the area in question, will be available. The smaller scale map sometimes may be a plate in an atlas. The map librarian may reasonably modify this principle as an act of further service to the reader. If she has, for example, bought a map of the world at a scale of 1:1,000,000 in order that a useful size map is in the library for some lesser known countries previously only represented by an atlas plate, then it would seem highly desirable that this conscious decision to provide needed maps should be made plain to users. No rule could be made about such a case, and it can not be decided by the cataloguer, it has to be a reflection of the use of the catalogue by the user as seen by the librarian in contact with the user. The librarian will then provide or ask the cataloguer to provide entries for sheets of that world map for those countries not previously represented in the map catalogue; if she deems this to be fruitful.

It is noted that PARSONS appears to make a ruling on this matter in his section on cataloguing, under additional entries (p 21), 'Additional entries are to be made for areas which are important in themselves, but which are included in a series of maps or a general map covering a larger area. These additional entry cards are replicas of the master cards with appropriate changes made in area heading. . . .

a) Continents or countries, whole or part, covered by world maps or series. For example, the *International map of the world* 1:1 M would require additional entries for each continent or part of a continent and also for certain countries or parts of countries covered. . . .

b) Countries, whole or part covered by a general Continental map or series . . . would require additional entries for the countries or parts of countries covered.'

However the apparent rule becomes more in the nature of a suggestion when one reads the second paragraph omitted from the quotation above, 'The size of the country and the scale of the series must be taken into consideration in the selection of additional entries'. It can be repeated that area entries should be provided in these cases on the basis of the map curator's assumption that they will be of value to the user of the catalogue and map collection.

Listing on a catalogue card the sheets held by a library might seem useful in terms of the sheets of the Ordnance Survey One-inch map or the 1:50,000 map which have numerical identification and designated area titles, but if one transfers the idea to even a part set of the 1:1250 scale map, identified by the coordinates making the National Grid reference number for the south-west corner of the sheet, the prospect looks rather different. Again there will be a policy for buying a number of sheets on this scale and that, expressed as a

146

geographical coverage, should be used as a note in the catalogue entry for this map to describe what sheets are or will be available. In all cases the true identification of the sheets which are held should be through the index map, an infinitely better guide for the reader, and for the librarian, than a listing of numbers. Coverage of a map can be seen quickly and the necessary sheet identification information can be read, in order to retrieve the appropriate sheet. It is common for a library to have only part sets of a map except for the very small scales, and the index map will be marked so that the sheets in stock are noted. This is usually done by drawing a diagonal line across the rectangle representing a sheet, or colouring it with a light colour probably yellow, with a felt-tip pen or similar. The index map is so frequently used it is necessary to protect it, probably by mounting on stiff card and laminating with transparent sheeting. When necessary different colours can be used to represent different additions, but if a new edition is produced a fresh index map should be started. In libraries where a catalogue entry is used as an accession record or shelf register, the marked index map has the same function.

It is probably a reflection of the cost, in money and time, for cataloguing by traditional methods in a general library, that when maps can be efficiently displayed for use there is a natural tendency not to catalogue them, in the belief that access to them will be through their 'visibility', rather than through the catalogue. An example is to have a library's collection of street maps stored in a prominent map case, fully accessible to the user and filed in a readily understood manner, probably alphabetically by name of town. The saving of administrative costs is obvious, but it is difficult to tell how much, if any, use of these plans is lost because they are not catalogued. A great deal must depend on the geography of the individual library but it should not be assumed that because the file is quite prominent and the staff members are fully aware of its existence that it is equally to the fore in the minds of library users. If readers requiring street plans frequently have to be referred to this file by the staff, there is a strong possibility that other potential users do not know the file and do not ask the librarian for assistance. An additional form of guiding is used by some libraries by the provision of a strip index to such plans, adjacent to the point of storage in the reading area. In the St Pancras Library of the London Borough of Camden, the map collection area of the reference library includes atlases, guide books, gazetteers as well as maps and a strip index is available which gives guidance to all of these. A traveller to New Zealand consulting the index has all the maps, guide books etc brought together under that name, the countries are arranged alphabetically. The index entries for plans, guide books, etc are typed on variously coloured strips according to their form, and reference made to their different, classified, locations.

Chapter references:
BOGGS; CURRENT; DDC; HORNER; PARSONS; PARSONS/ FATHERS; SMITH; WEAR.

9

Classification of maps

Any discussion on the classification of maps must commence from the premise that the most important single characteristic of a map is the area it depicts. 'It has been estimated that ninety five per cent of map reference requests require searching by area-subject entries. A survey of 360 map libraries in the United States made by a committee of the Special Libraries Association Geography and Map Division of the United States of America in 1953 revealed that in seventy two per cent of the libraries, maps were most often requested by area alone, or qualified by date or subject. They were seldom requested by author or by title', WALLIS. The filing of maps will therefore usually be expected to be on an area basis; a classification which relates a division of the earth's surface to districts which are a part of that division and also to the region which includes that division. The differences between published map classification schemes are primarily differences in detail on how this aim is achieved and also in the degree of detailed classification which is available in the published scheme. It is a false economy to chose a scheme where a broad outline classification appears to offer simplicity. As the collection grows, inexorably unless the library has an extensive policy for discarding which is unlikely, time that has to be spent retrieving single maps not differentiated from their fellows in a large group, far outweighs any advantage which might be gained from having a simple notation instead of a more complex one.

However detailed the scheme it is commonplace for any individual library to have to modify and extend the scheme in places where it does not reflect the interests of that particular collection. If a scheme is used which, whilst being fully international, originated in a country different from that where the library is situated, the scheme will be found to reflect the interests of the country of origin rather than the national interests of the library. In a public library with its very detailed and extensive local regional interests, no general scheme could offer the detail required. Similarly, other geographical interests of a map collection, most readily exemplified by the need to reflect the detailed emphasis of a lecture course on some regional or thematic aspect of geography will possibly require a more detailed approach for that area than elsewhere.

Area is a concept that, in classification, can be approached in two ways. The world or a continent can be divided into its constituent parts either by regions based on physical geography, or by the political divisions of countries or states. A classification for a library should not be designed to embody a theory but to arrange the materials that are collected. Consequently as most maps have a coverage which is relevant to the political divisions of the earth, it would seem that this should be the main arrangement. Nevertheless, maps are produced which owe little to national or other boundaries and it is desirable that means exist to classify these maps adequately, within a scheme giving full recognition to political divisions. Three broad categories of published map schemes exist, those which give emphasis to major geographical areas, those which give emphasis to political units, and the type, which is possibly of most value, which whilst emphasising political units relates them one to another in a manner which reflects the geographical regions to which they belong. There is another category of classification which can be called home-made and is based on considerations perhaps unique to one library. This latter is not to be confused with the practice in many map collections of adopting a published scheme and modifying and extending it sensibly and naturally to follow the assumed requirements of the library. Although most map classification schemes publish small scale maps on which the boundaries of a level of the classification division are delineated, for a scheme based on geographical area such an index outline is essential. The provision of such a map should also be prepared in a local library if an extension to a part of the scheme is made.

All map classification schemes to be mentioned have initially a division by continents, usually with a class for world, hemispheres etc. at the beginning and a class for oceans, Antarctica etc. In a few cases the scheme includes provision for map bibliographies and other books which might be expected to be filed in a map library. SMITH in discussing the classification scheme he has made for a specific university map collection, and for which he used the area classification schedule of the Library of Congress classification, has laid down three qualities for a workable area classification:

'1 It should be sufficiently detailed to encompass the considerable number of geographic and political units together with their major subdivisions.

2 It should be sufficiently flexible to deal with the unavoidable

compexities and changes, and also to allow classification of areas or grouping not specifically listed in the schedule.

3   It should be arranged in a reasonable progression from area to area, with due regard to hierarchical relationships, and it should be accompanied by some system of numerical designations for the areas.'

The following is a comparison of map classification schemes most commonly used in general libraries:

(IGU) International Geographical Union, Commission on the classification of geographical books and maps in libraries. *Final report* Bad Godesberg, Germany; Institut für Landeskunde, 1964. This report contains, *Draft of a regional classification according to physio-geographical areas of the earth for application in the Universal Decimal Classification* (UDC) by E Meynen, B Winid and M Bürgener, pp 121–132, and Annex 11, *Regional classification on physio-geographical areas of the earth . . . Common auxiliaries of the main units and further subdivision (Proposal).*

This classification is based on regions which are recognised physio-geographical areas and thus which are not affected by political or administrative divisions, but are relevant to geographical and scientific purposes. The classification is for geographical literature as well as for maps and has been drawn up to designate 'details of physio-geographic criteria' as much as to create a regional division of the earth. Thus a book on coffee growing in Puerto Rico is classified as 633.73 (7–9.925) the portion in brackets representing the physio-geographical unit. Similarly, to quote the report, 'the common auxiliaries of regional division by physio-geographical areas of the earth could be readily combined with the UDC common auxiliaries denoting the political divisions of the continents', which are similar to the Dewey Decimal Classification divisions noted below:
Examples:

(4–9.2)   British Isles and Atlantic France.

(4–9.221)   Cumbrian mountains and the Pennines (This includes the full length of the Pennines and Northumberland).

(4–9.1)   Fennoscandia (includes Scandinavia, Finland and Karelia region of USSR, but not Denmark).

(8–9.1)   Western Patagonian Andes and Archipelago of Tierra del Fuego, (approx South Chile and SW Argentina).

(8–9.2)   La Plata region (approx Uruguay, Paraguay and northernmost part of Argentina).

(8–9.3)   Southern Andes, Northern part and coastal region of central Chile.

All the above examples, except (4–9.221) are further subdivided on a physio-geographical basis.

151

This classification does not appear to be suitable for use on its own in general map collections because the bulk of maps there are topographical, frequently of offical surveys, and thus normally following the lines of political divisions. However, if the map collection were in a general library using UDC classification, the UDC common auxiliaries of the political divisions of continents would be used for the area classification, the physio-geographical divisions could then also be utilised where necessary. To quote an example in the *Final report* '(758–9.53), Georgia, USA, Blue Ridge'. For most countries however the divisions are not sufficiently detailed to do this effectively; in England, Lake District, Peak District, North Yorkshire moors, all national parks and common map units, would all have the same number.

Comment on division by subject etc will be made in the section on UDC. It should be noted however that IGU *Final report* contains 'On the classification of geographical books and maps and the application of the Universal Decimal Classification (UDC) in the field of geography' by E Meynen, pp 131–46, which includes 'special auxiliaries of place', and the common auxiliaries of form.

(BOGGS) Samuel W Boggs and Dorothy C Lewis *The Classification and cataloguing of maps and atlases* New York, Special Libraries Association, 1945.

Based initially on a division by continents, the political divisions, countries, are arranged within the appropriate continent on a regional basis with sub-divisions for each country. 'The general plan is like what one finds in the large world atlases.' The divisions within a country are often in the form of compass directions but these divisions are used according to the nature of the country, are not always used, and sometimes conform with a local physio-geographical region, eg 762.3 Western Ecuador, Pacific slopes and plains. 'The sequence of divisions in a country is mainly according to political and geographical relationships. Where a natural grouping is obvious, it is employed...'

Examples:

210 British Isles. 210.2 Great Britain.

211 England (Subdivided by regional groups of counties, eg southwestern counties).

225 to 229 Scandinavia (Norway, Sweden, Denmark) and Iceland.

740 South America.

760 South America: West coast countries

780 Southern South America; La Plata basin.

782   Chile.

782.6   Southern Chile.

This is a decimal notation but the published schedules are an abridgment in which subdivisions for the inclusion of minor administrative regions, cities and smaller islands have been omitted. With a table of nine compass directions including central, an appropriate notation is available for areas which can be subdivided in this way. Towns are classified under the last nine under the country number, following all regional divisions and arranged alphabetically. A notation is supplied for the alphabetisation of town names. A system is also available for the classification, within states of the USA, of counties and minor regions based on alphabetical order.

This classification has been adopted by many libraries, for example in Australia, and it does appear to reach better than most towards a true geographical arrangement of countries and provinces but always based on the political unit. Although countries such as Great Britain and Australia are not sufficiently subdivided in the published schedules, and are not suitably arranged for further subdivision by general sequence notation noted, there is a useful international basis to the scheme, no undue emphasis being given to the United States.

Further subdivision

BOGGS considers that the basic categories for classification of maps are area, subject, and date. Beyond this it is considered that cartographer and title may be called upon to make further arrangement of a large group of similar maps, and that the physical format will be taken into account when it is of such a nature that the map has to be filed separately from the normal sequence. A very detailed subject classification schedule is provided, using letters to distinguish them from the area numbers. The following is only part of a summary of the schedule. The summary might be sufficiently detailed for many general libraries, the expanded schedule could be used in any part of the summary where local interest required it.

a   General maps.
at   Travel, exploration, discovery.
b   Mathematical geography.
bd   Geodetic surveys, triangulation.
c   Physical geography.
caq   Geology.
cb   Geomorphology.
ce   Oceanography.
cf   Meteorology and climatology.
d   Biogeography.

153

df   Plant geography.
e   Human geography.
ec   Geography of population.
f   Political geography.
g   Economic geography.
gc   Agriculture.
gca   Soil maps.
gcac   Soil classification.
gm   Transportation, communication.
h   Military and naval geography.
n   History of geographical knowledge.
p   History.

A map showing oil shale areas of Alberta, Canada would be classified as, 614.7qbha.

In library practice a call number seeks to establish the location in the files of a single wanted map, as opposed to the classification number which seeks to bring together maps which have similar areas and subjects and which may, therefore, be checked together by the reader. BOGGS recommends a call number formed by the area-subject classification number and letters, with further 'the date of situation portrayed on the map, which is the date of survey in a general map if known or, in many distribution maps, the date of the statistical or other information portrayed.' If necessary, where a grouping would otherwise be large and undifferentiated, the cartographer's or publisher's initial can be added, or the appropriate symbols for the cartographer from the Cutter-Sanborn tables, and further still the first significant letter (lower case) of the title. Devices such as these, particularly cartographer and title letters, are not an integral part of a classification scheme but are a filing device and could be used as part of the call number in any map collection whether the BOGGS or any other classification number was used for the significant part of the arrangement. Similarly, BOGGS suggests location symbols 'W' (wall map), 'S' (sets of maps) etc which should precede the rest of the call number and which could always be extended with symbols relevant to local conditions, eg there might be several places in which wall maps have to be housed and they could be denoted as W1, W2, W3.

The use of dates, as in BOGGS, and of scales, which will be found in other schemes, whilst being filing devices have a virtue in the map file or in the classified catalogue and might be considered a further degree of classification because they can be relevant to the needs of the enquirer. They are in fact sometimes treated as part of the schedules in some more sophisticated classifications such as UDC. UDC also provides a form number for formats such as 'wall map', 'globe', 'folded' etc which will serve the same purpose as a location guide as are 'W', 'S' etc in BOGGS. However, they have far less mnemonic quality and a map curator might be forgiven for not recalling, in UDC, that (086.4) referred to relief maps which presumably are separately filed and this is the first thing to appreciate from the call number in retrieving the sheet for a reader. Form divisions such as those in UDC have the virtue of being fixed and unrelated to a particular library and (084.3–528) will always mean 'among the roll maps' wherever they are kept even when the present library has been rebuilt and all the storage is changed, whereas the examples of W1, W2, W3 made above will need to be altered.

(DDC) Melvil Dewey *Dewey decimal classification and relative index* 18th ed, 3 vols New York, Forest Press, Lake Placid Club Education Foundation, 1971.

A general book classification, widely used, with a notation on a decimal basis. 912 is designated the class number for 'graphic representations of surface of earth and extra-terrestrial worlds', and covers atlases, maps, charts and plans. An area arrangement is available for quite detailed subdivision, 912.3 to 912.9. 912.191 to 912.199 cover large areas but mainly oceans and seas. The main area classification commences with an arrangement for maps of the ancient world. 912.4 to 912.99 covers the modern world arranged first by continents, subdivided into countries arranged regionally, with further subdivisions. The country subdivisions have an arrangement which eschews alphabetisation, always being based on local regions, with a published notation for every recognised division.

Examples of area arrangement:

912.4   Europe.

912.47   Eastern Europe (countries, and administrative divisions both arranged regionally).

912.471   Finland.

912.472–.479   USSR areas.

912.48   Northern Europe (Norway, Sweden, Denmark).

912.8   South America (Order of arrangement of countries not readily apparent).

912.81   Brazil.

912.82   Argentine.

912.89   Other parts (includes Paraguay and Uruguay).

One enormous advantage of this classification scheme is that the schedules are revised and published at regular intervals, and additions may be published separately, prior to the publication of a new edition of the scheme. As an example of the value of this there are the recent changes which have taken place in the local administrative areas of the United Kingdom which have in many cases meant the creation of new counties, the division or combination of old ones, and a number of new names and the disappearance of names used for centuries. The changes first took place in the Greater London area and the 18th edition DDC provides a classification of the London Boroughs, administrative divisions of London, which takes into account this reorganisation of local authority boundaries and the newly created names. The further reorganisation of local authorities in the United Kingdom made it necessary to provide a fresh scheme for the rest of the country. These are now published in: *Dewey decimal classification. Additions, notes and decisions.* 3 (4/5) April 1974. Supplement. This contains the revised edition of area table—42 (England and Wales), and issue 3 (6), October 1974 which contains the revised edition of area table—41 (Scotland). These *Additions . . .* also made a necessary correction in regard to the classification number for British Isles.

Examples:

912.41   British Isles. Great Britain and United Kingdom are also classed here. 'Division is primarily by metropolitan and non-metropolitan counties, and secondarily by metropolitan and non-metropolitan districts . . .'

.411   Scotland (Division of Scotland is by region and district, Northern Ireland is by district alone).

.413   South eastern Scotland.

.413.2   Lothian region.

.413.4   City of Edinburgh district.

.42   England and Wales.

.428.7   Tyne and Wear Metropolitan County.

.428.79   North Tyneside, including Longbenton, Tynemouth, Wallsend, Whitley Bay.

DDC by its standard subdivision table of areas provides a detailed means of area classification for maps, simple to use in that the tables are fully expanded with notations. An examination of the tables in detail shows that although most countries have an adequate subdivision, the tables for the United States show a great emphasis on the country of origin. The area tables occupy 235 pages and 149 of these are concerned with the United States.

DDC tables are commonly used for maps in British general libraries as part of the classification scheme also used for the books in the library. The letter M or the word 'Maps' could be substituted as a prefix for the area tables, in place of 912, and in this form the notation would be acceptable in any separately organised map library.

Further subdivision

DDC reveals itself as primarily concerned with book classification when it is realised that it is not possible to further arrange maps under a country according to subject. No scheduled opportunity is given to provide any subject arrangement for maps unless the maps are arranged initially by subject, and then there is no facility for arranging by area within a subject.

912.1001 to 912.1899 is the part of the schedule where 912 'Graphic representations of surface of earth and of extra terrestrial worlds' can be divided according to specific subjects as 001–899 of the main schedules.

912.1553282 would represent a geological map of oil deposits, but no differentiation can be made for area. Similarly, although there are many subjects in the main schedules where subdivision takes place according to the area's subdivisions this is for the classification of books only, as at 554–559 the geology of specific continents countries and localities. The only exceptions are that historical atlases are classed at 911 and atlases and maps for navigation are classed at the specific subject, eg aeronautical flight guides 629.13254. A book on the geology of Alberta would be classified as 557.123, but no appropriate form division is provided to convert this number into one for a geological map of Alberta. Is it not to be expected that a librarian might locally provide an 'appropriate form number' say the prefix 'Maps', if she wishes to classify geological maps in the same department of the general library as geological books? Similarly, if a librarian using DDC and classifying all maps at area alone, eg 912.7123 for a map of Alberta, felt it necessary to subdivide according to subject as in many other schemes, a local extension to the scheme may be evolved. This may involve using the class numbers for subjects in the main schedules eg 912.7123, 550 the latter showing it to be a geology map, or by using a list of subject headings in alphabetical order, as 912.7123 geo(logy). If this is done it should be as part of the call number and not as part of the classification number.

912.7123   or   912.7123 so that if DDC officially changes any
   550   geo
numbers in the area schedules, as with the class numbers for United Kingdom divisions recently, then the library, still using the 'pure' DDC numbers for areas, can make those changes without possible conflict with the unauthorised subdivisions. For the same reason the use of terms like 'geo' in the call number, is less likely to create conflict with the DDC numbers, but necessitates the creation of a full list of subject headings for present and potential need which can be used as

157

an authority file for the future. It would be advisable to examine the subject headings for maps in a variety of map classification schemes before this was compiled and compilation must always be liberal in anticipating the collection's holdings in the future. Local amendments of this or any other nature, and whatever the map classification scheme, should only be made after the fullest thought has been given to it.

(UDC) *Universal decimal classification UDC 9, geography, biography, history* English full edition; Fourth international edition. (FID publication No 179). BS 1000(9): 1972. London, British Standards Institute 1972. *Index to the selection of common auxiliaries of place for use with UDC 9,* Supplement 1. London, British Standards Institute 1972.
Universal decimal classification Abridged English edition. (FID publication No 289). BS 1000A : 1961 3rd edition, revised 1961. London, British Standards Institute 1963.

UDC common auxiliaries of place, naturally show a family resemblance to the DDC auxiliary table of areas, but there are differences within the area classification as well as in the use of these auxiliaries within the two, mainly book, classification schemes. Libraries using UDC as the main library classification might be expected to use the common auxiliary of place, as appropriate, for the classification of maps, and it must be remembered that (IGU) is a scheme for physio-geographical areas which is proposed as an addition to UDC and could be used in conjunction with the common auxiliaries of place.

UDC area classification is a much less detailed classification than DDC in some sectors, particularly with regard to the United States, and yet provides class numbers for divisions elsewhere which are not in DDC. Generally UDC, like DDC, is based on continents, with a secondary division by countries arranged in geographical groupings and further subdivided by county, or state, or province etc. Normally this is the extent of subdivision in the published schedule. The UDC is continually under revision but in the example of the reorganisation and change of boundaries of the United Kingdom administrative areas it is later than DDC. *FID News Bulletin* 25(1) 1975, 5 reported that among the proposals for the revision of UDC issued by the FID Secretariat on December 31, 1974 was a note on changes for (421 / 426.7) on Greater London and the London Boroughs, for inclusion in *Extensions and Corrections to the UDC, Series 9:1* (mid-1975).

Examples of area classification, found to be very similar to, but different in detail from DDC:

(4)   Europe.
(41)   British Isles.

(410)   Great Britain, United Kingdom.

(411)   Scotland. (No reorganised areas catered for in this edition).

(43)   Germany. (Treated differently from DDC, possibly showing a more European viewpoint).

(430.1)   FDR   (Land subdivisions).

(430.2)   DDR   (Bezirk subdivisions).

(431/435.8)   German provinces up to 1934.

(48)   Scandinavian states.

(480)   Finland.

(481)   Norway.

(485)   Sweden.

(489)   Denmark.

(8)   South America (as a whole).

(81)   Brazil.

(817.4)   Brasilia (Main divisions of 8 similar to DDC).

The first major difference with UDC, compared with DDC, is the greater freedom for synthesis by allocating class numbers formed from the main UDC numbers in the schedules and the addition of common auxiliaries. Secondly the far wider range of auxiliary numbers provides an auxiliary of form, (084.3), for maps, charts and plans. This immediately opens up the prospect, not allowed for in DDC, of using the main schedule numbers, with the appropriate auxiliary, for maps.

(084.3) is the common auxiliary of form, for maps, charts and plans, but there are special auxiliaries of this number for further classification by scale, by types of map, by types of reproduction, and by format for types of storage. Examples are:

(084.3 – 222)   Bird's eye view.

(084.3 – 223)   Air photo mosaics.

(084.3 – 34)   Distribution maps, dot maps.

(084.3 – 42)   Blue prints.

(084.3 – 526)   Folded, in cover.

(084.3 – 528)   Rolled.

(084.35)   Wall map.

(084.4)   Atlas.

In UDC, which is basically a book classification, maps are classified at 912 'Non-literary representations of a region, pictures, graphs, diagrams . . . maps, atlases, globes' and these can be further defined by using the available common auxiliaries of place, time, form etc. The area classification examples noted above are part of the auxiliaries of place, 'non-literary representations' of Scotland would be classified as 912 (411). Further definition can be obtained by the addition of the appropriate auxiliary of form, see the examples above, so

159

that 912 (411) (084.4) is for an atlas of Scotland. An alternative arrangement is allowed by the subdivision of 912 in line with the (08) auxiliary of form as:

912.4 Pictorial, graphic and cartographic descriptions.

912.43 Maps, plans and charts.

912.44 Atlases.

912.643 Globes.

912.644 Relief models and maps.

The UDC facility of combining numbers by the use of a colon, allows maps also to be classified either at the number for the geography of a country, with the colon combination of the 912 division, or at the subject number within the main UDC numbers.

914.80 : 912 (084.3–223).

[Finland : airphoto-mosaics].

55 (489) : 912.43.

[geology (Denmark) : maps].

or, if the area is to be preserved as the main characteristic of classification,

(411) 631.4 : 912.43.

[(Scotland) Soil : maps].

Part of the special auxiliaries at (084.3) refer to scale, which provides the facility for using scale, and if necessary date, which is denoted by '. . .', as '1975', for filing purposes.

(LC) Library of Congress, Subject Cataloguing Division *Classification: Class G; geography, anthropology, folklore, manners and customs, recreation* 3rd ed Washington, Library of Congress, 1954.

Class G Geography including the form division 'maps', is another book classification concerned mainly with an arrangement of books according to their subject matter. Designed for use in a specific library, that of the United States, Library of Congress, the general classification is widely used in other libraries. Blocks of numbers are assigned to subjects and, for maps, to areas. All classification numbers consist of the class letter, G for geography and maps with at least four numbers. Some blocks of numbers are not used, to allow for possible expansion, which is also possible through decimal expansion. Atlases have numbers within the range G1001–G3102, the area arrangement within this range being similar to that for sheet maps. Once again the area arrangement is based on general maps of the world followed by a sequence of continents, which are subdivided by regions, natural features etc and by major political divisions such as countries. This style of subdivision applies to major geographical areas and to countries which would be divided by states, provinces, counties, etc. This area-subdivision is indicated by the following plan which occurs when two or more numbers are assigned to an area. The last numeral of each number represents:

0 or 5   General maps.

1 or 6   Division by subject.

2 or 7   Division by region, natural feature, A—Z when not assigned individual numbers.

3 or 8   Division by political division (countries, states, provinces etc), A—Z when not assigned individual numbers.

4 or 9   Division by towns, A—Z. (This is always a division under the country except for towns in the USA and Canada which are classified first under state or province.)

On this basis a general map of France would be classified G5830.

a map of the department Var, at G5833. V2. Cutter numbers being used to provide the alphabetical sequence, V2 = Var.

a street plan of Paris at G5834. P3.

Examples of area arrangement: G precedes each number.

G 5700–5702   Europe.

5720–5722   Western Europe.

5740–5742   British Isles and Great Britain.

5750–5754   England, and maps of England and Wales together.

5753   England counties, A—Z.

5753.L4   Leicestershire.

6905   Northern Europe.

6910–6912   Scandinavia.

6912.L3   Lappi (part of Finland).

6920 to 6954   covers Denmark, Iceland, Norway, Sweden.

6960–6964   Finland.

6965–6966   Eastern Europe (as a whole).

5200–5202   South America (as a whole).

5280–5384   is the block covering numbers for Venezuela, Columbia, Ecuador, Peru, Bolivia, Chile, Rio de la Plata basin, etc in that order.

Plans of towns of countries other than USA and Canada are in an alphabetical arrangement under the number for the whole country. This is a common practice in map classification schemes. The different arrangement for North America in LC shows the natural profusion of this material in the Library of Congress. It indicates the emphasis on the USA, another example being that numbers are assigned to all counties in each state. Unlike DDC, new editions of the schedules do not appear regularly, but LC, Class G, has been revised and is to be published in a new edition in 1975. Particularly, attention has been given to the revision of geographical/political entities in order to reflect current usage, for example, a divided Germany. There is a regular quarterly publication *LC classification-additions and changes* which publishes revisions and amendments to the full scheme. A commercially produced publication cumulated such changes for Class G; *Library of Congress Classification schedules: a cumulation of additions and changes through 1970. Class G. Geography, anthropology, folklore, manner and customs, recreation* Detroit, Gale Research Co, 1972.

Area class numbers which are of two or more digits can be subdivided according to the subject emphasis of the map or atlas. This is permitted and signified when the last numeral of the block of numbers assigned to the area ends in 1 or 6, a block usually consists of five numbers. A similar division can be made at an area subdivision for a map which uses a Cutter number. The subject divisions consist of seventeen major topics, which have a capital letter notation, divided into subtopics which introduce numbers; eg

Physical sciences C.

        C3   Hydrography.
        C5   Geology.
        C8   Meteorology, climatology.

A form division is included in this subject arrangement and all divisions are printed in the schedules.

    Special category atlases and maps A.

        A1   Outline and base maps.
        A2   Index maps.
        A3   Aerial views.
        A4   Photomaps etc.

Examples of the use of subject divisions—

    A map of the agricultural regions of Eastern Europe: G6966.J1, consisting of, E. Europe. Agriculture. Agricultural regions.

    A map of the coal-mines of Leicestershire: G5753.L4 H9.

consisting of   G5753   English counties.
           .L4   Leicestershire, Cutter number.
           H   Mines and mineral resources.
           9   Coal.

The LC schedules include notes on the call numbers used by the Library of Congress. It must be repeated that all the parts of a library's call number are not part of the classification scheme. These parts are a means of locating an individual map required and distinguishing it from its fellows which have the same classification number. Therefore another library may use the Library of Congress classification for maps as outlined above, and not use that library's means of further arrangement. However although few libraries in the world will ever have the problem of arranging as many maps as the

Library of Congress at one classification number, it must nevertheless always be remembered that map collections grow and it is much easier to provide a call number arrangement from the beginning than add it to a large library when it becomes absolutely necessary. In a large general library, Cutter numbers will probably already be in use in full for distinguishing books according to author or editor and therefore their use for maps, in a sub-arrangement by person responsible for the map might seem justified, although it may be thought that the arrangements by scale and by date of survey are more logical in a map collection. The LC call number for maps consists of the area classification number (area number and sub-area number if any), subject letter and number (if a thematic map), date of the map, Cutter number of the name of the responsible corporate body or individual. Sets of maps of a country or area are kept separately from other maps of a country and filed before them in scale, not date, order. They are distinguished in the class notation by 'S' after the area number, thus a 1:50,000 map of France would be G 5830 S 50 (1:50,000 less last 3 digits).

For atlases the call number consists of area number, person or body responsible, date of atlas.

Example of map call number using all elements:

G 3803   New York counties.
.M6 P2   Monroe County + subject, roads.
  1959   Date of survey.
  .A5   American Automobile Association.

(PARSONS) E J S Parsons *Manual of map classification and cataloguing, prepared for use in the Directorate of Military Survey, War Office* London, War Office 1946.

The major aim of this classification is simplicity and it is based on the collection of maps in a specialist library. The primary division is mainly by continents, the letter A—N are used for these and in the case of the Americas, three divisions F—H are used and J—L are assigned to the Pacific, Atlantic and Indian Oceans and islands. The continents are divided by political units, countries, but no attempt is made to group these on a basis of associated geographical areas, except for island groups and a few areas such as Scandinavia, Balkans, in Europe. With these exceptions all subdivision is by an alphabetical arrangement of countries. Within the countries subdivision is first by the accepted pattern of compass directions, Northern—to South Western—, followed by an alphabetical arrangement of states, counties or other administrative divisions. The countries are given a number in arithmetical progression, as are administrative divisions preceded by a colon. There is therefore little pattern of subdivision in arrangement or notation and every continent, country, subdivision is printed with its assigned notation. The exceptions are for the second division of every continent which is for adjacent seas and major lakes and for town plans which are always assigned a number at the end of the sequence under the country, several numbers not being used to allow for expansion. The town plans are to be arranged alphabetically, this could be done by the use of Cutter numbers.

Two alphabetical indexes are provided, one to continents, countries and seas, and the second is a very extensive index of islands and island groups each with its assigned classification number.

Examples:

C1   Europe (as a whole)
C2   European waters
(remainder alphabetical countries, eg).
C3   Andorra
C4   Austria ± Hungary
C15   British Isles
C17   England and Wales
C17:1   Northern England
C17:11   Anglesey
C17:12   Bedfordshire
C32   Portugal
C33   Scandinavia
C34   Denmark
C35   Finland
C36   Norway
C37   Sweden
C38   Spain
H1   South America   H2 South America, seas
H3   Argentina (and continuing alphabetically)

This classification is intended to be simple and because of the extensive use of alphabetical arrangement this is probably achieved as a filing arrangement. PARSONS is used by the Bodleian Map Library, Oxford University, with amendments, and in other British university libraries. Because of the absence of revision, libraries using the scheme will have found it necessary to make local amendments and it is the only published scheme seen to be in loose-leaf form which will facilitate such local alterations. A description of the use of the scheme and the associated cataloguing procedure is given in E J S Parsons and Betty D Fathers 'Map room, Bodleian Library' *Society of University Cartographers, Bulletin* 2 (2) June 1968, 1–7.

The arrangement of maps beyond the arrangement provided by the area classification number is, in PARSONS, different from any other scheme described here but follows a method which in one form or another is quite common in university geography departments. PARSONS offers no classification arrangement except area in filing maps, but in providing a catalogue to a map collection the scheme provides for a 'Subject File' which in the published scheme, provides a limited degree of subject access to the map collection, an access which could however be greatly increased by local expansion of the principle employed. Firstly, considering the arrangement of the maps in the files, PARSONS provides for the compilation of a 'handlist'. This has to be a loose-leaf collection of ruled sheets, each sheet representing one specific area number in the classification. When a map of that area is received it is noted on the area sheet in the handlist and assigned a sequence number, which for the first map will be 1), for the second 2), and so on. The area class number and the sequence number form the call number of that map, and of course, decide its place in the files.

The use of sequence numbers, or any form of running number, may well be justifiable in individual libraries. Additions to a file which depends on this method for arrangement, are entirely 'adding to the end' of the file or major part of the file. Any classification system which in the call number continues to arrange by characteristics such as subject, scale, date or author after the area number requires the intercalation of maps in the files, with consequent difficulties of physical expansion being regularly required at various parts of the file where room for physical expansion is not available. As PARSONS does not use a single sequence of numbers (but as many sequences as there are class numbers) this problem is not avoided. It would seem that the purpose in making sequence numbers is to provide an inventory in ledger form. Any map collection where it is felt that a map inventory should be provided is recommended to prepare an extra unit card when cataloguing for this purpose and file this set of catalogue cards in the same order as the maps in the cases, but to arrange these maps and the cards in a meaningful order, an order which provides subdivisions for subjects, where necessary, and an arrangement using scale, and date as required. This inventory file can have additional non-cataloguing information added to the cards, if desired, on such matters of record as price paid, supplier and stock-taking checks. If the library file has or intends to have a part of the map catalogue arranged in the same order as the maps in the cases there is no reason why this should not have the additional function of inventory. If the map curator thinks it necessary to have a unique number for each map, the order number can be brought forward on to the map on receipt, and noted on the catalogue card. If several maps are ordered on one order form the number of the line on the order can be added as well to provide provenance for the map from order to filing cabinet.

The PARSONS scheme does stipulate that with each area division maps in sets must be separated from single sheet maps, or maps completed in several sheets. The maps in sets or series, are to be grouped according to scale. In order to retain the use of the sequence number and yet bring together maps in series, the scheme has to allocate blocks of numbers in the sequences to be recorded under each area number for the numbering of maps of particular scales. Thus, within a country area number the sequence number 1–10 are allocated to series larger than 1:20,000, 11–20 for series of scales between 1:20,000 and 1:50,000 whilst the sequence for maps not in sets begins at 101. There is, therefore, a limit to the number of sets at a particular scale which can be added for a country before the system has to be altered.

(AGS) R Drazniowsky *Cataloguing and filing rules for maps and atlases in the society's collection* Revised and expanded edition. New York, American Geographical Society, 1969.

A classification, or map filing system, which has been evolved for use with the large collection of maps in the library of the American Geographical Society. The primary area arrangement is of continents, using nine divisions, but in a rather unusual order. I, North America, only covers Greenland and Canada. The United States has a primary division of its own, 8, far removed from Canada and adjacent to 7 devoted to Oceans. The area notation consists of three or four numbers, the latter using a decimal point, and many numbers are unused. Class 200 for Latin and South America has no class numbers after 267 although prior to that each number from 260 is in use for individual countries in South America. The first edition of this scheme, published as the *Manual for the classification and cataloguing of maps in the society's collection* 1947 used the two classes 280 and 290 for 'Research materials, drawings, and archives of society's maps of Hispanic America'. Perhaps in the society's files they are still used for that purpose, but the numbers would have no significance in a published scheme for the possible use of other libraries.

The division within continents is by countries, or in the case of North America by states or provinces, and their arrangement does not appear to follow a pattern. For Africa, the countries are grouped into northern, western, eastern and southern countries although these regions are not named; in Canada the provinces are listed from east to west, but this is not an unusual method of listing Canadian provinces;

166

and in South America the countries, and in USA the states, are listed alphabetically. Further subdivision is not catered for by a notation in the schedules, but general filing rules are made to cover the maps of lesser areas, and others. These are:

1 World, continents, parts of continents, countries. Filed chronologically under area-subject.

2 Sets of maps filed under area-subject, a letter 'b' is added to area number to denote a set, and then by scale, the larger scale first.

3 Any maps covering 'secondary areas', that is maps of any political, administrative or physio-geographical divisions of a country, together with maps of towns and their environs, national parks, international boundary maps, are filed alphabetically by the name of the division or area under the country. After the area number, a letter 'c' is added to denote these maps, and under any division name the maps are arranged chronologically.

4 Town plans are arranged under the country, in alphabetical order, the letter 'd' being added to the area number.

5 Wall maps are filed separately according to area-subject and are distinguished by a letter 'a' after the area number.

6 Atlases are filed separately, arranged by the same area number as maps but with the prefix 'At'.

Examples of area arrangements:

250   South America.

251–267,   alphabetical order for fourteen countries from Argentina to Venezuela, the Guianas all at G.

600   Europe.

610   Scandinavia   610.1   Lapland.

611   Norway.

612   Sweden   612.1   Gotland I.

613   Finland.

614   Denmark   614.5   Bornholm I.

615   Iceland.

620   British Isles.

621   Great Britain.

622   England.

No subdivisions are designated for the above, except as shown. In England, the counties, for example, must be arranged as noted in three of the filing rules above, any notation being devised by the library concerned.

This is a broad classification scheme and probably because of that it becomes complicated when a wide range of maps in a library is considered, primarily because of the absence of divisions under countries and thus the need to introduce Section 'c'. Again the 'English'

Channel Islands are selected to be islands in the Atlantic Ocean and are therefore classified 723.8 whilst England is at 622; but under 120, Canada, it is stated that 'Islands of the Arctic, Hudson Bay, and Northwest Territories . . . area code number 120-c. Islands in the Atlantic and Pacific Oceans . . . area code number of the nearest province'. This rule covers Baffin Island.

PARSONS offers a similar type of filing arrangement for areas, and because of the far more extensive schedules seems to be more simple in use. AGS has been issued in three editions in 1947, 1952 and 1969 so revision has taken place regularly. However it is a broad classification and so many political and administrative boundary changes which may take place have no effect on the published schedules, they are not sufficiently subdivided. Some libraries would consider this as a favourable point.

AGS provides a helpful means of subject division within the area classification. Thirteen subjects are listed in the tables, provided with a notation of capital letters. Examples of the subjects are:

D Transportation and communication.

Maps showing roads, airways, railways, and other types of transport. Also maps showing other media of communication such as television, radio, telephone, radar.

E Economic.

Maps dealing with natural resources, minerals, forestry, fishing, thermal energy, recreation areas, national parks, conservation, agriculture, vegetation, land use, land tenure, trade, finance.

These subject divisions obviously offer only very broad groupings. AGS suggests further division, using numbers, but the sub-arrangement is not tabulated, it is left to local librarians. AGS recommends that the subject classification symbol be always given as a second line below the area number.

R Drazniowsky in the AGS scheme gives a very useful comment on the matter of subject classification which should be quoted here in some detail. 'To choose the proper subject or subjects for cataloguing [and initially for classification], the cataloguer must have a knowledge of map reading, among other qualifications, and should be well acquainted with the collection. Insufficient knowledge may result in over-or under-cataloguing. As a guide to the cataloguer for subject selections the following suggestions may be helpful. [Consider:]

1   The purpose for which the map was prepared.
2   The purpose for which the collection was established.
3   Types of users.
4   Material available in the collection.
5   Specialisation of other collections located in the vicinity.'

It could be added that when such matters have been taken into account, when either for classification or for cataloguing, the decision which was made should be recorded, so that in future there will be consistent practice on that point.

AGS, like BOGGS, recognises that much of the material in a map collection appears in sets of maps, often from official surveys. The sets of maps are distinguished in AGS by the addition of the letter 'b' to the area number which allows them to be filed together and not with single sheet maps filed among them. BOGGS provides a prefix 'S' to the call number which also signifies sets, and implies also that they will not only be filed together but kept in separate storage apart from other maps. The BOGGS scheme will, of course, create a duplicate classification arrangement in the storage, but the AGS scheme merely separates but keeps sets and single sheet maps of the same area in adjacent positions which many libraries might find to be the most acceptable solution.

(RGS) Royal Geographical Society arrangement.

The large collection of maps owned by the Royal Geographical Society is one collected and arranged for the benefit of members of the society, but since 1854 the British Government has made a small annual grant to the Society in return for which the Map Room is open to the public. CRONE records that in 1960, 9,000 sheets per annum were being added to the collection. With this in mind, and the knowledge that use by the public as well as members will create a wide variety of demand, it is perhaps salutary to realise that this map collection is filed according to a system which, except for the usual initial arrangement by continents, is entirely an alphabetical filing arrangement with no pretensions to classification as such. Maps of the various countries are filed under the name of the country within the appropriate continent, and the countries are arranged entirely in alphabetical order. Each continental group, but not the world, and each country has subdivisions which are,

General maps.

Divisional maps, (a major part of a continent or country).

District maps, (administrative districts, as county, state or province).

Special maps (various, including large scale maps of small areas, boundary surveys, geological maps of a small area, town plans etc.).

There are no detailed schedules, and no notation for countries although G, Div, D, and S, are used after the name of the country to signify the sub-groups.

Each of these groupings can be further subdivided by some twenty

169

nine subject headings, with additional headings such as 'Communications, sea routes', for the world section. The subject headings cover both subjects, such as Climate; Communications, road; Communications, railways; Geological; Soils; Vegetation, and forms, such as Chart; Topo. (1:500,000 scale and larger); Wall maps.

The (RGS) filing arrangement is used, with minor changes, for the University of Hull map collection, part of the Brynmor Jones Library, but housed in the Geography Department. FERRAR writes on map classification in the light of the RGS arrangement in 'The management of map collections and libraries in university geography departments' *Library Association record* 64 (5) May, 1962, 161–165.

(RGS) by its very broad classification and the resultant necessity for creating non-scheduled sub-divisions has a similarity to the (AGS) arrangement. (AGS) in the 'C', secondary areas subdivision, offers no further arrangement other than chronological, any grouping within 'C' would be that made by an individual library. Similarly in (RGS) groupings 'Divisional', 'District', and 'Special', further sub-groups, other than the subject headings, would appear to be called for so that all maps covering one district were together then perhaps arranged by date, and in the 'Special' section all town maps might be together, probably then arranged alphabetically. The practice at the society is to assign an accession number for the map, so that everything within the group is filed in order of receipt. This is not helpful for searching whether done at the map cabinet or more probably at a catalogue arranged in 'shelf' order.

A broad classification, if published, leaves many problems of filing unresolved. Problems of assigning places to areas include such matters as mentioned in the notes on (AGS) in connection with islands. Baffin Island, Channel Islands, are they filed (RGS) in the alphabetical sequence as countries? When does an island adjacent to the mainland of a political unit become part of that unit for filing purposes? This type of decision has to be made and must be made to avoid confusion in any library. AGS has Sicily a main area entry in the catalogue, PARSONS has Sicily filed in the islands section of 'Italy and Sicily'. In any individual library, if such decisions are not made by the published map classification scheme used, a register of locally-made decisions has to be compiled for future guidance. A library can not long survive as an efficient and developing service if these decisions, and similar problems that have been sorted out to the satisfaction of the local users, are only part of the so-called 'know-how' of the current map curator. Therefore if they have to be recorded for areas, that would be more efficiently done by creating a more detailed classification scheme with rules for classifying. '[A] classification system needs at the outset to provide the framework for inclusion of every likely map subject, though it need not give an absolute location for the less common subjects . . .', BOGGS.

Local modifications
It would seem inevitable that in any substantial map collection within a university or public library it will be found necessary to modify the general classification system used for maps. The primary reason is that libraries reflect the interests of their users and there will therefore be an emphasis on national, regional and maps of the area around the library which provides a special depth to the collection which can not be represented in a general classification scheme covering the world. Another reason can be that the general scheme is not sufficiently up-to-date to accept in a meaningful order, changes within political boundaries or, for example, the advent of new types of maps. General schemes for books and other materials which are commonly used, as L of C, DDC and UDC do have regular revision of their area schedules and, at intervals, new editions are published as well as amendments to information between editions. An example of such an amendment, and of the need for it, is the change made to the area classification in DDC for the new local political boundaries in the United Kingdom. AGS has appeared in three editions, but the two specialist map classification schemes which are most popular PARSONS, and BOGGS LEWIS have no updating, which should compel the local map librarian to make his own adjustments for geographical and political changes.

SMITH in producing a manual for classifying, cataloguing and processing maps in the University of Kansas gives information on the reasoning behind the procedures adopted and in particular the choice of L of C with minor area amendments and an expanded subject arrangement. This is a most useful book to stimulate thought on the modifications which might be made in other libraries whatever classification is being amended. It is always worthwhile, when departing from a published scheme, to remember that without great care one may create unforeseen difficulties and the wise map librarian will try to make this a very remote possibility not only by exercising great care in the construction of the modified section but also by considering how other map librarians have tried to overcome similar problems.

In Great Britain, the quite common use of PARSONS in university map rooms has led to some publication on local amendments. PARSONS/FATHERS describing the Bodleian Library, Map Room give a brief outline of the general classification scheme used based on the PARSONS scheme for use in the Directorate of Military Survey and only modified slightly. At Edinburgh University where there are two map collections, a general reference collection in the main university library and another collection for the teaching requirements of the geography department both use PARSONS modified. WEAR describes the collection in the geography department and gives one or two instances of PARSONS being out-of-date in detail, eg no number for the USSR as a whole and no number for Pakistan. David P Ferro, of the Map Area, Edinburgh University Library, also points out, in a letter, the need to provide a number for the Republic of Ireland.

BOGGS is the classification favoured in Australia and it is used in the Mitchell Library, Public Library of New South Wales. The library had to make a number of changes, most significantly in expanding and, as a result, changing the schedules for Australia, New Zealand and Oceania. The National Library of Australia, Canberra also uses the Boggs and Lewis schedules as extended by the Mitchell Library and has prepared index maps for each state and Papua New Guinea where the boundaries of the new area divisions and the appropriate classification number are marked. *Australian maps*, the Australian national map bibliography published by the National Library uses the amended scheme. The Boggs and Lewis scheme is also used for the map collection in the University of Sydney but detailed modifications and extensions for Australia have been made by Dr E F Kunz.

Chapter references:
AGS; BOGGS; CRONE; DDC; FERRAR; IGU; LC; O'REILLY; PARSONS; PARSONS/FATHERS; PRESCOTT; SMITH; UDC; WALLIS; WEAR.

10

Cataloguing maps

Many people or families, have a small map collection at home, the individual map being bought normally for what was a need at the time, or town plan, a walking map, a motoring map for a foreign country. In some persons' lives they are the background to a life story, the period when the owner walked and climbed in this country's hills and mountains, the motoring map when he took more to the road, the approximate dates of travel abroad and so on. Mention a route and the owner of the map might go to his shelves and produce a sheet which will assist, even if not quite up-to-date. He probably knows whereabouts to find it but even if it is misplaced it does not take too long to trace it, because one can soon leaf through the whole collection. In a library the collections are much bigger, but however big they are one can still find a map required, if there is one relevant to a reader's need, by examining the collection from first to last until an appropriate sheet is found. The introduction of a classification system is to reduce such a search to an examination of one or two groups of like maps which might answer the requirements. A catalogue should be provided to identify this group or a few groups, and, if possible, the map or maps within those groups, which seem most appropriate, and sometimes select a map which might also suffice but is elsewhere, for example in a set covering the world, or within the pages of a book. 'Cat and class', or indexing, are techniques which are designed to answer the question beginning 'have you got a map—which . . .' as clearly as possible, and if the answer is 'yes' to direct the librarian to the location of the sheet or sheets.

The question may be qualified in many ways . . . a map of the Netherlands, a canal map of the Netherlands, a map of the Netherlands before the completion of the Great Enclosing Dyke, a land use map of the area between Amsterdam and Utrecht, a recent map of the Netherlands showing motorways, a large scale plan of Utrecht etc, etc. The arrangement of the maps cannot alone hope to satisfy all these questions. They may be kept in area order and so to discover maps of the Netherlands is possible but it would not provide any facility for finding, say, Arrowsmith maps. As the major characteristic in users' requests for maps is for the area covered this is the primary consideration to be taken into account and so map collections will normally arrange their maps on an area system. Too often this arrangement is the only means that users have in order to provide an approach to the sheets they want in the labelled storage cabinets. Often if a card is made for each map and filed in the same order as the maps in the cases this does not provide an alternative means of access, it is not a catalogue but a 'shelf-list' merely requiring the user to consult the cards instead of the actual maps to trace a wanted sheet.

A catalogue makes use of the possibility of making more different approaches to the map collection, different approaches which are designed to answer the different questions of the reader such as, a map of the Netherlands, maps by Arrowsmith, geological maps. The construction of a catalogue requires the librarian to consider the current and the potential needs of her readers. Potential also because the map library will grow, because of this and because better access is being made to the collection by cataloguing, the use of it will increase and be more varied, one might say that these are laws of librarianship.

The catalogue of maps must always be judged in all its parts as how it will be helpful to the readers, both in the approaches to the maps which it offers, and the information, the description of the map it provides in an individual entry. There is regretfully a tendency in cataloguing to create a bureaucracy, the chief bureaucrat being that inanimate catalogue, demanding adherence to rules for the sake of rules, and the purpose of its existence can be forgotten. Rules are absolutely essential for uniformity of practice within a catalogue, to record what is decided is probably the best practice in problematical situations, to allow the user to follow the cataloguing pattern with comprehension, but wherever a rule, logical though it may be in a theoretical situation, appears to be operating against the interests of the majority of users, that rule must be modified and a rule made on the modification. This means that the map cataloguer must be the map curator constantly in touch with the map users, or the map curator must have a governing influence over the development of map cataloguing. A catalogue can also serve as an inventory with perfect success, but this is secondary to its function as an aid to users.

Much has been written about the differences between maps and books. The acceptance of these differences has not led automatically to the realisation that this means there should be a difference in their cataloguing. Map curators involved in special map collections naturally catalogue for maps, but map librarians in a general library find maps catalogued as an unusual type of book; one imagines for the sake of the uniformity of a catalogue. WOODS, and others, have written most interestingly on this curious dichotomy. Curious because the difference is generally accepted but not acted upon and the prime consideration of cataloguing, the assistance of users, is thus ignored. Suffice to note that the British Museum, Department of Printed Books, which has enjoyed world renown for about a century for the authority of its author catalogue, has always treated maps differently. The BM RULES states, 'Every atlas, map, chart, plan or view has its main entry under the name of the geographical or topographical area which the work represents . . . Supplementary entries are made, where possible, under the name of every author, draughtsman, engraver, surveyor, or compiler'. This in general terms is the view of specialist map libraries, the area depicted is the main incontrovertible characteristic for all maps. For books, the author provides the main catalogue entry, and in general libraries maps are catalogued in that same pattern, so that in AACR 3 pages and 2 rules are devoted to establishing the author of a map.

Map curators and map librarians knew from experience what was confirmed by a survey conducted by the Special Libraries Association, Geography and Map Division, Committee on Map Cataloguing, that the majority of requests for maps are from the area approach. The survey showed that seventy two per cent of libraries replying to a questionnaire expected maps to be requested more frequently by area, or area with subject and date qualifications, than to be requested by author and title. Such factors persuade map librarians that the main entry for maps must be the area entry.

This, however, continues to be evaded by cataloguers. The cataloguing rules for non-book materials published by the CANADIAN LIBRARY ASSOCIATION in 1973, includes maps, the British Library Association equivalent excluded maps because they were so 'obviously like books'. The Canadian rules state under, Main entry, 'If a media centre wishes to have an integrated catalogue in which all media, book and non-book, are interfiled, the same rules of entry must apply to all materials. Entry under title will occur more frequently for non-book materials because authorship can not be established as readily for many non-book items'. The section on maps keeps the picture of an integrated catalogue, 'Main entry. Maps are entered under title', but its value in assisting a user to find a required map is a little less obvious. WALLISCH strongly criticised this rule in a review of the preliminary edition of the Canadian rules published in 1970, and the 1973 edition of the rules contains an appendix A, 'Alternative method of cataloguing a specialised non-integrated collection of maps'. . . . 'included at the request of several map librarians' which includes—'Main entry—Maps are entered under the name of the area covered, subdivided by the predominant subject matter illustrated, with a further subdivision for the date of the situation depicted, eg, (US—national parks and reserves—1971). This supplied main entry is enclosed in square brackets. Maps with no predominant subject matter are entered under area subdivided by date eg (Ontario—1930).'

This rule apparently written by Miss J Winearls and other map librarians, naturally has a resemblance, but is not identical with, the suggestion for main entry headings, made by the SLA G & M Div, Committee on Map Cataloguing. The committee suggested, the main entry entered under area, followed in the heading by date, and then subject division, with the further addition of scale and size.

The above notes on choice of author, or title, or area as the main entry in a catalogue of maps, shows that map librarians are aware that 'area' is the obvious choice to users but that other cataloguers are persuaded differently by the supposed incompatability of this in a catalogue also concerned with books or other non-book materials. Are both sides 'tilting at windmills'? The crux of the matter is the term 'main entry'. Ask a catalogue user if he has looked at the main entry and no doubt he would not know, but he would appreciate the meaning, in relation to a map, of author catalogue entry, area entry, and thematic or subject entry because they have functions in providing access to the map collection. When typed cards or printed catalogues are used, the main entry will contain the full entry that a descriptive catalogue can supply, with other entries providing briefer identifying information only. Now in card catalogues, there is a unit entry which is reproduced mechanically as often as necessary for the various headings to be used, and in a computerised catalogue the same information, though perhaps in different order, is repeated at different entries. Where is the main entry in such a card catalogue? Its only function in such catalogues is as a means of recording the tracings or the record of the other entries for that map. No librarians, in say a general library using a book classification, will suggest that one can not provide entries for maps in the classified section of a classed catalogue, under area as a name in a dictionary catalogue or in a subject/area index in a classified catalogue, or under subject in a dictionary catalogue or in a subject index for a classified catalogue. These factors are the only ones which concern the use of the catalogue. It is reasonable to expect that for the sake of administrative convenience the tracings in a general library catalogue will be put on the author 'main' entry card for a map, as for a book, and in a separate map catalogue they will be added to the area 'main' entry card. This implies however that there will be author entries for cards in the general library, and that area entries are provided as 'added' entries in an integrated catalogue.

Consideration must now be given to the different headings to be used to provide the variety of access which may be needed to the collection. In order to do this it is necessary to identify three broad categories of libraries which will contain maps. There are general libraries, university, college and public, which will contain maps as part of a larger collection of books and other materials. These libraries will compile either a dictionary or a classified catalogue of the whole stock. There are also map collections, usually within the geography departments of universities, which will provide a catalogue mainly of maps, the books in the department being only ancillary to the use of maps. These catalogues could also be dictionary or classified but more commonly the curators who have full catalogues appear to favour keeping separate the different indexes which make up the complete catalogue. In some geography departments the 'catalogue' is really a 'shelf list' alone but this is not suggested as a category to be considered as it adds nothing as a means of access to the collection except to reduce the handling of the maps. A shelf list could however be the nucleus of a classified catalogue.

Area entry
All authorities agree that the majority of approaches to maps in a collection is through the area covered. All catalogues should therefore have an 'area catalogue' which will include cards, for every map, each card having a heading, being the name of the area by which the file would be arranged. Maps of countries will be represented by a name of the country heading, continents by the name of the continent and so on. A map may however show a substantial part of two countries, in which case there will be two area cards, one under each country heading. This is an example of the major difference compared with the arrangement of the maps themselves. A map can only be filed at one country placing, the catalogue can provide, if necessary, as many cards as are appropriate. Similarly, if, for example, a set of maps is added to the collection and it covers several distant countries at a scale larger than any previous maps of these countries represented in the collection, then the map librarian may wish to provide area entry under these countries for that set as well as the area entry, world or continent as it may be, for the set as a whole. This will be a departure from the norm, a map represented by a set of sheets will usually be catalogued as a whole as it is classified, but the catalogue allows the

177

librarian to bring it to the notice of users if it is thought that will serve a useful purpose.

The form of name to be used in the area heading requires careful consideration and a set of rules should be followed consistently. The simplicity of the direction in PARSONS is deceptive, 'The name of the area is to be that mentioned in the title of the map, or in the absence of a title, that illustrated by the map. The name will be in the vernacular form except where there is an accepted anglicised form', and is matched by the BM 'Every . . . map . . . has its main entry under the name of the geographical or topographical area which the work represents, the generally accepted English form of the name being adopted'. Yet PARSONS would provide an area entry: GERMANY dist BAVARIA, whilst the British Museum would enter: CUMBRIA : COUNTY, or DELHI : CITY. This illustrates the use of either 'indirect' or 'direct' entries for area.

BOGGS makes a direct entry of 'the most significant area name', and uses the anglicised form of names. WALWORTH CO, WIS, and SAO PAULO, BRAZIL (State).

RGS uses indirect entry like PARSONS for areas smaller than a country. The entry is under the name of the country followed by the abbreviation 'Dist' for 'District' and then the specific name of the county, state or province, eg FRANCE, Dist VAR.

AGS provides direct area entries in the catalogue for those countries, provinces etc for which area numbers are provided eg NEW JERSEY; NEW SOUTH WALES; NEW ZEALAND. But areas without individual area numbers provided in the AGS classification scheme are considered secondary areas, and are entered under the main area name eg ENGLISH CHANNEL IS, JERSEY; GREAT BRITAIN, CITIES, ST HELIER. Obviously a province or state in for example, USA, Australia and Canada, have direct entries whilst divisions of other countries such as South Africa, Union of; Germany, etc, have to be entered indirectly under the name of the country. This is an arrangement which lacks consistency and would be confusing to a user who would not consult the copy of AGS *Cataloguing and filing rules* before consulting the catalogue. Of course references would be made eg HESSE, see: GERMANY, SECTION. HESSE, but a map user learning from this example may well later expect to find an entry: AUSTRALIA, SECTION. NEW SOUTH WALES and be disappointed.

No doubt general libraries will follow the practice of direct or indirect entry prevailing for similar entries in the rest of the general catalogue, but otherwise a consistent rule must be made and the practice of direct area entry is most in favour, and is, for example recommended by SLA. Users of AGS or PARSONS for map cataloguing rules would be following the indirect system of area entry. The AGS rule that 'the names of geographical divisions, historical, political or economic units with individual area numbers (ie AGS classification numbers) are used as the catalogue's main area entry', means that an established thesaurus of area names is to be used, all areas not in this list being entered, as secondary area entries, as a 'section' of the country or state containing the named area. A similar arrangement is followed by PARSONS, although the country name is followed by 'dist(rict)' not 'section' but the names to be used are not laid down. BOGGS provides guidance on the choice of area names, which because of the vagaries of transliteration, may appear differently on different maps of the same area. BOGGS, PARSONS and other indexes to area classification schemes might be used as a nucleus of the area names to be used, but many more will be required as the library develops, and as political changes are made in some countries, and the library must itself establish an authority file of area names used. For guidance a standard gazetteer might be considered, but a more appropriate reference source and one which would lead to standardisation of transliterated forms, would be the national volumes published by the US Board on Geographical Names and the complementary volumes of the Permanent Committee on Geographical Names for British Official Use of the Royal Geographical Society, London.

Other difficulties occur in entries using place-names. In the case of islands, PARSONS suggests 'Maps of islands belonging to a country are catalogued under the name of the country followed by the name of the island prefixed by the abbreviation "Is", thus following the indirect form of entry.' Island groups however bring agreed action from PARSONS and AGS in that individual islands with island groups are entered under the group name eg Caroline Is followed by the name of the island. BOGGS makes no mention of these and so presumably would retain direct entry.

Geographical features covering more than one country are entered under the name of the feature in AGS, as NILE VALLEY; whereas all geographical features are treated in PARSONS as districts of countries or continents, therefore the example would be, AFRICA dist NILE VALLEY.

Boundary maps are especially considered as a difficult problem for area entries and the BOGGS ruling is the more detailed and requires that if the boundary mapped is between two countries only the entry should be under both with a heading 'Country A—Boundaries—Country B', which is reversed in the Country B entry. If the map

179

shows the boundaries of one country in relation to several adjacent countries, the entry is under the one country. AGS provides for boundary map entries under both countries although only one entry will appear in each heading, and PARSONS is similar, both adding the compass division including the boundary after the country name.

Of course entries will be added which deal with other types of areas eg NATO and similar area groupings, but a library should be able to arrive at a reasonable decision regarding the form of entry if the policy of cataloguing under indirect or direct area names is kept in mind. Every library has to make decisions concerning these and other problems in cataloguing and in classification as new maps are received and it should be normal practice to consider critically what published schemes and other libraries have decided for similar cases.

The area entries in catalogues will take different forms according to the type of map catalogue in use or to be compiled. If the map catalogue is part of a general library book catalogue the maps will be classified as allowed by the general classification scheme, eg UDC, DDC, L of C. When a classified catalogue is in use, area entries for maps will appear as classified entries in the general catalogue or in a map catalogue, the catalogue cards being arranged by area but following the classification notation which thus should be in a prominent position on the catalogue card, probably in the top left-hand corner preceding the area name also in the heading. Area entries arranged in this manner require to be indexed in order that a user may establish the classification number for say, Canada. The index to the classified catalogue is an alphabetical listing of names, not referring to specific maps but to the notation, eg (in DDC) Canada, 912.71. In an integrated catalogue the index cards for maps will be intercalated with index cards referring to the book section of the catalogue and so some distinction should be made, eg Canada:maps, 912.71. This would not be necessary for a classified catalogue of maps alone. It is noticeable that an index to a classified catalogue is usually the weakest part, entries being made in the classified section for which no index card is prepared. An index card is required for every area represented in the classified catalogue by a classification number and great care must be taken to ensure that when a classification number is used for the first time an appropriate card is added to the index. Further index cards are necessary even within the same classification number, for example if town maps are all classified at class number for the country or at the class number for the appropriate county or province, each area, in this case town, having an index entry referring to the general class number. In some libraries, depending on the space and equipment available, it might be considered possible to have an

180

index map on display which demonstrates the areas covered by the classification numbers of the scheme used. Two such maps would probably be required one for the world, and one of a larger scale for the country in which the library is situated.

In some map collections an arrangement of area entries exists following the filing order of the maps but not using a notation. All known arrangements first group according to continents, ocean areas etc, and so even if within continents the countries are arranged in alphabetical order this may not be a straight forward arrangement for the user, who will only find it acceptable by custom and, particularly, fairly regular usage of an area of interest. The alphabetical arrangement is also probably not a simple sequence as curators tend to break it for maps of areas such as Iberian Peninsular, Scandinavia, Great Britain and Northern Ireland, and bring them into conjunction with the individual countries which comprise these geographical and political areas. Without a notation it is not possible to provide an index to such an arrangement, and so it is not a practice to follow.

An alternative arrangement for the map catalogue is that of the dictionary catalogue, which is probably more acceptable to users who in general resent examining an area index to find a class number which then must be consulted in another part of the catalogue to find the record of maps available which show the area required. In the dictionary catalogue the area entry cards are arranged in alphabetical order, the classification number, which will be on the catalogue card but not part of the heading, is part of the location or call number but plays no part in the arrangement of the catalogue cards. The cards are arranged entirely by the names of the areas in alphabetical order. In this case entries for related areas are not brought together if direct entries are used for area headings, for example maps of French towns appear under their names and not under France. It will be necessary therefore to add to such a catalogue a reference card which will remind users of the possibility of other wanted maps being elsewhere in the arrangement, eg under FRANCE, 'see also under names of departments, cities'. Similarly, and also in the index to a classified catalogue, reference should be made under alternative forms of name to the form of area name used. This will occur in a different way for changes of name. The country of Zambia has been previously called Northern Rhodesia, but maps of that area whatever the area name will have the same classification number and therefore appear together in any classified catalogue. When the change of name took place the only alteration to be made in a classified catalogue was the addition of an index entry under the new name of Zambia. In a dictionary catalogue however the maps before and after the change of name will appear at the two different places, Northern Rhodesia and Zambia. A reference is required at the front of the card sequence under each name, the one informing the map reader that maps published after 19.. are filed at Zambia and a companion 'see' reference under Zambia referring to Northern Rhodesia. Thus although in a dictionary catalogue no index is required there are exceptions to this statement for certain categories of entry. A virtue of a dictionary catalogue is that it offers an alternative approach to that of the classification scheme by which the maps are arranged.

As will be seen later, dictionary and classified catalogues accept in the one sequence cards relevant to the different approaches to the map collection, area and subject. Some map curators, with a separate map catalogue, prefer to keep the cards relevant to each section of a catalogue in separate arrangements; and probably alphabetical. There does not seem to be any good reason for this generally and it would appear to be more valuable to provide all entries in one alphabetical catalogue if a classified catalogue is not in use.

Subject entries

In many libraries and map collections a high proportion of the maps in the collection will be general maps of a topographical or geographical nature, and one can say of them that their subject is the area. However in other maps the area shown is a base map on which is illustrated the distribution of some other factor such as average rainfall, mineral resources, and these are the subject of the map. In other cases features which appear to some extent on a general map are emphasised in special maps to be more informative and to carry a greater amount of information about that feature than would be the case on a topographical sheet, eg a canal system map. Such subject maps require catalogue entries which will allow access to these special subjects. Unless this is done the interested subject specialist has no ready means of discovering the map coverage of the subject in the library. In many map classification systems the subject of the map will be a part of the classification number or letter following the area part of the classification. In UDC it is possible to reserve the normal 912 section of the scheme for general maps, and classify subject maps according to their subject, sub-dividing according to the area, if it is desired to show the location of, say, geological maps in the same section of the library as the geological books. DDC has no arrangements for allowing maps to be arranged primarily by subject, unless local amendments are made. A librarian should not be inhibited by DDC or any other scheme from locating the storage of groups of maps where he believes they will be of most value to his readers, the call number can direct the user to the appropriate part of the library or a different department.

In a classified catalogue using UDC the entries for maps under subject numbers will take their appropriate place in the catalogue with added entries under the areas concerned. In all other schemes noted here subject classification is a subdivision of the primary arrangement by area. In all classified catalogues, other than those based on UDC using subject arrangement for maps, it will therefore be necessary to provide a subject index to the subject entries. It can not be too frequently stated that the comprehensiveness of the index in the classified catalogue is an essential component of the catalogue. There must not be any suggestion that because, in a **very** simple broad subject classification the letter X represents Geology and is always filed after the area cards for any country, with alphabetical arrangement of subject letters, that this is almost intuitive knowledge to the map user as it might be to the librarian using the collection every day. Index cards must be provided in this case for 'Geology', with at the very least the statement that maps on the geology of an area will be filed at X in the subject sequence under the area card. Much better however would be a listing on the 'Geology' card, or cards, of those countries with the full area/subject class number, for which geological maps existed in the library, so that a geologist could look at the listing quickly and obtain an overall view of the geological map provision for that library.

With a dictionary catalogue the problem does not arise. The 'dictionary' is one alphabetical sequence of cards, area headings, subject headings, author headings and any other form of catalogue entry thought necessary for access to the collection, all being amalgamated. Subject entries therefore take their appropriate place according to their heading and are unit cards with a subject heading, as Geology:Zambia, whilst in the same catalogue another unit card for the same map carries the same information except that it is filed under the area heading, as Zambia:Geology. In those map collections where different catalogue sequences are kept separate there is no cataloguing difference to the practice for dictionary catalogues, the only difference is that the user has to check which section of the catalogue he is consulting instead of making a direct check into the one alphabetical sequence of a dictionary catalogue.

The published map cataloguing systems, with the exception of BM, being considered in this section all provide a list of subject headings for maps. These are very extensive in the case of AGS and BOGGS, and based upon the classification schemes. PARSONS, however, names only six subject divisions, one Communications having six further subdivisions, which are used for subject entries

only as a subject division of area entries and not as a subject catalogue, this gives a catalogue very similar to a classified catalogue,
except that areas are filed purely alphabetically, but bringing maps of
every type under the area name. RGS follows a similar pattern,
although using many more subject divisions under area, and so
neither scheme can provide a catalogue which will allow a reader to
see what subject maps, for example 'geological', are available in the
library except by examining every area heading. No doubt the majority of requests for geological maps are coupled with a particular
area, but there must be occasions when the overall view is required by
a reader, particularly a lecturer in geology. The lists of subject headings provided by BOGGS and AGS are not meant to be exclusive and
AGS is careful to note that 'subject entries can, of course, be expanded
to accord with cataloguing needs, in the manner shown in this list'.

Author entry
Where the map collection is part of a general library the cataloguer
will consider the author entry for maps as the main entry, in conformity with the practice for books in the integrated catalogue. A reflection of the importance attached in this way to author entries are the
pages devoted to maps and atlases in the *Anglo-American cataloguing
rules* although the bulk of the information concerns rules for 'description'. This attitude to author entries is not shared in cataloguing
codes which are designed purely for map collections but most of them
do make provision for author entries in the map catalogue, an exception being PARSONS. It must be agreed that generally the use and
value of author entry for maps is much smaller than that for area entries but there are occasions when the cartographer or publisher of
maps is the significant characteristic that is required by a user. An
obvious example is with regard to early maps and it is significant that
the Bodleian Library (PARSONS/FATHERS) in its use of the PAR-
SONS scheme, which was created for a significantly different type of
library, provides an additional author file of entries for authors,
engravers and publishers of maps produced before 1850. A reader requiring a map of the English county Derbyshire would not expect to
receive a sixteenth century map of the county by Saxton, if he required
a Saxton map it would more probably be to examine the work of this
Elizabethan cartographer, and which county maps were available in
the library would be somewhat immaterial. The user in such circumstances would expect to examine the catalogue under the cartographer's name and not to check through all the areas of England
and Wales to find which Saxton maps, if any, were available. The
'cut-off' date used in the Bodleian Library, 1850, is the approximate

end of the era of the private cartographer. The more anonymous official map produced by a department of state or local authority or public institution may nevertheless, in the future, if not now, achieve a similar importance as an author in the history of cartography. The student of cartography may wish to see the cartographic style of a map producing agency at a particular period, just as a student of book printing should be able to consult a library catalogue to discover books in the library printed by John Baskerville, access being by the printer's name not from the authors and titles of books. This has, in fact, already occurred in Britain through historical needs in general rather than cartographic history, when the sheets of the Ordnance Survey *One inch to one mile map* first edition, were reprinted by David and Charles Ltd. Any request for them will most probably be via 'author' and title of the edition, followed by the area required, rather than first by area. Cartographic interest of a comparative nature will also encourage author approach to current maps. It does seem, therefore, that there is little to be gained and something would be lost for some map users, if the author approach to the collection is omitted.

What, however, is to be understood by the term 'author'? In 1970 a Commission of the International Cartographic Association decided to try to prepare a comprehensive definition of the term 'map author', (SPIESS). The recommended definition is 'Individual, group of individuals or agency who conceives the idea of a map, participates in its design and in the decision about its definitive presentation and who is primarily responsible for its informational content'.

BM RULES take a comprehensive view and make entries for every author, draughtsman, engraver, surveyor and compiler, if known of course. AGS considers that anyone indicated on a map as having some responsibility for it should be considered as an author, whilst BOGGS similarly calls for entries for every person or institution which appears to have contributed significantly to the 'content' of the map, both sets of rules considering the author to be usually the private surveyor or corporate body which produced the information available in the form of a map. The person named in the heading of an author entry should always have a distinguishing description added, eg cartographer, publisher, etc.

The AACR should however be the main source of guidance regarding the choice of heading in an author entry. These rules cooperatively developed by committees of librarians representing the American Library Association, The Library of Congress, the Library Association and the Canadian Library Association, provide comprehensive guidance for author entry in whatever variant of 'author' may be involved, for titles, and for descriptive cataloguing. The British text of

AACR is prepared by a committee which had the assistance of four specialists for the rules concerning maps, and this text differs significantly from the American text on maps. The AACR naturally refers mainly to books but the rules 210 and 211 concerning author entry for maps are introduced by a note acknowledging the distinctive characteristics of maps, and continues 'Most map libraries make the main entry under the name of the area depicted by the map. Rules 210 and 211 determine the choice of entries which shall be compatible with author entries for books in an author and title catalogue. They will be used particularly for main entries in catalogues of historical collections and for added or index entries for catalogues arranged primarily by area depicted.'

For a map which has informational content other than geographic, a thematic or subject map, the author is the person or corporate body responsible for the non-geographic information, and the same rules concerning author entry as used for books apply. If the geographical nature of the map is its principal feature a different rule applies which is relevant to the different types of persons responsible for the appearance of a published map. This rule, 211, has been evolved to give guidance for the many maps where it is difficult to decide which person should be considered primarily responsible. If the responsibility is stated on the map or the map is noted as being compiled by a named person, or there is a personal or corporate body's name included in the title, then this person is recognised as author. If a commercial firm (eg a petrol company), other than a map publisher, is included in the title, this is disregarded for map authorship. When the authorship is not explicit, the author entry is chosen according to an order of preference of potential authors, namely, 1 surveyor; 2 cartographer; 3 engraver if known to be also a cartographer; 4 corporate body that prepared the maps, including a map publisher; 5 title.

It should be noted that AACR is providing a ruling to establish a main (author) entry. In a library where an area entry is considered to be the main entry, the application of this rule is somewhat unimportant, the significant part of it is that added author entries will be provided for every 'person or corporate body that has had a significant share in the responsibility for the work'. Little need be said about the file of author entries. It has to be a separate file in a classified catalogue because of its alphabetical arrangement, but in a dictionary catalogue author entry cards will be filed in the one sequence with the area and subject entry cards.

Other types of catalogue entries
A library may choose to provide additional means of access, via the

medium of the catalogue, to the maps in the collection; presumably this is in response to a known demand, for the area, subject and author approaches must cater for nearly all requests in the typical general map library. However, there are always maps the use of which will benefit from an approach to their cataloguing which is exceptional and not followed for all other maps in the collection.

Title entries, for maps for which no named authorship can be attributed, will be used in lieu of author in catalogues where the author entry is considered a main entry. Obviously very few maps will be of this nature because the bulk of maps are produced by official agencies and map publishing firms whilst many of the remainder are produced for a specialist need by a specialist agency which is clearly stated. Early maps are more frequently in this category and this will be considered in discussing the cataloguing of early maps. BOGGS does allow the possibility of other title entries in certain cases namely 'a) Maps with distinctive titles and b) Old maps, usually'. In the case of b) as it is followed by the statement the 'titles for old maps may sometimes by abridged' this seems to destroy any value the title may have as the only remembered detail of a required map by a map user who then has to find it via the title. Obviously reproductions of the *Vinland map* would be sought for through the medium of the title rather than a facsimile publisher's name, but that would be covered by the initial suggestion that anonymous maps receive a title entry, or more generally by a policy of providing any entries, additional to area, subject and author, under headings which would appear to be of value to a map user in tracing a required map. Such a policy should guide a map librarian in all aspects of cataloguing and this would lead to the provision of an entry *International millionth map of the world (IMW)* because it is a well-known title, not an area description, not a national scale, which will often be requested.

A set of sheets, however many there are forming a map, is not a series. A series is a number of maps of an individual nature bearing a series title and necessarily showing similarity in format, style and cartographic characteristics. A series is often formed by maps all of one area with each map showing distribution of a different phenomena, a thematic map, but this is not an essential condition.

Form entries can refer to the physical format of a map for example 'wall map' or to the cartographic form. In any educational institution it is probable that teaching sets are kept, duplicate sheets for class use, and perhaps files of maps or more probably parts of maps which have been used for examination purposes. These maps should not be classified according to area but filed together as convenient and provided with form entries so that they can be located through the catalogue if that becomes necessary. Similarly, and particularly for educational purposes but not solely so, a student of geography or cartography may wish to see a map using the prime meridian of Ferro, or with the top of the sheet east, or a particularly good example of hachuring and many other unusual features. It should not be the occasion for exercise in memory or constructive guesswork by the map librarian but a mere consultation of appropriate form entries in the catalogue where, as all good librarians should attempt to do, examples have been catalogued, using a form entry, in anticipation of such requests. Obviously, such cataloguing does not follow a rule, the entries will be provided selectively, following the principle of service to the clients.

Analytical entries
If the map collection is to offer the greatest possible service to map users it is essential that an enquirer can find in the map catalogue guidance to all the maps of value that the collection and the wider general library possess. This means that not only will maps be catalogued if they are present and filed as sheet maps, wall maps etc but also if they are published as part of another form of record such as a book or periodical. Maps folded and put in pockets, fold-in maps, and maps as plates, will all occur in books and periodicals. The books and periodicals containing such maps are most probably filed and catalogued in the several parts of the general library and a system of cooperation must be devised so that the map cataloguer is aware of these maps which would not otherwise come to his attention. These maps are catalogued in the map catalogue and the process is known as analytical cataloguing. In most libraries a degree of selection must be exercised so that only maps or plans are catalogued which are particularly important in themselves, or which because of their nature and the interests of the map library have potential interest for the map library's present or future users. Selectivity has to be practiced even within the American Geographical Society's map collection where the provision of analytical entries is an especial feature of the map catalogue as it is recognised to be of great importance for research.

Analytical entries for maps in a periodical may be for a map which is the first accurate map of a recently explored area, reported in an article in the journal by one of the exploration team. A book may include maps of distributions relevant to the theme of the book, distributions which have not previously been recorded in map form in this library. It is also valuable however to provide analytical entries for maps which are part of material kept within the map collection, the maps concerned not being sufficiently displayed in the catalogue by the normal entry for the material of which it is part. Significant individual maps in an atlas, particularly unexpected thematic maps in a general atlas, or inset maps, perhaps a good town plan included in a map of a wider area. These latter will be mentioned in a note within the descriptive entry for the larger map but this on its own might not be sufficient. A sheet or sheets of a set forming for example, a map of the world may be analytically catalogued to draw attention, probably selectively, to their presence 'within' the world map.

An analytical entry consists of the appropriate heading, and a normal cataloguing description of the map or plan so analysed, and this must be followed by the relevant citation of the containing volume or map, which (AACR; AGS) is preceded by 'In'. AACR, in rule 156 with reference to books; AGS; and BOGGS all refer to analytical entries for the types of map noted above; whilst PARSONS refers to analytical entries for inset maps alone. BOGGS suggests, and AACR mentions the possibility, that some map collections may prefer to give further added entries using the unit card for the containing work but with headings referring to the map analysed. This is possible, but the cautionary footnote to AACR, rule 156, should be observed. This cautions that if this is done the unit card must include, either in the body of the descriptive entry or in a note to it, (which could be added) a reference to the map analysed so that the catalogue users can connect this reference with the heading for the added entry. AACR further notes that 'analytical entries are generally preferred . . . 1 if the added entries would be so numerous as to make the unit entry tracings too cumbersome and 2 if the part analysed required its own added entries and therefore its own tracings'. The headings for the analytical entry should be allocated as if the map were an individual sheet map, as area, subject and author if required. In a classified catalogue the map analysed will be classified according to its own characteristics and the card for the entry in the classified catalogue will be filed according to the resultant classification number. The call number on the card will however remain that of the book or map which contains the analysed map. In other types of catalogue, there will be no necessity to classify the analysed map, apart from the choice of area heading.

Description

In this chapter on cataloguing the assumption has been made that the map catalogue will be one formed by cards, the type of catalogue which is currently used in the vast majority of libraries. Some cards in the catalogue will be guide cards serving as signposts to the contents of the drawers, guide headings being printed on parts projecting above the normal cards, others will be cards providing *see* or *see also* references. Most of the cards however will contain descriptions of individual maps, the cards being filed under the various forms of entry discussed above. The information given in the description of the map now must be considered. The information has to be noted systematically and to provide sufficient detail about the map to allow the reader to deduce with reasonable certainty whether the map described will answer his needs or not. This description is normally typed or printed on a card, and the card is reproduced in sufficient copies to be used for each heading under which a catalogue entry for the map is to be filed. Further copies may be made of course for a map catalogue to be housed elsewhere, for incorporation in a general catalogue etc. The card bearing the description is a unit card, to which appropriate headings are added for filing in the different sequences.

AACR, AGS, BOGGS and PARSONS each provide rules or guidance for the information to be included in a unit card and the order in which it is to be presented to the reader. The layout of the details on a card should be the concern of the library making the catalogue in the light of local conditions, but the copies of cards shown in the pages of some schemes should be noted, their example being conducive to the establishment of good style in cataloguing. The style of layout, the positioning of entries on the card, the punctuation, should be recorded carefully in the map library's manual of procedure and adhered to, so that a uniform system is achieved throughout the catalogue and thus clear communication established with the user of the catalogue. PARSONS provides a detailed set of rules regarding description which are significantly different from the other schemes, these rules are often used in British university geography departments, and so the system will be considered separately later. (See pp 193–195.)

AACR and BOGGS give extensive guidance regarding the action to be taken in regard to the possible variations that can occur within the above items, and these should be studied in full by every cataloguer. Certain common practices in any map description can however be observed.

The title is given in full and is taken from the face of the map. AACR gives title preference to one in a cartouche, before one in the margin, BOGGS follows titles in uncommon languages by a translation. As in all cataloguing, if anything is omitted, such as uninformative words in a long title, it should be marked by the inclusion of . . . if anything is added such as a translation of a title it is placed in square brackets [ ]. For some maps it may be necessary to supply a title, in square brackets, AACR gives order of preference for source of titles, but one created by the cataloguer should include the area shown, and in the form used on the map. The author is included in the title sentence.

Order of items in description

AACR	AGS	BOGGS
Title	Title	Title
Author statement		Author statement
Scale	Scale	
	Projection, if indicated	
Edition		Edition
	Author and/or publisher	
Place of publication	Place of publication	Place of publication
Publisher		Publisher
	Edition, publisher's serial no	(Place of printing/ engraving)
Date of publication	Date	Date of publication
		Scale
No of sheets	No of sheets	No of sheets
Size of sheet	Size	Size of sheet
Series statement		
Supplementary information	Short description	Supplementary information
		List of entries
		Added copies

Scale should be given as a representative fraction. The scale may have to be calculated from a scale rule drawn on the map. If no scale is given, it must be calculated from measurements made on the map, and noted, along with the statement 'no scale given', in square brackets. Occasionally, a map will not be drawn to scale, or not uniformly to scale, and that should be stated. AACR has a footnote, p 213 'Commercial natural scale indicators are available by means of which a representative fraction can be approximated from a graphic scale expressed in miles, kilometres, or yards, or from the parallels of the map projection grid'. BOGGS reproduces copies of these two types, which are not known to be commercially available in Great Britain.

Edition is a term which it is attempted to define in BOGGS. AACR usefully notes that 'Official map series may combine the edition statement with a "standard series designation", and this should be transcribed in full'. For current maps this 'Edition 1' etc is the type of statement to be given, but many large official survey editions have frequent reprinting with revisions and additions of individual sheets. The individual sheets are, of course, not catalogued, and the map has its edition number. The index map, if used as a stock list or inventory, can be used to record the addition of new issues of individual sheets in the edition, and the new issues should be filed in the storage cabinets with the previous issue of the same sheet of that edition. Here a sequence number can be given, and written against the call number on the map sheet only, for issues of each sheet, and the actual sheets filed in order with the largest sequence number, the latest issue, at the front. In order that the latest issue is retrieved when that sheet is required, the sequence number of the earlier issues can be ruled through to inform the librarian that it has been superseded.

BOGGS gives the printer and place of printing and/or engraving in the order noted above, if it is different from the publisher and of particular interest.

The date of the map is capable of being differently interpreted. For geographers, and most other types of map users, the date of the information shown on a map is the significant date, but for bibliographical purposes, mainly of interest to cartobibliographers and librarians, the latest date relating to the printing of the map is important. The BM in its catalogue shows, where possible, first date of survey and then date of printing. Wherever a date is used in a catalogue heading for arrangement purposes this should preferably be the date of survey. For the catalogue card description, AGS, reflecting a geographer's interest, gives the following order of preference for date; date of compilation, of copyright, of publishing, of edition. This is a matter in which the presumed interest of the library's users should be taken into account, but in a general library catalogue integrating entries for books and maps, the date of publishing should be given for uniform practice, the date of survey if known and if different, can be supplied in a note.

The collection statement of the number of sheets can indicate if they are coloured. If the sheets in a set are published over a period of time, it is common, in a typewritten catalogue, to leave space for the number of sheets to be added when the total is known, a similar method being used for the date note when only the commencing date of publication can be shown. The measurement of sheet size is normally given by height before width, the practice with the systems being discussed. AACR and BOGGS use centimetres but the BM practice of using millimetres would appear to have more in common with metrication in Great Britain where centimetres do not appear to be normally used for linear measurements in industry and trades.

192

The notes which can be added at the end of the above systematic description are, of course, valuable for bringing any relevant types of information which might be on the map to the attention of the user. BOGGS precedes general notes by giving the projection used for maps of the world and the prime meridian if other than Greenwich. These items should always be noted here or in general notes. BOGGS divides the notes into general items as:

a) relation of the map to other works eg analytical note

b) 1 Descriptive notes on content of the map eg air routes, hachures. 2 Reproduction if any, eg mss copy

c) Carto-bibliography notes, eg railways added to September 1939

d) Additional notes on map sheet, eg index on reverse

AACR offers opportunity to record the same type of additional information both geographical and carto-bibliographical in a determined order. Particular attention should be given to the note that a physical description of the map is to be included if it assists in showing its suitability for a reader's purpose, eg it is a photocopy. Details of a facsimile copy would be given here, whereas BOGGS would note them immediately after the imprint data which would be for the original. AACR specifically rules that a note of the date of situation (information shown) should be given here. In all libraries, if, for a map which exists in a set of many sheets, only a selected area is to be covered this should be given in the notes. In some cases the area covered might be best described in words, the details of which sheets are in the library being better illustrated by the index map. The rules for description and comments on them are very detailed in AACR and, whatever form of cataloguing procedure is used in a particular library, the map cataloguer will find it beneficial to be fully acquainted with the thought and guidance succinctly stated in AACR.

Description—printed card system

PARSONS *Manual of map classification and cataloguing* 1946 includes a copy of the catalogue card base to be used in the Directorate of Military Survey, for which the *Manual . . .* was written. The catalogue card is ruled to provide a number of compartments on the face, each one being identified by a descriptive name. The card being divided in this way directs the cataloguer in siting the information put on the card, and the compartment headings are both an aide-mémoire to the cataloguer for the information to be supplied and as guide to the catalogue user.

The design of the card is based on one which was used by the then Army Map Service, USA, and similar cards, usually showing a family resemblance, can be found in many libraries housed in universities. The Bodleian Library, Map Room uses the Parsons card with very slight changes, principally the omission of some information. Some map libraries provide a set of named compartments on the catalogue card for the description in the body of the card, leaving space above for the addition of the varied headings required; the Parsons card does not permit a blank space for variant headings. The Public Archives of Canada uses printed cards of this type 'Descriptive entry card', but much larger (3x) than the normal catalogue card, and using both sides of the card. As will be seen later the principle is not unknown in public libraries for use in a special map catalogue where detailed description might be required, but it is rare in general libraries.

The practice appears to have a great deal to commend it, not only in special map libraries but also in general libraries with integrated catalogues of books and maps. This catalogue card immediately declares itself to be for a map which will help the assistant filing catalogue cards by drawing attention to any different filing procedure which is required. It is not unknown, when a filing order for maps or atlases is different from books, for the world atlases, for example, to be filed in another incorrect order when a guide card at the beginning of the sequence informs the reader that the atlas cards are filed by date of publication. The reader too is to some extent informed of the meaning of the different items of information on the card and, if using maps fairly regularly, soon knows how to follow the pattern of information for an item of interest. The size of the 'compartments' limits the amount of information which can be given which therefore has to be concise, and it is desirable that careful attention is given to the compilation of a thesaurus of descriptive words to be used for describing the contents of a map, and that these words, when relevant, are used in a given order. The information is all contained in the readable area of the card and not 'lost' at the bottom as often seems to occur with typed cards.

The Bodleian variation of the Parsons catalogue card gives the following compartmentalised information:

Top line: Area (Country, + Dist, or + Town); Scale; Date (of compilation)

2nd entry: Ref no; Publishing body or author (and date of publication if different from that of compilation)

3rd entry: Title (Exact title as on map; with titles of additional maps on sheet, if any, introduced by 'On reverse', 'Inset', 'Also', 'Together with', as appropriate, or for an analytical entry 'In')

4th entry: Shows (This is a frequently used term in a printed card system and is immediately understood by any reader. Here are noted any of the following present on a country, or country: district map. Projection, prime meridian, grid, international and administrative boundaries, contours (int 50ft) and heights; Railways, roads (eg)— three categories, tracks. The presence of the following are noted on a town plan: Street names, principal buildings, railways, bus routes, parks, administrative boundaries, contours and heights, grid, any other information)

5th entry: No of sheets; Source

The printed 'Descriptive entry card' used by the Public Archives of Canada for maps, has sixteen entries as follows:

Along top line: 1 Author, 2 Call number, 3 Subject

Further entries: 4 Title, Area (if not described in title), 5 Insets and views, 6 Surveyed by, 7 Drafted by, 8 Other signees, 9 Imprint, 10 Additional information

On reverse: 11 Brief title, 12 Location or source, 13 Description A) Manuscript, B) Print, C) Blueprint, D) Photocopy, E) Microfilm, F) Original, G) Copy, H) Coloured, I) Scale, J) Dimensions—whole map dissected into .. sections—one map of .. sheets each .. —one set of .. sheets each .. 14 Features (an alternative for 'Shows' in Bodley card) 15 Cross-references A) Area, B) Author, 16 Remarks.

Filing of catalogue cards

Within each sequence in the catalogue, classified area, classified subject, alphabetical area, alphabetical subject, author, etc depending upon the catalogue used with a collection, the cards will be filed by the arrangement of the appropriately added heading in numerical or alphabetical order. In classified catalogues the numerical ordering should be easily achieved. It must be clear to assistants filing cards however that the cards are arranged by the classification number alone, and not by the call number which includes it. There should be no difficulty in selecting the classification number from the rest of the call number for the heading for filing in a classified catalogue, in some collections the classification number may be underlined in order to prevent any possibility of error, but more helpfully, the call number will be included in the body of the entry in a unit card or at the top right, the classification number being added as a heading to the left for filing order.

Where an alphabetical arrangement of headings is used rather more possibilities for a lack of uniformity occur, but using a standard set of rules as the *ALA rules for filing catalog cards* will obviate this. These ALA rules will also give guidance on the arrangement, alphabetically by a chosen factor, of cards having the same heading of name or classification number. For books the arrangement of cards with the same heading is by author, unless it is the author arrangement where the sub-arrangement is usually by title. For maps however this does not create a particularly meaningful arrangement, and means must be found to arrange maps in a manner which gives more guidance to the catalogue user. An author arrangement for early maps may well be meaningful but that is considered in another section.

The factors in maps which may be used for arranging cards in a map catalogue are area, subject, date, scale, author, title, size, and any of these, or a combination of them in a specified order, may be added to the heading for a catalogue entry to specify the arrangement of cards for maps which are all classified at the same number, or have the same area coverage, or the same subject, so that a further helpful choice is available for reader selection. Too often, and particularly, but not only, in general libraries largely of books, the lack of defining a selected order for map entries results in what can be only regarded as ludicrous arrangements of cards. Within an author catalogue, maps and books by the same author, usually the official survey—a corporate author, should be separated. Typical of what can be found in the author section of a map catalogue, under the name of the national official survey, would be the following for a British library under the heading Ordnance Survey. This is quite obviously an unhelpful order.

Frome: sheet 166/Scale 1:63,360 (7th edition) 1972.

Gazetteer of Great Britain: giving the national grid references to all features named on the seventeen Ordnance Survey quarter-inch maps. 1972.

The history of the retriangulation of Great Britain, 1935–62. 1967.

Isles of Scilly: map Scale: 2″ to 1 mile (5th ed 1960)

Map of Hadrian's Wall. Scale: 2 inches to one mile. 1964.

One-inch map of England and Wales, 1925–1947. National grid. (New popular edition).

One-inch map of Great Britain. 7th edition. 1952–73 190 sheets. Scale: 1 mile to 1 inch. National grid.

One-inch map of Scotland 1925–1947. National grid. (New popular edition).

Quarter-inch map of Great Britain.

Report of the progress of the Ordnance Survey to 1936. 1939,

Second land utilisation survey of Britain: index to 1:25,000 series. Scale: *ca* twenty miles to 1″. 1964.

The three peaks, Whernside, Ingleborough and Pen-y-ghent; showing part of National Park boundary and Pennine Way. 1:25,000 outdoor leisure map. 1973.

These titles are selected from two library catalogues which follow the alphabetical by title sub-arrangement. In all but the very smallest map collections the listing together of books and maps by one author can only cause confusion to the catalogue user, particularly when, as often occurs, map titles do not have the same definitive character as titles from a book's title-page. The normal rules for author entry arrangement should be followed when an official survey, for example, both produces books or pamphlets and maps, and also in a dictionary catalogue when there is the same heading, the name of the survey, for a subject entry when a book or article has been written about the survey.

Heading: Surveyor.

Sequence: 1 Maps by the Survey. A suitable order for maps, eg area/scale/date but not title (see example at end of chapter).

2 Books by the Survey. Title order.

3 Books about the Survey. Author order.

The various possible filing arrangements for map catalogue cards were considered by SLA, Special Libraries Association, Geography and Map Division, Committee on Map Cataloguing, which circulated a questionnaire to map libraries to help prepare the 1956 report on map cataloguing. This questionnaire revealed that map librarians thought the factors of most concern to map users were area, subject and date, in that order, but the committee decided upon area, date, subject as the order for the heading which would guide card filing. BUFFUM in opposition to the SLA Committee's report gave reasons for prefering area, subject, date.

The SLA Committee considered that these three factors would determine the filing position of most cards, whilst BUFFUM suggested that three factors are as many as any filer should be asked to keep correctly arranged. This latter suggestion is debatable because a filer deals with one factor for arranging at a time, only going to the next factor when the group arranged by the preceding factor has been found. The SLA Committee provided for the further factors of scale and size to be used for filing and therefore added to the heading in the same order. SMITH uses area, subject, scale in the University of Kansas map collection, so it can be seen that among practicing map librarians in the USA there was, no doubt is, a divergence of opinion as to what constitutes the better filing order. In no case however is author (or authority) or title suggested as being within the first three useful factors for filing within a group of maps.

The implication in the use of the above factors for a filing order is that there is always a subject, for many maps this would be 'general' or 'topographical', BOGGS however, also using area—subject—date headings, recognises that many maps will be considered to not have a subject and rules that area—date, precedes area—subject—date, as:

Sumatra—1937 *before* Sumatra—airfields—1937. This arrangement is logical on the 'nothing before something' principle in filing and would be recognised by a map user.

These A-D-S, A-S-D, and A-S-S headings are all with reference to an area file within a dictionary catalogue. By implication the SLA Committee expected the A-D-S heading to be the arrangement under every section, ie under area, subject, author etc entries, in the catalogue, when writing '. . . would make subject added entries file by subject, area, and again by subject'. There seems to be no reason why in such a case the order would not be subject-area-date, instead of repeating subject, and continuing by scale if necessary.

In considering a filing order within a heading it is worthwhile considering the majority of the types of maps which have to be filed under one country, the country of the library usually providing the most in number and variety. There will be official sets, commercial sets, and maps in one or few sheets. If it is thought desirable to separate sets from individual maps in the map storage cabinets, mainly because the bulk of sets 'hides' interfiled single maps, there is no need to continue this in the catalogue where they are probably represented by one unit card each. The respective call numbers will differentiate their locations in the map files. The catalogue entries will represent many different scales, for Great Britain probably from 1:1,000,000 to 1:500, and in a general library will have been published over a number of centuries, 175 years for Ordnance Survey maps alone. In arranging entries for these under area, and arrangement by scale, and within scale by date would seem to be the better solution. If subject maps are considered also, the user would expect to be able to see their entries together, if he first consulted the area entry he required, and so the arrangement under area would then be by subject-scale-date, with the arrangement of subjects being in alphabetical order, following the area entries for general (or non-subject) maps.

Whenever scale or date arrangement is followed this should be by numerical order and not by the alphabetisation of the words represented by the scale or date number, ie

correct	not correct:
1:500	five hundred
1:1250	five thousand
1:5000	million
1:63,360	one thousand, two hundred and fifty
1:1,000,000	sixty three thousand . . .

198

The numerical order is seen to be logical and relevant by a user who can immediately go to the correct place in the file for a selected scale. If the scale, chosen mentally by the catalogue user, is not represented, this is obvious immediately and the user can select the nearest scale, a simple process which is far from obvious if the word arrangement were to be carried out. The same principle will, of course, apply to dates which are arranged chronologically. For most users however, a reverse chronological order would here appear to be the most suitable. Catalogue users do not normally look through the whole group of cards representing a number of similar maps and then go back to a chosen map, remembered in passing. There is a tendency to select, within the suitable group, the first map to give reasonable correspondence to the users' detailed interest. Most users would prefer the latest map on their interest, so let the recent dates be filed first in every date grouping.

Filing cards under headings in a classified catalogue involves other considerations not present in the comments above concerned with dictionary catalogues. The main arrangements in a classified catalogue are the area entries arranged by the notation for the appropriate areas in the map or general classification scheme used; and the subject entries, where desirable, also arranged by the notation for the subjects. The classified catalogue is frequently used for the area arrangement in a map library catalogue because it presents the map entries to the users in a geographically logical arrangement. With the changes of names of countries which take place over the years, there is no essential change in the classified area entry, the class number stays the same although the country name it represents is changed, and its geographical relation to the other countries of the continent remain the same in the catalogue. A reader may well find it more convenient to discover the maps he requires of, say, an African country by following his geographical knowledge in the classified catalogue than by trying to remember a changed name in order to consult an alphabetical area index to the classified catalogue, or a dictionary catalogue. In the classified catalogue of course the cards referring to maps of the country before and after the change of name will all be filed together under the same classification number. Similarly, the user of a map collection and also the librarian can more readily assess the strength of the map coverage for an area of the world in the library when the maps are arranged according to geographical proximity of the whole area and the various countries within the area and adjacent to it, than can possibly be done through the medium of 'arbitrarily' arranged cards in an alphabetical area sequence.

The subject arrangement of catalogue entries for maps of thematic content is less frequently found to be classified in special map libraries, although it will be in general libraries using a classified catalogue. A general classification scheme (UDC) offers a subject classification which is acceptable in practice for a classified catalogue but a detailed map classification by subject (BOGGS) appears to be less acceptable. The alternatives practiced seem to be an alphabetical subject arrangement, or an arrangement which owes something to the idea of subject classification, by attempting to group similar subjects together but without the aid of a fairly detailed scheme and notation, this creates more sub-groupings under the main subject divisions which cannot be arranged by detailed subject content. An examination of examples of subject arrangements of this type will suggest that new users of catalogues with such arrangements must find using the catalogue something of a mystery and call upon the memory of the map curator. If that does not occur it will be because the subject arrangement is so broadly based that the complete set of headings used can be quickly covered, and therefore many undifferentiated entries have to be examined by the reader under each broad heading.

When a classified area catalogue is used in conjunction with an alphabetical arrangement or a broadly classed arrangement without notation, it seems unnecessarily complicated for catalogue users to find the subject arrangement is different. Map librarians ought to make far more use of the subject catalogue, particularly the classified subject catalogue, than is common at present. It must not be considered as the vehicle for the subject approach to broad categories of thematic maps such as geology or land use but as a vital tool in a developing information service. It can provide information about the presence in the collection of very specific subjects represented by maps filed in the collection or by maps in books and periodicals analytically catalogued. Further it is possible to provide added subject entries for special features in a map which are not usually shown, a subject entry can be made for this feature even though the map is a general, non-thematic map. As an example the collection may contain many maps of fairly large scale covering limestone regions, but only one or two may plot the entrances to pot holes. A subject entry under pot holes, or in a general library, a map subject entry for pot holes adjacent to the subject entries for books on pot holing will be helpful. Speleological journals with regular articles on pot holing will include plans of particular pot holes or cave systems, these can be given a reference in the map catalogue, a direct area entry under the name of the cave system, and a subject entry for pot hole maps.

The subject entry for a map of a particular cave system, will in a classified catalogue commence with the classification number for

200

caves, cbnc if BOGGS were used (and 551.44 for UDC). This will be followed by the area for subordinate arrangement of the 'caves' entry. If the cave system were that known as 'Gaping Gill' in the English Pennines, the area statement would in UDC, be (427.4–15), for Yorkshire West Riding, unless further local subdivision were made, providing a classified subject-area entry of 551.44 (427.4–15) which could be further arranged by the addition of scale and date in the heading. A similar map classified using the BOGGS system would be; cbnc 212. [Caves; England and Wales, Northern Counties] but this is apparently a most unusual way of using BOGGS in map libraries where alphabetical subject catalogues are more commonly provided. In that case the entry would be; Caves: Gaping Gill, Yorkshire. In this connection Dorothy PRESCOTT in a paper on map classification at the Map Keepers' Seminar and Workshop, National Library of Australia, 1973, notes that 'in order to maintain a logical subarrangement of areas it is necessary to practice indirect entry (which) leads to very long and unwieldy headings for small areas'. Indirect headings would give an entry; Caves: Great Britain, England, Yorkshire, Gaping Gill, Dorothy Prescott makes the very interesting suggestion for the adoption of a true classified subarrangement, 'to avoid this situation . . . by the expedient of using the area notation for subarrangement, which results in a very neat heading'. Our example would be, for a library not using BOGGS as a classified catalogue, but using the BOGGS classification for map filing; Caves: 212 (This class no does not of course, define the specific place, Gaping Gill) Although it is stated in the paper that a numerical file of area numbers will have to be provided in order to interpret the notation, and that readers are quite happy about using this system, one wonders why a normal classified catalogue should not work for readers at least equally well without the mixed alphabetical-classified heading. If the entry alone were 'self-indexing' for the reader, one could see an advantage, because there is no doubt that the need for an alphabetical subject index to a classified catalogue is seen by most catalogue users as an unnecessary hurdle, but an index is said to be provided. No alphabetical subject index is required because the subjects, eg caves, are in alphabetical order. No alphabetical area index is required for the subject catalogue entry; if Gaping Gill cave system is wanted by a reader, the area Gaping Gill will appear in the name index to the classified area catalogue, or in the area sequence of a dictionary catalogue. This will refer to the area entry but that will have a subject division ('caves') in the heading of the entry. If the reader makes the subject approach 'caves' then he is presumably wishing to know what maps the library has concerning caves, and browsing through the cards he will see in the descriptions the areas that are represented by the class numbers in the heading, and theoretically it might be possible to omit the numerical file of area numbers which was suggested, particularly as the file would have to be in a separate sequence or a separate listing on sheets. A readily visible, if less detailed alternative, would be to provide guide cards generously for some areas in any large grouping of cards within an extensive subject heading such as 'geology'.

Analytical entries

There are many occasions when an analytical entry has to be made. A common example is when a map is printed on part of the sheet containing the major map. This happens when a tourist map of a country includes inset maps which are street plans of selected towns. Another example is when it is felt necessary to bring to the attention of catalogue users a sheet of a map of a large area, or even a plate in an atlas, which provides information not otherwise well represented in the map collection. In both cases analytical entries will be added to the catalogue, giving entries describing the inset or sheet or plate and citing the larger map, multi-sheet set or atlas containing it. A general library, or even in the materials of a library confined to geographical subjects, can provide a large number of further analytical entries for the map catalogue, by the cataloguer producing analytical entries for maps which are significant but are included in books or periodicals. These entries are very useful, they add a new dimension to the stock of a map library, the maps analytically catalogued would otherwise often be 'lost' to the user and to the librarian assisting him. Something of the importance of analytical cataloguing in assisting to make the fullest use of a library stock can be gauged from the fact that the American Geographical Society *Index to maps in books and periodicals* First supplement Boston USA, G K Hall, 1971 contains 12,000 entries for maps catalogued in this way during the period 1968 to 1971 alone. The *Cartactual* publication service, from Cartographia, Budapest, should be a natural candidate for analytical cataloguing along with geographical and geological journals, but arrangements should be made for librarians involved with books and periodicals in other subject fields to draw the attention of the map librarian to concealed maps in these subject fields which would not otherwise be known in the map library. John G Fetros for example, has noted in SLA Geography and Map Division *Bulletin* No 92 (Jun) 1973, 53 that the *Statesman's year book* contains useful maps such as, in the 1967/8 edition a map of Belgium's linguistic frontiers. Sometimes up-to-date information is found on maps in official and international publications such as those of the United Nations, Security Council records, before they appear on other more generally available maps.

Inset maps etc may be noted in the catalogue by the provision of added entries using the main map unit card and appropriate heading, because the existence of the inset map should be noted on the main map unit card. Analytical entries for maps in books etc will normally require separate cataloguing as the map analysed will probably require added entries of its own.

Specimens of common types of entries for maps, for different types of catalogues and using different classification schemes.

The maps to be classified and catalogued are:

1 Great Britain. Geological Survey. Geological map of Great Britain. Scale, 1:625,000. Two sheets. Second edition. Chessington, Surrey. Ordnance Survey, 1965

2 Region Niagara Tourist Council. Region Niagara: regional municipality of Niagara. Fredk Paul, cartographer. Scale ca 1:145,000. St Catharines (Ont), Region Niagara Tourist Council, 1974

3 University of Glasgow, Department of Geography. Cairngorms recreation map. Scale 1:35,000. [Glasgow] University of Glasgow, 1974.

Dictionary catalogue, BOGGS classification and cataloguing rules:

Map 1 Unit card with area entry heading.
    210.2 GREAT BRITAIN—GEOLOGY—1964
    caq
    1964 G. Geological map of Great Britain; Geological Survey. 2nd ed., with minor emendations, Chessington, England, Ordnance Survey. 1966 1:625,000 two sheets, 82 × 103 cm. Ordnance Survey 'Ten mile map of Great Britain' second edition, 1957; reprinted with emendations, 1964; reprinted second impression, 1966.
    Index, sedimentary formations and igneous rocks.

    1 Geology—Great Britain—1964
    2 Geological Survey
    3 Ordnance Survey, 'Ten mile map of Great Britain'

The area entry card is filed under GREAT BRITAIN, after cards with the same area heading but with no subject. The card is arranged alphabetically in the subject sequence and then chronologically by date of situation portrayed on the map. If there are more cards with the same heading they are arranged according to title, and by edition if the first edition of this map had the same date. The subject entry is similarly filed in the same alphabetical arrangement in the dictionary catalogue. The author entry would only have a sub-arrangement by title, the author heading replacing, area-subject-date, and this is generally most unsatisfactory, as noted earlier. The subject and author headings would be printed as tracings at the bottom of the unit card. The author entry GEOLOGICAL SURVEY will only refer to non-current maps because Geological Survey of Great Britain was incorporated with the Overseas Geological Surveys and the Museum of Practical Geology to form the Institute of Geological Sciences. Now geological maps would appear under the name of the institute. There would be a reference filed at the entries for the institute, referring catalogue users to consult the catalogue under Geological Survey for maps produced before the date of amalgamation and vice versa.

The call number on the left hand of the heading consists of area-subject classification, followed by date of map and initial letter of authors name as a means of filing the maps themselves in sequence.

If a classified catalogue is used in a map library using the BOGGS classification, the area entry would be filed according to the class number: 210.2 caq [Great Britain : geology] The subject entry in the classified catalogue would be filed at; caq 210.2.

Map 2
613 NIAGARA (ONTARIO) mun.—TOURIST—1974
atu
1974 R Region Niagara; Regional Municipality of Niagara.
Fredk. Paul, *cartographer*. St Catharines, Ont, Region Niagara Tourist Council, 1974.

ca 1:135,000, 36 × 54 cm

Roads (2 categories), routes, sites of tourist activities. Table of addresses of 10 tourist information offices.

1 Tourist—Niagara—1974
2 Regional Municipality of Niagara
3 Paul, Fredk. cartographer

The class number consists of 613, Ontario, and atu, tourist map. The map shows no topographical information, it is basically as noted.

There are two author entries for this map. BOGGS requires that 'entry should be made for every person or institution responsible in any significant way for the content of the map'.

Map 3
221.2 CAIRNGORMS, Scotland—PARKS—1974
gbbg
1974 U Cairngorms recreation map; Department of Geography, University of Glasgow. [Glasgow], University of Glasgow Press, 1974.

1:35,000, 77 × 49 cm irreg. fold. to 11 × 19 cm

Inc. Cairngorms National Nature Reserve, Glenmore Forest Park. 4 classes vegetation, railways, ski-tows, chair lifts. Location of recreational activities (eg climbing), huts, reindeer pasture. Aerial photography, Hunting Surveys Ltd. Margin. Eng. equivalents of Gaelic words used in place-names; Cover, *The mountain code for Scotland* prepared by Scottish Sports Council.

1 Parks—CAIRNGORMS—1974.
2 UNIVERSITY OF SCOTLAND, *Dept. of Geography*.
3 Hunting Surveys Ltd.

The BOGGS class number consists of;
221.2 Northern Scotland
gbbg Reserves, parks, etc.
A decision would need to be made as to what types of areas were entered under Parks, and the decision recorded in an authority file. This map is of a specialist variety designed primarily for the use of walkers, climbers and skiers, and the notes describing it are arranged according to the order prescribed in BOGGS.

This, in the area entry, is an example of how the classification order used for filing maps usefully complements the dictionary arranged catalogue. The area entry CAIRNGORMS is a direct entry, of value for the reader who requires a map of the Cairngorms. If it is necessary to know the variety of maps of Scotland, or of Northern Scotland, which are in the collection this can be seen by examining the map file.

Classified catalogue, UDC classification and Anglo-American cataloguing rules
In the UDC classification scheme maps may be classified within the

class 912 with other forms of graphical representation of information, this is in line with the practice of the Dewey DC scheme where maps are isolated and arranged according to area. Because UDC has a method of distinguishing a map from books and other forms of record, by common auxiliaries of form, it is possible to allocate maps to subject numbers as used for books. This method allows general maps of a country to be associated in the classified catalogue, with geographical books on that country, or subject maps to be associated with the relevant books. There is no necessity to break up the collection of maps according to subject departments if this style of classification is followed, and all maps would have one entry under the general area number in the classified catalogue. This procedure will be followed below, and the full classification number will be provided, although all libraries would not wish to create such a detailed classification.

Map 1
    914.10:55 GEOLOGICAL SURVEY
    '1964'
    (084.3-M625) Geological map of Great Britain; Geological Survey. Scale 1:625,000 2nd ed., with minor emendations. Chessington, Surrey, Ordnance Survey, 1966.

                2 col. maps, 82 × 103 cm. Ordnance Survey 'Ten mile map of Gt. Britain' 2nd ed. 1957; reprinted with emendations, 1964; reprinted, 2nd impression, 1966.
                Index—sedimentary formations and igneous rocks.

TRACINGS   1 Geological Survey
             2 55 (410) '1964' (084.3—M625)
             3 Series title

Class number consists of:
914.10 :55 '1964' (084.3–M625)
Gt Britain Regional Geology. Date. Maps. Scale 1:625,000
    In the classified catalogue the map entry is arranged by area-subject, and the sequence filed date, scale, and by subject-area and the sequence arranged the same. Either date or scale could be omitted if desired, or both of them. The order of notations which are common auxiliaries of time and form, and in the subject-area entry of area which is there a place auxiliary, is ruled by the order in which common auxiliaries are applied, ie Place, Time, Form.

The form 'map' (084.3) would always have to be present in the classification numbers above, but M625 representing scale could be dropped. Scale is expressed in this example by omitting the last 3 digits, '000', in the representative fraction and 1:625,000 became M625. An alternative method is to use a code available for groups of scales in UDC, when (084.3–15) would represent scales within the range 1:250,000 to 1:1,000,000.

The classification numbers are, in the isolated position of these examples, quite incomprehensible in appearance, and a similar comment could be made of the BOGGS mixture of numbers and letters if used for filing map entries. The class numbers are, however, not incomprehensible when consulted in the context of the whole classified catalogue.

The author entry for the author catalogue accompanying the classified catalogue, is considered the main entry in AACR. The series entry brings together all the maps in one series, this particular series formed a type of national planning 'atlas' for Great Britain and the series entry would have attracted a number of catalogue users.

The AACR section for cataloguing maps, which is extensive, up-to-date and compiled by the committee with the assistance of specialist map librarians, could of course be used for the descriptive cataloguing, that is the body of the entry excluding headings, whatever the classification scheme in use.

Firstly there must be a comprehensive alphabetical subject index to the classified sequence, which must be admitted as an additional step towards tracing a map. The subject index would have entries:

Great Britain 914.10

Geology 55.

These entries do not refer to the map catalogued but to the class numbers, and equally can be used to trace categories of maps filed to locate them as groups of similar maps within the storage cabinets. Secondly there should be a generous provision of guide cards within the classified arrangement identifying class numbers with names so that although catalogue cards in the classified section commencing with 914.10 do not have a heading GREAT BRITAIN, as they would in a dictionary catalogue, a guide card with the superior heading 914.10 GREAT BRITAIN would provide the guidance for all the cards in that particular section of the sequence.

Map 2
917.13:711.2 REGIONAL MUNICIPALITY OF NIAGARA
'1974'
(084.3-M135) Region Niagara. Regional Municipality of Niagara; Fredk. Paul, cartographer. [Scale ca.
1:135,000] St. Catharines, Ont., Region Niagara
Tourist Council, 1974.
Map 36 × 54 cm
Shows roads (2 classes), routes, sites of tourist activities, e.g. camping grounds. Includes table of
addresses of 10 tourist offices
1 Regional Municipality of Niagara
2 Paul, Fredk, cartographer
3 711.2(713) '1974' (084.3-M135)

917.13 : 711.2 '1974' (084.3-M135)
Ontario, Regional planning, Date, Map, scale 1:135,000.
In this example an additional author entry is required for the car-
tographer.

Map 3
914.12:796.5 UNIVERSITY OF GLASGOW; Department of
'1974' Geography
(084.3-M35) Cairngorms recreation map. Department of Geography, University of Glasgow. Scale, 1:35,000
(Glasgow), University of Glasgow Press, 1974
Col. map, 77 × 49 cm irreg, fold to 11 × 19 cm
Aerial survey by Hunting Surveys Ltd. Shows
Glenmore Forest Park, Cairngorms National
Nature Reserve and adjacent areas SE of Avie-
more; 4 classes of vegetation, roads, railways,
ski-tows, chair-lifts. Location of recreational activities, huts, reindeer pastures. Margin: Eng. equivalent of Gaelic words used in place-names; cover,
The mountain code for Scotland prepared by Scottish
Sports Council
Tracings 1 914.12:796.5
2 796.5(412)
3 Hunting Air Surveys Ltd.
Analytical 4 Scottish Sports Council.
5 796.5 entry for 'Mountain code . . .'

914.12 : 796.5 '1974' (084.3-M35)
Scotland, N. Central—Touring, walking, mountaineering,—Date—
208

Map—Scale 1:35,000.
This has been classified for a general library and by the use of 796.5 the map is associated with books and guides on mountaineering etc, specifically in the north central area of Scotland. If the map were filed in a university geography department as an example of cartography for recreational purposes, or for national parks, it would be possible to provide a different subject entry, or an additional one which would emphasise this function:

711.2	Regional planning
(234.65)	Scottish Highlands, Grampians
'1974'	
(084.3-M35)	

In the above example (234.65) is a form division for 'physiographic designation' and is not a 'place' auxiliary.

Map 3 AGS—catalogue and classification
Area entry:

SCOTLAND, Section	624-c
Cairngorms, 1974	E-1974

Cairngorms recreation map
1:35,000
University of Glasgow, Dept. of Geography [Glasgow] 1974. 27″ x 18″ irreg.
Recreational facilities, walking, mountaineering, ski-ing etc. in Cairngorms National Nature Reserve, Glenmore Forest Park and adjacent area

Subject entry: Add, PARKS, National as heading to above card, placing heading at top centre.
Author: Add, University of Glasgow, Department of Geography, immediately above area in unit card. Author cards are filed alphabetically, then by area, chronologically.
The AGS call number at top right of card is for the classification and filing of the maps, and in the American Geographical Society map library is not used for a classified catalogue. The call number consists of—

624 —Scotland (For a British library this would be too broad a class, a local extension would need to be created)
c   The Cairngorms is a subdivision of Scotland
E   Economic, AGS subject classification to include National Parks
1974 Date

The area catalogue heading shows Cairngorms treated as a secondary area entry. AGS treats all maps of divisions, administrative or otherwise as secondary area entries, thus bringing together all the main political units, usually countries, as SCOTLAND, which is a different practice from that usually prevailing for a dictionary catalogue.

Map 3. PARSONS Classification and cataloguing
PARSONS, and libraries using the scheme or amended schemes eg BODLEIAN Library, University of Oxford, use a catalogue card printed with ruled spaces each identified eg scale. The rules and identifying words have been omitted from the modified example shown:

SCOTLAND
dist. CAIRNGORMS   1:35,000   1974
C18:2(11) University of Glasgow, Dep of Geography
Cairngorms recreation map
Gridlines 1 km apart; boundaries of nature reserve and forest park; contours (10m), hill shading, spot heights, 3 lines of magnetic North across sheet: railways, roads, tracks, ski-tows, chair-lifts, recreational facilities eg car-parking, rescue posts, huts; reindeer pastures, 4 classes vegetation
1 sheet   [Source obtained]

The PARSONS catalogue combines area, broad subject file etc in one sequence of areas arranged alphabetically. This map would have:
Area entry: SCOTLAND dist CAIRNGORMS which would appear in the section, Scotland dist (guide-carded) then alphabetical by districts.

Subject entry: Another copy of the same card with a changed heading would be put under one of the eleven headings provided by PARSONS, or more in a locally developed scheme. The only appropriate heading in PARSONS, if one were used for this map, might be Economic and the subject heading might be SCOTLAND—National Parks. Subject cards follow those of the area file under the broad subject heading eg ECONOMIC. Scale file follows the subject file where maps are arranged by scale. The master entry card is used with scale underlined in red. No author entry is suggested by PARSONS, the Bodleian Library provides one for early maps defined as dated before 1850.

DDC scheme, with classified catalogue, using AACR for cataloguing. Classification 912.412.

This scheme does not allow for the classification of maps by subject as well as by area, although local amendments may achieve this. The

210

basic subject index entries which would lead a user to this map and maps of the same type would be:

      Scotland: maps 912.41

      Cairngorms: maps 912.412

It is possible to classify subject maps to be arranged according to subject in 912.1 by adding the appropriate subject number from the main schedules to that base number, eg 912.15541, geological maps of Scotland. It is only possible to provide area following subject however where the main schedules offer a regional division, as 554–559 regional geology. If it were desired to associate the Cairngorms map with the subject 'outdoor life', for which as a recreational map it is designed, the class number could only be 912.17965 which is 'outdoor recreation maps' with no opportunity to provide an area division. Subject maps classified at 912.1 are not associated with books of the same subject in the classified arrangement but the index cards for the subjects can be associated together alphabetically as:

  Geology, Scotland   554.1

  Geology, Scotland. Maps 912.15541

This is not possible for a normal subject index entry to direct a reader to a 'recreational map of the Cairngorms' as there is no class number for reference.

    Recreational maps 912.17965

    (and other similar appropriate entries)

Is all that can be provided, unless a technique using a subject-area-reference card (BOGGS p 78) is practised. This can be adapted to provide a means of subject guidance where a general classification scheme has no facility for the classification of maps by subject. Assuming all maps are classified in DDC by area which is the primary intention in the scheme, then the recreational map of Grampian mountains would be at 912.412 and a similar map of Snowdonia, Wales would be classified 912.42923.

    In the subject index the normal references would be from the areas Cairngorms, maps 912.412

            Snowdonia, maps 912.42923

but a subject-area-reference card, entered under the subject

eg   Recreation:maps

  or Mountaineering:maps

  or Walking:maps

could be provided which does not give a classification number for the subject in the heading (there is not one) but lists the area classification numbers of those maps which have that subject;

        Recreation:maps

        Cairngorms   912.412

Snowdonia 912.42923

(etc)

As in all subject index entries this card does not direct the user to the specific map but to the classification group which contains the map.

Arrangement of author catalogue

The catalogue entries for this map would be the classified entry or entries as outlined above, and the author entry which would be considered the main entry as compatible with book entries in the same combined catalogue. The arrangement of cards under author entry would therefore be by title which has been shown to be an inadequate arrangement for map catalogue entries. The method used in author entries by the AGS would appear to be a considerable improvement which would be welcomed by map users consulting author entries for specific maps. The AGS master card has the area entry towards the top left and when an author card is required as an added entry the author is added above the area entry. The card is then filed in the author sequence according to the author's position in the alphabetical sequence and the cards referring to the same author are further arranged first by area, and then by date, ie the original area entry. This is a significant arrangement for map entries unlike the purely arbitrary, and often extremely confusing, alphabetical arrangement of titles. A reproduction of an author entry in the map collection of the National Library of Scotland is given on p 124 K G B Bakewell *A manual of cataloguing practice* Oxford, Pergamon Press, 1972. This author entry is like the AGS, an author heading placed above the area entry and so the arrangement of cards under a particular author is by area-subject-date. A caveat must be made however for the use of this AGS system. Although area-date is the arrangement also given approval (for a dictionary catalogue) by the SLA Committee a sub-arrangement of author entries by area-scale-date would seem to be more valuable. The largest grouping of author entries for most map libraries will be under the name of the official survey of the country of the library, because the library normally possesses a large number of maps of every type for its own national area. The need for the survey's maps is normally expressed by scale, and the latest date of that scale assumed. An enquirer checking under eg Ordnance Survey would therefore appreciate a scale arrangement. SMITH at the University of Kansas map collection promotes scale arrangement to follow area-subject, in a dictionary catalogue, and in justifying the arrangement suggests that a scale approach is especially necessary for geological, general, road, and topographical maps, which of course form a high proportion of any collection. The equal importance of official survey

212

sets confirms this judgement for author entries, and it might also be used with advantage as a subordinate arrangement in the classified catalogue. SMITH would arrange by scale by the order of larger scale preceding smaller scale. Similarly, it seems most helpful to the catalogue user when arranging by date to use an inverse chronological order so that the latest maps appear at the beginning of any particular group. Catalogue users do not examine every entry under a subject heading, or classification number, and then recall which seemed to be the better for their purpose and return to it at its position in the file. They usually in a general collection note the first map which appears to satisfy their need—this ought to be the latest of the class and so the maps should be arranged modern first, older later.

Classification schemes and cataloguing practices are not necessarily combined in the ways noted above, although these are common combinations. There is no reason why a library should not use, for example, UDC for filing the maps, have a dictionary catalogue, and for the area and subject headings use a system of sub-arrangement as suggested in the last paragraph for author headings. But, a degree of uniformity between map libraries in their technical processes would be beneficial, even more particularly when computer-produced catalogues are more common. Such uniformity would have to be achieved by agreement, it might be noted however that the items to be included in descriptive cataloguing, and the order in which they are entered, are strikingly comparable in AACR and BOGGS and a new map library would be well advised to adopt one of these codes for the unit catalogue cards. Headings should be provided for area, subject and author entries but as has been seen they differ widely in how to achieve these entries, but any computerised system should be able to generate whatever forms of headings and arrangement are selected. It must be said that in libraries outside the major map collections, there is a more urgent need than a machine produced catalogue and that is to have a system which will be able to cope effectively with very much bigger map collections than there are at present, and more varied collections in main libraries than are normally available in present collections in university geography departments, and in the book-orientated general libraries to recognise the different needs in classification and cataloguing of map users. No doubt the spur of the possible production of a mechanised catalogue for which the cataloguing system, or lack of it, in use is found to be inappropriate will be the occasion in many libraries for taking a new look at such processes.

Chapter references:
AACR; AGS; ALA; BM RULES; BOGGS; BUFFUM;

CANADIAN LA; FETROS; FINK; HORNER; PARSONS; PARSONS/FATHERS; PRESCOTT; RGS; SLA; SMITH; SPIESS; UDC; WALLISCH; WOODS.

11

Classifying: early and local maps

Early maps, until recent years sometimes often referred to as old maps
by writers on map cataloguing etc, may in some cases be thought to be
those maps which are no longer in current usage, but more specifically the dividing line will be for maps before land-surveying became
the work of government agencies on a national scale. BSI DRAFT
(1973) defines an early map as 'normally a map made before 1825',
whilst the Bodleian Library, Map Room selects maps before 1850 for
special cataloguing. It will be useful in most libraries to select a date
as a defining principle for an early map so that these maps are readily
observed and treated accordingly. One must always be clear however
why a particular procedure is followed, otherwise the date, be it 1825
or 1850 or any other selected, becomes merely a point in a meaningless ceremonial. The demarcation line to be chosen is that between
maps to be treated as early maps and those to be treated as modern
maps. For maps published prior to the chosen date it is desirable to
give more extensive descriptive cataloguing, particularly of a cartobibliographical nature, because these maps justify such treatment.
This type of knowledge is a major reason for some users interest in
examining them. If a map is received in a map collection, bought or
donated because of its cartographic historical interest, but dated
later than the library selected terminal date for early maps, it should
still be treated as fully as an early map. 1825–1850 are the kind of
dates usually adopted in British libraries for a primarily European
view of the history of cartography. The similar early period of map
production in other countries might reasonably differ significantly in
dating, and it must be remembered that interesting cartographic
examples from all parts of the world may appear in any good map
collection, at least as a facsimile publication.

Local maps are those maps covering the area of specialist area interest, probably local to the location of the library and whose coverage is of a small area using medium and large scales. Local maps are
more particularly seen to be those maps which are collected in public

libraries and the area depicted covers, or is within the area of local interest as decided by the acquisitions policy of the department of local studies. The definition of local map must vary from library to library. In some, local maps may be more correctly described as 'early local maps', although in Great Britain at least, it is normal in this connection to consider 'early' as including all maps, and this does not omit Ordnance Survey sheets, produced up to 1900. Elsewhere maps in a library's local studies collection are all maps of places within the local area of interest including currently produced maps. For the purposes of this chapter, local maps will be considered to be those maps of the area of local interest to the library which were produced before 1900.

It will be found that most of the literature on early and local maps is concerned with printed maps and the problems of cartobibliography. In a library collecting at this specialist level however there will be numbers of manuscript maps and plans, even if the archival repository for the area is not associated with the Department of Local History. Manuscript plans will therefore be discussed when appropriate.

Classification: early maps
There would appear to be no advantage in creating a special classification scheme for early maps and the classification used for current material can be followed. Thematic maps will probably be represented among the collection of early maps, Edmund Halley had published his map showing the distribution of ocean trade winds in 1686, and this was probably the first example of what is now understood to be a thematic map, but except as local maps they are probably not very numerous in the map library until comparatively modern times. It is therefore probably unnecessary to provide subject divisions within the area classification, any matters of subject interest can be brought to the attention of the map user by the catalogue.

It is inimical to the principles of preservation to allow early maps to be handled unnecessarily and so it is not expected that there will be any browsing among maps in their files. With this category of map therefore the classification is more particularly a means of locating an individual wanted map identified in the catalogue, and also for the construction of a classified catalogue if that is used. In the classified catalogue several entries can be made for any map and so the absence of any qualities thought desirable for the cataloguing of an early map which are not present in the general classification used, can be overcome. The call number will probably be more complicated than usual, by the addition to the classification of filing symbols, probably prefixes, describing the location of the file holding the map. Early maps should not normally be filed with current sheets, so that more attention can be given to the provision of appropriate storage methods for their better preservation, and to reduce the handling which would result from their being filed with frequently consulted current maps. The format of a map is an important factor to be considered in preservation, and early maps are found in more varied formats, and drawn on different mediums, which require their own selected storage.

Classification: local maps

Maps and plans form a very important class of record in most aspects of local studies, and in public libraries the large majority of early maps are obtained because of their connection in some way with local interest or studies. The interest may be the cartographer's connection with the locality. Christopher Saxton, the Elizabethan surveyor and map-maker known as the father of English topography was born in the Leeds area and this was an important factor in the purchasing of a copy of his 1579 atlas for the Leeds City Library. Birmingham City Library possesses a rare Saxton map because of his importance in the history of English cartography, but in the libraries of both cities the early maps are mainly of areas within the field of interest of their respective localities, and this category of map is probably an even higher proportion of the early maps in libraries outside those which are metropolitan districts such as Birmingham and Leeds. In Sheffield, another metropolitan district, the wonderful Fairbank Collection came to the city library because the maps, plans, field books and ledgers are the business records of an old Sheffield family of surveyors working for about a century after 1750. The maps in this collection are spread over areas within at least three counties, Yorkshire, Derbyshire and Nottinghamshire, but naturally with their greatest concentration in the Sheffield district.

It must be remembered that a library will collect and preserve for local studies today's Ordnance Survey sheets and other current maps of the locality as well as any old maps which come into the market or become available as gifts or in the form of photocopies of unique or rare maps kept in other collections. The current map is some library's local map, but, as has been noted earlier in a discussion of storage methods, no library would wish to provide the same physical conditions for a sixteenth century estate map drawn on vellum and a sheet of the Ordnance Survey 1:1,250 scale map published this year and covering the site of the estate, although both must be adequately treated and housed to ensure the possibility of permanent preservation.

Departments of local studies in British libraries commonly contain

217

hundreds of local maps in thousands of sheets, and the number of maps and plans will easily reach four figures if manuscript maps in the university or public library archives department are also included. As all these maps and plans will be concentrated within a small area of the earth's surface it is obvious that a normal map classification scheme arranged by area to cover the countries of the world will not be able to provide a sufficiently detailed analysis to differentiate between these local maps.

Local collections, taking a public library as the guide, will cover the area of the library authority, an administrative region of local government in Great Britain, and some adjacent areas depending upon the geographical distribution of the influence of the region. This is measured by an appreciation of commuter traffic, road network, siting of government offices, etc, and by the boundaries of non-government administrative areas. The administrative authority responsible for the public library within a region varies in Great Britain and Northern Ireland, but in England the libraries are administered by metropolitan districts and non-metropolitan counties. The metropolitan districts, which are in conurbations, have well-established local studies departments and historically have always accepted a role of acquisition of local materials for their surrounding rural areas, beyond the conurbation, up to the area of the county prior to the change in boundaries in 1974. Counties, which do not as library authorities include metropolitan districts, accept the role of acquiring the maps of their county and to some degree small-scale maps of surrounding areas. Since 1974 many counties have incorporated previously independent borough libraries, many with first rate map collections for their locality. The county of Leicestershire can be expected to collect all maps of the county as a whole, and the maps and plans of towns, villages, rural areas, estates etc within Leicestershire, and some maps which cover Leicestershire and adjacent areas such as a nineteenth century map designed to show the areas of the various hunts in the shires. Any general map classification scheme can only provide a class number for Leicestershire within its published schedules, which has to suffice for all the categories and areas of the Leicestershire maps noted above, with the exception of the shires map which would cover a greater area. If the Leicestershire County Library were to classify using the (LC) Library of Congress scheme almost all local maps would bear the same class number, Leicestershire maps, G5753.L4.

G5753.L4 would be an accurate classification for one category of local map in Leicestershire, the county map. The county was, for over two centuries until the advent of the Ordnance Survey, the major unit for printed maps in England and Wales. Local studies departments have sought to collect all their county maps, and should have collected all editions of them. Leicestershire in (LC) is distinguished from the other counties in England by the counties being arranged, after the class number for England, in alphabetical order and then the abbreviated Cutter number to signify the name of the county, eg L4 Leicestershire, is added to G5753. This method of further subdivision can be continued, whether the classification uses this, like (LC), or whether it does not as in (DDC). For (LC) it would however produce a clumsy classification number if G5753.L4 were to be followed by letters and numbers. Since there would be many more place names to be designated within the county than there are counties to be designated in England, there would have to be more detailed Cutter numbers of the order of G5753.L4 H235. However nearly all maps in the local collection would commence with G5753.L4 so that could be left understood and omitted from the records and replaced by for example ML to signify Maps, Leicestershire. In a classified catalogue ML would be classified as G5753.L4 and the same would occur whatever type of general classification is locally extended to provide depth for a local area.

A local classification scheme should then not continue to use L4 as the class symbol for maps of Leicestershire as a whole. This can be considered as the general area to be further subdivided, and so the substitute symbol ML can be used for maps of the whole county of Leicester. Maps of adjacent counties or areas larger than the county will be comparatively few but if filed in the local studies collection they should not be classified by the general map classification scheme, but classified as part of the locally developed extension. So maps of counties adjacent to Leicestershire, and of any areas within these counties kept in the Leicestershire Local Studies map collection, might be designated

MD   Maps: Derbyshire
MN   Maps: Northamptonshire

If as in the case of Leicestershire two adjacent counties have the same initial letter in their names a further distinction would have to be made, as: MN1   Maps: Nottinghamshire

Districts within Leicestershire would be treated in this mythical sample scheme, as subdivisions of ML and a notation provided. One method is again to arrange all districts in one alphabetical sequence and the notation will then once more be provided by the full Cutter number for the district as: ML   B 486

Leicester, the one large city in this particular county, may have to be considered differently as it might be expected that there will be numerous maps of parts of the present city area, parts which may at one time have been independent communities. A cartobibliography, Bonser and Nichols *Printed maps and plans of Leeds, 1711–1900* Leeds, Thoresby Society 1960, lists 374 printed maps of that city, and a local studies department would possess many manuscript plans as well. Leicester therefore might be represented by MLe alone and the subdivisions, the Leicester districts would be classed by their Cutter numbers as: MLe G 123

What are the districts into which the English county should be divided? Preferably, as in similar areas elsewhere, they should be divided by smaller administrative units which together make up the whole county and for which boundaries are known and an index map can be provided. The accepted division in this way would have been by parishes in rural areas and by boroughs in more populated areas. The boroughs would be further subdivided, possibly by recognised district names, often the names of historic townships which are now part of the borough or city. County councils usually prepare maps which identify parishes, and administrative areas maps are published by the Ordnance Survey for each county and metropolitan county showing all districts and civil parishes, either could be used as an index map. A detailed index map is necessary in order that very small areas, for which maps might be available eg a map of land ownership in the eighteenth century, an estate map of just a few closes, may be identified with the appropriate modern district in which it is situated.

Recent changes in local government areas of Great Britain mean that many local areas, usually larger than the parish, have had boundary changes and sometimes changes of name. This is most easily recognised by the appearance of maps with new area names, at county level 'Avon', and at district level 'Charnwood' in Leicestershire, which do not conform to previous areas or names. If division of the maps is alphabetical by name, the new maps will appear under the new names. If there has been a change of name for approximately the same area, the catalogue will have to link the old name with the new name, but the many local maps of the old administrative areas remain and earlier names must be retained in the catalogue. It would soon become confusing nevertheless to retain the old names alone for the notation division of the classification. It will be necessary where new area names have been created and where area boundaries have changed, to examine the local classification scheme which is in operation, whatever the type, and to supply new divisions which will provide for maps of new areas. These maps will probably not be individually a significant element in the future mapping of the area. Except for some maps purposely designed to show the boundaries of an administrative area or the planned work within that area by the district council, local maps are of a social-community area frequently the town and its environs, the village, property ownership in a small area—sometimes a very small area indeed in property sale plans, or parts of the national survey with sheets owing no allegiance to any local boundary or interest.

The position of all British and Northern Ireland public library local studies collections should be under review as a result of the 1974 and 1975 amalgamation of library authorities. For England and Wales, (DES) the Department of Education and Science, Libraries Division *The public library service: reorganisation and after* London, HMSO 1973 recommends as a prime consideration the creation of a strong central local studies department for the needs of research, but with recognition of local needs at the various population centres within the county area which will have built up in the past, as an independent library service, a good local studies collection. However this is interpreted, the central collection is paramount, and where duplicate copies of maps are not available the dispersed local collections should have photocopied maps relevant to the 'branch' area, the original being in the central collection. This obviously implies that for most areas there will have to be a complete reorganisation of the classification and cataloguing of local collection materials, including maps and plans, as it is not possible that the, in many ways unique, local systems of classification which were used in the various previously independent libraries can otherwise be brought together with any reality or efficiency. The map librarian responsible for local maps and plans has then the opportunity to devise or adapt a scheme which is truly classified and not dependent on alphabetising place-names. A scheme which will group the areas and places concerned according to their geographical affinities within the county. Villages and towns in the northern part of the county should, if possible, be located within the same part of the classification scheme and separated from the areas which have affinity with one another in the southern half of the county, although these divisions should be concerned with natural community area relationships, not compass directions. Then the plan of the nineteenth century landowners park and house in the parish A will be classified with the eighteenth century enclosure map of parish A, and they will be adjacent to the smaller scale map of town B and its environs, the environs including the twentieth century parish A which is now a dormitory of B, and all within the notation for the region which covers, for example, a nineteenth century map of the proposed line for a railway to join town B with the county town C and passing through parish A. Because of the possible different physical nature of these maps and plans they will not necessarily be filed together but

221

the classification used should in greater or lesser degree associate them together, the main purpose of classification. This association is perhaps seen best by the use of a classified catalogue which displays the material as a substitute for browsing within the maps themselves filed in similar order.

The classification scheme for local maps is based on area. In a department of local studies the books share this primary characteristic for arrangement, area. Unlike the remainder of a general library the books which are added to the local studies department are acquired, whatever their subject matter, because of a local area connotation. This is the reason for their existence in the local studies collection and so the primary characteristic for classification with books of topographical significance is area, just as it is for the maps. Although the book classification scheme used may be further subdivided to take account of the various subjects represented by the different books, every consideration should be given to the books and the maps sharing the same area classification scheme with obvious mnemonic value, but perhaps more importantly, to bring together in a classified catalogue a book and a map on the same village. In a dictionary catalogue there should be an area entry for all books with topographical significance to achieve the same end, the catalogue cards distinguishing between book and map.

Map librarians may create a local area classification scheme based upon the known needs for a defined local area. If a numerical notation is used, or a letter symbol not composed from the name of a district in an alphabetical order, later changes in name will not affect the classification, although the alphabetical index for the classification would need to record the reference from the new name. The devised scheme must be capable of extension, there must always be the facility for adding a new class number, or letters, for a new area at the reasonably appropriate position in the notation. Other difficulties can however occur and anyone devising a new local scheme should learn the lessons of the problems facing other libraries.

Numbered or lettered subdivisions can be allocated but the areas represented by these class numbers must have agreement with the areas mapped in the past and which will probably be individually mapped again in the future. A logical classification arrangement makes this easier to accomplish for the future, unlike an arbitrary arrangement of names. Units of area have however to be identified and this can prove difficult when attempting to give the scheme permanency. This difficulty can possibly be best exemplified by an examination of the local classification for maps adopted in the nineteen thirties by Sheffield City Library for a very important and well administered collection.

Sheffield City Library used a simple scheme for maps in the department of local studies.

A   General
B   Yorkshire (general)
C   Yorkshire (North Riding)
D   Yorkshire (East Riding)
E   Yorkshire (West Riding)
F   Derbyshire
G   Nottinghamshire
S   Sheffield

[Sheffield in the extreme south of Yorkshire borders on the northern boundaries of Derbyshire and Nottinghamshire.]

It will be noted that the areas around the city of Sheffield no longer conform with the modern counties of the Yorkshire area which are

West Yorkshire
North Yorkshire
South Yorkshire
Humberside

In no case are these areas the same as the previous Ridings and the new area, Humberside, includes a portion of the old county of Lincolnshire on the south side of the River Humber. Yet the many early county maps of the individual Ridings are still in existence, to be classified, just as the many maps of Middlesex remain after the county ceased to exist as an administrative unit, but fresh maps of, for example, the new South Yorkshire have appeared.

The subdivision of the Ridings in the Sheffield local classification is by reference to the number of the 6" to 1 mile Scale Ordnance Survey sheet which covers the area of the map classified, noted in curved brackets. A district which was in the West Riding might be classified:

E (288)   288 being the OS 6" sheet number

Not only has local government reorganisation altered the currency of this class number, but 288 refers to a 6" map sheet of the pre-1939 county sheet lines which has been superseded since by sheets of different boundaries and numbering based on the National Grid.

Similarly the divisions within classification 'S', city of Sheffield, must be considered. The city library has a vast collection of maps not only of the city as a whole, and the city has covered an increasingly large area over the years because of population growth and subsequent boundary alterations, but also a collection of plans of districts and small areas within the city. The classification scheme provided for the division of the city by area units which were the city electoral wards, arranged alphabetically, as:

223

S	Sheffield (general)
S(1)	Attercliffe ward
S(2)	Brightside ward
S(3)	Broomhill ward
. . .	
S(24)	Walkley ward
S(25)	Woodseats ward

The ward boundaries were as shown on a specific map, Roberts *Map of Sheffield* 1931, because the wards also have changed over the years, both in area and name.

With hindsight it can be seen that the use of area units based on local administrative boundaries has not the permanency one would wish to have in a classification scheme, and that arrangements using area names, as within Sheffield or for the counties, must in some way allow for extension, but more probably that arrangement also becomes out-dated. The arrangement of divisions, of counties in this example, by the use of OS map sheet numbers would seem to be the better method, but even this has changed within the last forty years. Nevertheless in Great Britain this latter method would seem to provide the greatest possibility of permanency, now being based on the structure of the National Grid system.

A tentative examination of the possibility of basing new local classification schemes on the National Grid, for the maps previously classified in the example outlined above, suggests a scheme on the following lines.

General

Derbyshire [General maps of old and present county, further subdivided for maps of smaller areas, eg Chesterfield]

Nottinghamshire [General maps of old and present county, further subdivided for maps of smaller areas, eg Worksop area]

Yorkshire [Old county maps and new maps of areas larger than the new administrative counties]

North Riding [Old county maps]

North Yorkshire [New admin county maps, further divisions for towns, villages]

East Riding [Old county maps]

Humberside [New admin county maps and subdivisions]

West Riding [Old county maps]

West Yorkshire [New administrative county and subdivisions as eg Leeds Metropolitan District]

South Yorkshire [New administrative county and subdivisions, excluding Sheffield]

Sheffield [Maps of the district area, further subdivided by districts

224

of Sheffield area]
A prefix will be required in order to distinguish the broad areas
named above. Letters might be used as in the old example, subdivision could then proceed on a system based on the National Grid. The
divisions of the National Grid which might usefully be used for this
purpose are the areas covered by sheets of the Ordnance Survey
scales:

Scale	Area covered	Sheet size
1:10,000	Whole of Great Britain	Represents 5 km square
1:2,500	Britain, except mountains and moorlands	1 km square (but sheets to be produced 2 × 1 km)
1:1,250	Urban areas, 20,000+ pop.	500 m square

In the example chosen it is possible, except for the Sheffield district,
that sufficiently detailed subdivision will be achieved if the 5km
square is used as the area unit. This could be read from the grid lines
printed on any 1:50,000, 1:25,000 or 1:10,000 sheet covering the area,
and for subdivision within Sheffield the subdivision could be taken a
stage further to define a 1km square. For a given library the notation
used for the classification might be a simplification of the normal
National Grid reference numbers but nothing should be done to destroy the National Grid sequence otherwise the advantage of a 'permanent' arrangement, proof against name or boundary changes,
would be lost, together with the facility to use Ordnance Survey maps
to identify local maps containing a place designated by the coordinates which are the National Grid Reference.
An example of the resultant notation, not using any simplification,
can be given for Nottinghamshire and urban areas within that county.

Scale/square used	Grid ref	
5 km square	SK 53, NW	An area SW of Nottingham city centre, Wollaton, Beeston.
1 km square	SK 5438 – one of 25 divisions of SK 53, NW	

The 5km sq Grid Ref does not distinguish between Wollaton and
Beeston, the 1km sq reference chosen identifies an area in Lenton,

225

Nottingham largely occupied by part of the campus of Nottingham University. The notation (National Grid reference) of the latter is not readily seen to be a division of SK 53 NW, and if other 5km squares within SK 53 are considered the 1km square notation would be as follows:

Within SK53NW 1km squares numbered SK5035 – SK5439
Within SK55NE 1km squares numbered SK5535 – SK5939
Within SK53SE 1km squares numbered SK5530 – SK5934
Within SK53SW 1km squares numbered SK5030 – SK5434

Remembering the names involved it is realised that maps classified in this way and then filed alphabetically would destroy any attempt to grouping by 5km sq areas. The National Grid Reference number consisting of two letters and four digits is therefore probably the best unit to use for the classification of local maps in a substantial collection. A plan of an area smaller than the 1km square would take the National Grid reference number of the 1km square, whilst maps of the whole of larger areas, districts like Beeston and Wollaton, would be given the six-figure reference number relevant to the central 1km sq grid area for their area. The same procedure could be followed for larger areas up to county level, except that towns and districts which have developed from an historic centre should be allocated the National Grid Reference number for the 1km square containing the historical site of the town and this should be the classification number for the town as a whole through all the developing stages of its existence. This will probably be now the site of the main central shopping area which might not be at the geometrical centre of the present administrative area. In all cases the map of the whole county, or area of local interest, would have to be examined and a National Grid reference number allocated to the full list of familiar or historic divisions of the county and to new administrative areas if they differ.

A substantial part of any local map collection will be the relevant sheets of all Ordnance Survey maps, and these will form an increasing proportion. These sheets of OS maps, if filed separately in a local map collection, will be filed and classified as units and access to them must also be by the National Grid reference. Sheets of such a map, and 1km squares of the grid, are identified by the reference to the SW corner of the sheets or of the square, and so curators and map users fully acquainted with the National Grid can achieve access to maps of a smaller area from its reference as read on the index map or as a reference in an alphabetical index which would be provided for all the more obvious place names to which National Grid references had been allocated. All smaller scale Ordnance Survey maps act as an

226

index map if their system of classification is followed. It is a more truly classified arrangement in that the numerical sequence does partially associate adjoining areas, and, given one 1km square Grid reference, the adjacent sheets can readily be deduced without resort to an index map. It is as permanently acceptable as any arrangement could possibly be, with national application, and should therefore be comprehensible to, and it could be uniform with the practice in, other local studies departments. It is a means of identifying maps by coordinates, which in the future will probably be the accepted means of identifying a map in a library so that it can be automatically retrieved.

Further arrangement of local maps beyond the area division should be by date which is a natural arrangement for early maps displaying the resources of the library in covering the development of a particular area. Some librarians introduce an arbitrary number after the area classification to provide a unique number for each map or sheet, so numbers would be as:

SK 5135 (1)

SK 5135 (2)

Here the number in brackets is a sequence number given to the maps in the order they are added to the collection at that area classification. More usefully the call number will contain a storage location prefix, area classification, and the date of the information portrayed on the map or the sheet, as

SK 5135 (1781) or '1781'

SK 5135 (1815)

Mention has been made in this chapter of manuscript maps, and well-founded local studies collections will have substantial numbers of manuscript maps and plans. In the last fifty years manuscript local maps have probably been more frequently associated with county record offices, but the, often earlier commencing, library departments of local history and associated urban archives repositories have had an important role in the preservation of archival documents. In England and Wales the administrative arrangements which divided the various local resources for research in local history have now disappeared, and it is to be hoped that the various collections become as one. A local map classification should therefore be as capable of classifying a sixteenth century manuscript plan as a sheet of the 25″ Ordnance Survey at the beginning of this century, and there should be the one bibliographical record for an enquirer to examine which will refer to all local maps. It may well be that certain categories of map or plan will not only be dispersed from the main collection because of storage requirements but some also will be separated in order to preserve the archival unity of collections of documents. These latter

227

must have a call number which identifies their location, perhaps even in another building, and it would not be useful to classify them to provide a notation as suggested above, but they should still all be recorded together in a union catalogue, and if a classified catalogue is used they must be classified according to the local scheme for maps if only to provide their location in the classified catalogue. In this way an enquirer can see all extant maps, be they printed or manuscript, recorded in one catalogue, and be directed to where needed copies can be examined.

Chapter references:
BONSER; BSI DRAFT; DDC; DES; LC.

12

Cataloguing: early and local maps

It is not necessary to attempt to distinguish between the cataloguing of early maps in general and local early maps, as there is a common core of principles to be observed in each case. Some differences of detail do occur because of their sometimes varied functions in libraries and these will be treated in turn, in cataloguing the necessary detail is most probably given within notes after the basic description of the map.

As in all technical processes in libraries, or administrative processes, the purpose of the process must be kept in mind in order to accomplish satisfactorily and efficiently the service required by the map user, and so the reasons for the existence of early and local maps in the general library must be reiterated. In some major libraries of national stature and international importance, early maps are obtained as important evidence in research in the history of cartography, in the case of many national libraries, being added to nucleus collections which have earlier been in the possession of royal families, aristocrats or wealthy merchants. Not all important map collections are in national libraries, as exemplified by the existence of the Hermon Dunlap Smith Centre for the history of cartography in The Newberry Library, USA, and the wealth of atlases and maps in the libraries of the Netherlands described by KOEMAN (1961). The maps and atlases may be mediaeval or comparatively modern but they are guides to man's knowledge of the world at a particular time, or contemporary descriptions of the topographic details of a particular place, and they are important examples of cartographic development. These are the type of reasons for the British Museum in 1969 purchasing 3500 maps from the Royal United Services Institution, 140 of them having belonged to Field Marshal Amherst who had been British Commander-in-Chief in North America from 1758 to 1763 and his military maps concerned wars with the Indians and French there, and similarly the purchase of the 1800 maps in the Tooley Collection of Australian early maps by the National Library of Australia.

General libraries of universities and public libraries similarly may obtain similar acquisitions by gifts from local benefactors, and by making purchases, perhaps of more modest importance though of considerable interest, which will enhance the resources of the early map collection to provide an insight for the student of the work of cartographers of the past. The growth of facsimile publishing of atlases and maps has greatly improved the possibility of a general library being able to develop a reasonably balanced small collection displaying the development of cartography.

Universities and public libraries have however a very important role to play in providing evidence on the development of the cartography of their own country by creating or augmenting a microcosmic collection, one of great range and depth for a limited area of interest. This type of collection complements the knowledge of the work of the famous cartographers, land surveyors and cartographic publishers, and illustrates whether the provincial surveyor copied or emulated them, and often contributes examples of the work of a nationally known cartographer which are not known in a national library, a fact vividly demonstrated by the range of map collections used as sources of information in Eden *Dictionary of land surveyors* 1974.

For most educational purposes, not necessarily of a formal nature, library ownership of facsimiles of famous atlases or important early maps, are the finest form of illustrative example, but for research purposes and for the cataloguer and map librarian suggesting new paths for cartographic research, they are less important. It is the early original material, even rather unregarded and possibly unknown to the expert, which properly catalogued and recorded may provide new evidence towards the solution of an old problem. The facsimiles are of well-known material and the library's copy, whilst being locally valuable for educational purposes and possibly providing 'first-aid' assistance for research by bringing together copies of important material which a scholar may not easily travel to see, cannot however contribute new knowledge. An original copy of John Speed *The theatre of the Empire of Great Britaine* an atlas well-known throughout the cartographic world in many copies, may nevertheless be discovered to possess maps which are variants; an estate map by some unknown seventeenth century schoolmaster may provide fresh information on local standards of linear and areal measurement. It is the cataloguer's and bibliographer's role to record these maps accurately so that the appropriate scholar, student or interested person is guided to them.

Identifying the main uses of maps collected for historical study it is found that there are important differences of need. To some users they are graphic illustrations of certain aspects of the life of a community, or part of a community, at a particular point in time, and if there are a number of these maps the reader can see a development or decay of that aspect of community life. This is helpful to one studying the history of that area, and is probably the most popular single use of such maps. Another student, using the term in the widest possible sense, will not have an interest in a particular area but be concerned with the history of a topic which is capable of being represented on a general map or a form of thematic map in the collection. His wider subject interests should ensure that any separate department containing these maps is called 'Local studies' and not 'Local history', for he may be a student of field names on a national basis, of pre-enclosure agriculture, of the existence of wells as a factor in the location of breweries, or a student of medical geography. To these map users a particular map collection is only one collection among many others which provide, in sum, a national library of local and regional record, not matched, but supplemented by, the true national collections. Similarly other, fewer, users are interested in the history of cartography, and allied studies. To these also one map collection is only one unit in a chain of collections, which might provide further evidence of the work of a cartographer, of the development of conventional signs, of the accuracy of land surveyors in land measurement, of the development of engraving, of engravers' decoration etc. To all these users the information contained in the catalogue is of great importance. The maps they wish to use should not be handled more than necessary, some are very old and others in good condition would have their life expectancy considerably reduced by unnecessary handling. A good catalogue is in fact an excellent aid in the preservation of early maps. As no browsing can be permitted, the catalogue or a published index should allow a proper selection to be made by a user for his particular interests based on the catalogue description. The usual book-type of cataloguing found in general libraries is not normally adequate for all types of local and early maps, it is not 'geared' to provide the information needed by the variety of map users.

Too often writers appear to suggest that the sole purpose for the study of early maps is cartobibliographical. This is probably because much of great worth has been written in this field by curators of national map libraries who by their research are seeking to elucidate the background of surveying, map-making, and publishing which might affect map users use of the maps. Even this study develops other research topics in specialist fields such as the development of printing, of book, map and print selling, of the art of lettering, drawing and engraving, and calligraphy. Knowledge acquired through the content of the early map has its importance too, as exemplified by the study of

231

the changes in topographical features like A P Carr, 'The growth of Orford Spit: cartographic and historical evidence from the sixteenth century' *Geographical journal* 135 (1969) 28–39 and knowledge of exploration. The representation of buildings, of ships, contributes to social history. Early local maps also contribute to such studies and otherwise to the history of agriculture, town development, building of canals and railways and many other topics, which are important evidence for the geographer, historian, and in many ways numerous other scholars. Lloyd A Brown *Notes on the care and cataloguing of old maps* 1941, writes, pp 31–32, 'Readers who consult old maps are usually interested in confirming or supplementing textual data. They are interested in either a minute point such as the location of a city, river, fort, the spelling of a place name, or they are interested in compiling all available information relating to an area during a period of time. A scholar who is studying the history of the province of Georgia wants to see every map of the area made during the period on which he is working. He is interested in the changes in the boundaries and in the outlines of smaller political subdivisions. He wants to trace the development of the road system and the location of taverns, estates, meeting houses, and fortified points. A comparative study of a representative collection of maps of an area will furnish the reader with an excellent cross-section of the region'.

The cataloguer must provide, for the maps within his library, the necessary access that users require in order to trace and establish the usefulness of the maps in that library for these different purposes, and to bring items to users attention which might be of value to the user/scholar who was not however deliberately seeking that information. The catalogue must give full accurate information on the essentials of description, and indicate further possible interests. The cataloguer preparing a printed catalogue for wider circulation must provide the same information, but must also be descriptive about matters which may be relevant to further research interests rather than merely to note their existence. The user of the library catalogue on site can examine the map itself if he has his interest aroused by the catalogue entry, but the user of the printed catalogue may be far distant and needs further description of the map in order to establish if it is worth while travelling to examine it. The bibliographer has a function allied to that of the creator of the printed catalogue but the bibliographer is concerned with the maps and atlases in a number of map libraries and map collections. He has to seek out the material wherever it may be and present to the reader that which is relevant to the stated purpose of the bibliography. An important aspect of the bibliographer's role is the enumeration of the material traced by an exhaustive search, but in recording the results of the search, the bibliographer must equally provide exhaustive information about the maps, but with the addition that he must give a comparative description where several, apparently similar, maps and atlases are traced.

An examination of the cataloguing of early and local maps must recognise these differences, although all might be expected to be practised by map curators and librarians. The preparation of a library catalogue can be expected to be part of the duty of a map curator, the preparation of a printed catalogue for the early and local maps section is something perhaps to which one should aspire. The preparation of cartobibliographies is work for a specialist, not necessarily part of the librarian's professional role, but at least the librarian/cataloguer may assist in the work of cartobibliography by the provision of good accurate catalogues. The need for distinctive attention to be paid to the cataloguing of early and local maps is because of their interest to cartobibliography and, for historical/geographical purposes, they do not follow the modern norms of content and publication. The needs of the different types of user represented in the previous sentence are not always compatible, and this could create difficulties in cataloguing. In general terms the map library catalogue should seek to satisfy the historical/geographical purpose, rather than the cartobibliographical, primarily because there are more enquiries of a historical/geographical nature and the needs of cartobibliography are unlikely to be fully met within the confines of a catalogue card, or cards because there is no reason why a catalogue entry of length should not continue on continuation cards. Further the cartobibliographer examining the catalogue will understand the 'pattern' of early maps and readily comprehend accurate succinct catalogue descriptions provided, whilst the historical/geographical enquirer could have little specialist understanding of early maps and therefore is requiring more obvious guidance.

Observation of the cataloguing of early maps in a number of general libraries prompts the thought that at the moment the needs of neither broad category of user are adequately satisfied. Cataloguers do not appear to recognise the need for a distinctive approach to the cataloguing of early maps, the maps are catalogued by general cataloguers who do not necessarily have cartographical knowledge and errors of fact of a most elementary nature are made. No attempt is made to especially satisfy the interest of the cartobibliographer, in imprint for example, which is also of importance to the map user only interested in the map contents. Cataloguing of maps and atlases in a general library should be the concern of a subject specialist who has some understanding of the interests involved in early printed or

233

manuscript maps. The cataloguer may have this knowledge but otherwise the evidence regarding the maps to be catalogued must be assembled by the map librarian or curator for the cataloguer. Such arrangements would, hopefully, lead to the cataloguing of early and local maps to provide a descriptive entry and headings which would recognise the uses made of such maps, which would provide catalogue entries as accurate as possible in factual detail, which may have to be supplied, and which would be efficient in providing notes which would prevent users having to discover the same information time and again. The importance of date to the map user may be taken as a key example for these points. Too often it seems that university and public libraries are happy to note [nd] meaning no date, whenever a date is not printed on an early map or is not written on a manuscript map. The historical/geographical user should be given the date of the information contained in the map so that he can use the map properly; the cartobibliographer is concerned with the date of printing of that particular copy of the map and possibly the date when the plate was originally used for reproduction. Here we have two different needs, which in many cases are concerned with two different dates, the date of situation being different from the date of the impression. The date of situation may not be in fact a simple date, if the survey from which the map was drawn lasted two or three years to cover the area of a county, then the information provided would have to be the first and last dates of survey. The historical/geographical user would like to know, if possible, which area was surveyed at the earlier date and which at the later. The cartobibliographer needing information on all impressions of the map which is not necessarily the same as the date which might be printed in the title from a plate which could have been engraved fifty or more years ago, and updated by alteration which makes different states for the plate through the years. From one single copy in the library the cataloguer could not deduce the full bibliographical history of the map, but can avoid the more flagrant errors and give what information is possible.

In a library catalogue the date of situation should be given in the heading, and this date is that used for the subarrangement of cards when arranging cards within one heading of area or author, and the date of printing is given with the imprint information in the body of the entry. This is in general agreement with AACR rule 212 J 8 which is 'If the date of situation depicted by the map is known to differ from that shown in the imprint and has not already been given in the heading or title it is given in a note'. This rule however, whilst necessarily permissive, underlines what has been written above that cataloguers do not take every opportunity to provide the information which, in its

234

absence, users or the map librarian might have to discover time and again, and under pressure at the time it is needed. In other words, in cataloguing an early or local map, dates should not be taken at their face value, a check should be made by the map librarian to see, (paraphrasing the AACR rule 212 J 8), if the date of situation depicted by the map appears to differ from that shown in the imprint.

The early and local maps should be given a detailed examination on receipt by, if necessary, two librarians, one with an understanding of the area and contents of the map and one with an appreciation of cartobibliography. The map analysis which results should be recorded and made available for future use, the relevant details of the analysis being extracted for use in the catalogue entry. The obvious rejoinder from some librarians to such a suggestion would be that they did not have the time to do this, the short answer to that would be 'Why buy an early map or local map if it is not going to be properly prepared for use?' For there is not the slightest doubt that when such a map is consulted such an analysis has to be made in order that full knowledge of the map is available. The general library cataloguer may not have the time and most probably would not have the necessary knowledge, so such an examination would fall upon the map specialist and, for local maps, the local history specialist. Part of the knowledge must be available before the map was received, unless it was a minor gift, a knowledge and appreciation of this map which resulted in it being acquired by the library. Then the map librarian, and indeed all other members of the map collection staff, will examine the map to be conversant with this new addition so that they know their stock. The addition of such a map is not an everyday occurrence and is different from the addition of yet another sheet from a state survey. At the moment in many general libraries this is done, but, after the map has been catalogued in the general cataloguing department. The suggestion is that this necessary examination is before the map is catalogued, the results are recorded systematically, and any relevant information from the analysis is incorporated in the catalogue entry.

Catalogue entries
BOGGS (p 50) makes a general statement on the cataloguing of old maps but does not develop it in detail, 'Old and rare maps, similarly to old and rare books, should be described in more detail than current maps, as to small particulars on the map, and details of appearance, such as kind of reproduction, colour, illustrations, colophons, panels, and location of title'. The crux of the matter is of course how to record the necessary further details, in what order and in what form. Work is proceeding on schemes for uniformity of map description, although

these are concerned with maps in general not merely early maps. At the fortieth General Council Meeting of the International Federation of Library Associations, Washington, 16–23rd November, 1974, it was reported to the Geography and Map Libraries Sub-section that IFLA's Committee on Cataloguing and the Geography and Map Libraries Sub-section have established a Joint Working Group for the purpose of developing an International Standard Bibliographic Description for maps. The British Standards Institution produced in 1973 (Document 73/80194 DC) *Draft British Standard recommendations for bibliographical references to maps and charts in accessions lists*. This latter, whilst being designed for maps in general, does recognise the different needs of early maps and where necessary stipulates different recommendations for early printed maps and manuscript maps from those for modern printed maps. It must be noted however that this is only a draft standard and it may be extensively altered before publication, probably in 1975. A wide variety of possibilities are available to the cataloguer and bibliographer at the moment, but the words of BROWN (p 61–62) will probably always be relevant, 'The type of notes selected for inclusion on the card will vary with the collection and with the type of questions asked by investigators using the catalogue and the collection. These factors will also influence the number and kind of added entries to be made for each map. Some cataloguers will choose to stress bibliographic data such as printers, publishers, delineators and engravers, while others will consider geographic data such as scale, projection and prime meridia of foremost importance. The order in which notes should be set down on the card is debatable, but for the sake of uniformity, some order should be established and adhered to'.

In recommending, earlier in this chapter, that a record should be made of the detailed analysis to which every early map and local map should be subjected, it is recognised that although the resultant information will be of value in the descriptive cataloguing of the map, more information will sometimes be available than can comfortably be housed on catalogue cards. A description may continue on a further, or extension, card but such extended entries should be kept to a minimum. BROWN (pp 72–73) suggests that 'Rather than make one or more extension cards containing abridged or outlined information, it is better to make a sheet catalogue, which can be expanded indefinitely and which need not follow so closely the outline form selected for the card catalogue. In fact the sheet catalogue, which need be only a plain sheet of paper filed with the map itself, should be considered the place to set down bits of additional information about the map as they are acquired, or an extension or amplification of the catalogue

"Notes".' This must be recognised in general terms as good library, map or book, practice—recording and filing all the information traced about an early, and therefore somewhat exceptional, map or book, adding notes of other information that may come to the curator's attention through the years, all readily available for the user of that map at the time of use. A common example of the kind of additional information which would be added regularly is a record of any sales of other copies of the map to show date, sale, buyer, and most importantly the price and condition of the sale copy, in other words not necessarily the type of information normally associated with a catalogue. The Brown suggestion that the sheet record should be kept with the map is understandable, the information is then readily at hand when the map is removed from its file for examination, but library conditions may often indicate a preferred system of filing such sheet records separately. Any well organised map library, or general library, orientated to provide an economical, full efficient service to its readers and map users will find it desirable to construct information files over and above the provision of a good catalogue. A sheet record file for early maps would just be one of these, but some convention must be established for an instant reference from the catalogue entries and from the map itself to the sheet record, if needed. The type of thing which would do this would be using a particular coloured card for early maps and any other map for which additional sheet records were available, and a sign, perhaps a small label of the same colour, could be attached to the cover for the early map itself.

The sheet record should however have a form of entry of its own which bears resemblance to the more abbreviated catalogue description. Rules for description, plan of layout of the information, not only give a useful uniformity so that a user is aware of what to expect, but it both acts as an aide-mémoire for successive map librarians in completing the entry, and the absence of any particular information can be understood as a 'nil return' rather than a possible omission. Mr R Cooper, previously Borough Librarian of Chesterfield, Derbyshire, compiled for use in the Chesterfield Borough Library a sheet form to record information which could not be supplied on normal cards for cataloguing maps. The form itself emphasises cartobibliographical information, but of course the descriptive cataloguing on cards could give an emphasis to historical/geographical interests. Mr Cooper's form is ruled to establish compartments of various sizes and the information to be recorded is put under the following headings (p 238).

Unit card description
Many general and university geography department libraries will

237

catalogue maps in accordance with the rules of AACR or BOGGS, and these codes appear to offer the most acceptable directions for early and local map cataloguing. They also differ very little, the most

Local history collection – Inventory of maps

Cartographer Date(s)	Subject	Title	Date
Engraver Date(s)	Scale	Additional text	Evidence re date
Publisher Date(s)	Details shown	Variations	
Printer Date(s)	Colouring		
Containing work	Ornamentation	Reverse	Border Size
Plate number			
Method of printing Reproduction	Paper	Framed or mounted	Accession no
			Class no
		Folded, cased, rolled	Location
Quality of impression	Plate	Source	References

significant difference being in the position of the scale statement in the entry, AACR having scale immediately after the title and author statement, whilst BOGGS puts 'scale' much later after the details of imprint. The order of items on the cards laid down for these codes has already been listed in the section on current maps. The discussion of the map description which follows is conducted in the order of AACR for maps, but the points raised about each item would be relevant for maps in any system of descriptive cataloguing. The discussion below is based on an examination of many codes or published cataloguing practices and the consensus is given, or where that is not possible the author's preferred practice.

Title
The title is to be given literally and in full with the exception of unnecessary phrases. Spelling and punctuation should be copied. Apparently incorrect spelling can be indicated as being on the original by following the word with [sic], but catalogue users do not need such editorial notes for, say, the spelling DARBIESHIRE instead of the modern DERBYSHIRE. The omission of superfluous phrases must be indicated by . . ., and this should not be used as a means of abbreviating the title. The type of phrase which can be beneficially omitted is when a title includes a dedication, a flowery word of thanks to a benefactor. The title dedication must be included but the more obsequious phrases can be sensibly left out. Early maps frequently employ a plethora of capitals, in cataloguing this is excluded, if thought desirable an initial capital letter for a word can be used to indicate a word wholly in capitals in the original.

Titles often contain the name of the person responsible for the map, it is better to preserve fully such a title rather than to put the name of the person responsible in a separate author statement. Many plans, particularly estate plans both printed and manuscript include in the title land owners' names and, where relevant, a reason for the compilation of the map, eg as evidence in a legal dispute. Preserve such statements in the title, they are important aspects of the description of a plan and are better situated in the place given to them by the draughtsman than being included in the notes on the catalogue card.

Occasionally it will be found that the map does not bear title, this is not uncommon when a map has been extracted from an atlas or some other volume. Then a title is supplied and is put within square brackets in cataloguing. The supplied title should be as short as possible, based on the area displayed and the type of map if a particular feature of information is emphasised. AACR reminds the cataloguer that the map may have been referred to in reference sources, and in this case the title then supplied should also be used by the cataloguer.

Author statement
Who is the author of an early map may in some cases provoke an involved discussion but the cataloguer should not be too pedantically concerned by this. The important principle to be followed by a library cataloguer is that every person named as being involved in some way with the production of an early map or plan has an importance which

must be recognised in cataloguing. Often the author, commonly the cartographer in a printed map and the surveyor in a manuscript plan, is well established by the way his name is identified, 'A map of . . . by [cartographer]', '. . . surveyed in the years 1825 and 1826 by . . .' etc. Where libraries believe it advisable to have an author entry labelled as main entry, such phrases on early and local maps can be taken to identify the 'main' author. In the catalogue description all cartographers, surveyors, draughtsmen, compilers, publishers, engravers, printers etc will be identified. Sometimes any one of the above could be established as 'author', but usually it will be a cartographer or surveyor, others assisting in the production of the map will be named in the imprint information whilst the remainder not already listed will be identified in the 'notes' following the basic catalogue description.

BROWN (pp 37–45) has interesting notes on the authorship of early maps. The role performed by identified persons in the production of a map must be stated in the author heading, author statement, imprint or notes as appropriate. BOGGS (p 30) reminds the cataloguer that if the author's name has been supplied from anywhere other than the face of the map this should be noted by the use of square brackets, a convention which should be observed for any supplied information in catalogue entries or bibliographies.

Scale

The scale is sometimes written on the map or plan as a statement usually accompanied by a scale bar; on other maps the scale bar appears alone, and on others no scale statement is made. The scale should be quoted in the catalogue entry in the form given on the map. A statement on a plan might be: Scale twenty four feet to an inch. A statement accompanying a scale bar might be: Scale of chains and links by which the map is plotted 24. The latter will be followed by the measurement of the scale bar in square brackets, as: [Chains = 15.3 cm] Measurements made by the cataloguer should now be made in metric measurements. All cataloguing codes using metric measurements use centimetres, sometimes measuring only to the nearest centimetre, but in Britain there appears to be the possibility of the centimetre being hardly used elsewhere, textiles, furniture, building materials etc all being measured in millimetres or metres, and it may be advisable to use millimetres in cataloguing.

After the statement of scale as on the map, there should be given the approximate representative fraction, although if the scale is a well-known one as one inch to one mile, that is 1 : 63360, it should be given accurately. Scales which have to be measured from a scale bar can only be approximate and in early maps, particularly local maps and manuscript plans, complete reliance cannot be placed on the scales said to be used. The cataloguer should compile a reference table for use in cataloguing early maps which will record the computation of the typical scales used and equate them with the representative fraction to be quoted. ADAMS in preparing the published catalogue of the plans in the Scottish Record Office has printed a guide for converting from chains, both Scots and Imperial, to representative fractions. The guide for Imperial chains is:

Imperial chains to the inch	Representative fraction	
	True	Reduced
1	1 : 792	1 : 800
2	1584	1600
3	2376	2400
4	3168	3200
5	3960	4000
6	4752	4800
7	5544	5500
8	6336	6300
9	7128	7100
10	7920	7900
11	8712	8700
12	9504	9500

The cataloguer must be aware of other linear measurements which are used in early maps, on English maps for example, links; rod, rood, pole or perch; furlongs; paces (or pases); and a variety of miles. All should be listed in a representative fraction reference guide.

The statement of scale is an example of the information which must be carefully examined by the map curator before cataloguing. Early, and local, map scales must not be assumed to be the same as their modern equivalent because, at least in England, of the existence of customary measurements before statute measurements were uniformly accepted and used. Thus Robert Morden in preparing maps for *Camden's Britannia—newly translated into English* . . . by Edmund Gibson . . . 1695; used scales showing three customary miles, a long mile of eleven furlongs, a middle mile of ten furlongs and a small mile of nine furlongs. A rough manuscript plan *A Mapp of the division of Malcalfe Moore* . . . *1691 By me Charles Kyrke jun* in the John Rylands University Library of Manchester, has a note that 'each chaine is thirty two yards or four roods'.

It should therefore be a requirement in cataloguing an early map that a check is made on the scale by making measurements between points on the map for comparison with appropriate modern maps or plans. No completely accurate deductions can be made in this way because an early map has possibly suffered shrinkage, perhaps when printed if a printed map or during storage, and this is not always uniform in all directions. Mounted maps may also have suffered in this manner. For the same reason measurements for scale cannot be made from a contact photocopy, nor from a photographed copy unless the reduction of the latter is known, and because of this any photocopied or photographed original for addition to the collection should have a measuring rule included in the reproduction.

Some early maps, or more particularly plans, have different scales for N-S and E-W in order to emphasise a particular feature; others are more truly sketches and are not drawn to scale at all. Such distinctions must be noted. Whenever a map is drawn to scale but the scale is not given, or is not immediately comprehensible, measurements should be carefully made of several distances on the map and the measurements compared with the measurements between the same points on a map of known scale. The relation between the two sets of measurements can be written as a proportion, and thus the unknown scale can be deduced from the known scale. When a scale is given but cannot be understood it is usually stated in a form such as a scale bar with divisions which are not identified by the cartographer, or a statement such as ' . . . according to twenty in an inch'.

A scale as a representative fraction must always be calculated and noted in the catalogue entry within square brackets whenever no scale is given on the original, except in the very few cases where the map is not drawn to any consistent scale.

Edition, is the next item for entry according to AACR but this is not appropriate a position in the cataloguing of early maps. Any information about editions is preferably given as a note within the section as in AACR rule 212 J9 'Sources and bibliographical history'.

Imprint: Place of publication, publisher, date of publication.

For manuscript plans or maps it would be appropriate here to make the distinction with printed maps and plans in a combined catalogue by noting, [manuscript], before any information known about the production of the plan is recorded.

The place of publication should be given as printed in the language of the map: DRAFT BSI rules for manuscript maps specify that the place where the map was executed should be given if it is known. Early printed maps may give a fully detailed address in, say, London, the catalogue entry need only give the town of publication in this case.

Some early maps do not have a publisher stated, the role having been filled by a man, or group, stated to be printer or booksellers, as:

'Sold by J Tinney at the Golden Lion in Fleet Street London 1753' which would give an entry of London, J Tinney, 1753.

Date of publication is a point of importance which might require considerable work in order to establish as correct an entry as possible. This will be discussed at greater length later in this chapter but here it must be said that it is another matter for which careful examination by the map librarian is required before cataloguing. If an entry is eventually marked as [nd], ie no date, this must be looked upon as a failure to provide essential information, which must be rectified whenever any further information about the map comes to hand. It should also be noted here that if the map is contained in, or has been extracted from, an atlas or book, the imprint of the atlas or book is not to be understood as the imprint for the map. Early maps were often in existence for a long time and being sold separately before a number might be collected together and reissued in atlas form or within a topographical work. The existence of the imprint in the book can of course be of considerable assistance in establishing the probable date of publication of an undated map. Often for undated maps, the internal evidence of the map will be used to assist both in dating and in suggesting the place of publication.

The possible entries that may be given for the deduced date of an undated published map are best illustrated by the following list of possibilities adapted from a similar list in AACR. It is of course the more satisfactory the nearer the cataloguer can get to the probable date, but even if an exact date can be established, eg noted within an accompanying pamphlet, or a newspaper sale notice for the map, this must still be entered in square brackets as it did not come from the face of the map.

Date entry

One or two years uncertain	[1792 or 3]
Probable date	[1792?]
Approximate date	[ca. 1792]
,,	[between 1706 and 1712]
Decade uncertain	[179–?]
Only century established	[17—]
Century uncertain	[17—?]

Manuscript plans often include the full date of drawing or completion of survey, and this, day-month-year, can be noted.

If there is more than one date on a printed map, the latest date, in accordance with BOGGS, which could be the date of a reprint should be given. Particulars about editions, reprints, reissues etc should be included in the notes, cartobibliographical section. This does not apply to a photocopy of a printed or manuscript map made at a later date, the original date is given, as with a later drawn copy of a manuscript map. In these cases details of copying will again be in the notes, among the other details of the individual copy possessed by the library.

Collation

The collation refers to the number of sheets composing the map and the size of the single sheet map or the size of the individual sheets making up the map. AACR rules that single sheet maps shall be named 'map', or 'col map' if coloured. In many cases it would be unnecessary in a map collection to establish that the catalogue entry was for a map, and the number of sheets would only be noted if there were more than one. In a combined map and book catalogue however it is probably a wise precaution to state clearly that an entry is for a map, although collation would appear to be a comparatively insignificant place to make this known. If any other distinction is made, eg 'Map' is introduced as an item in the heading or different coloured catalogue cards are used, then there does not seem to be any value in noting 'Map' for single sheet maps. 'Col map' is also not an effective way of describing many coloured maps, particularly hand-coloured early maps, and this information is more effectively given in notes, physical description. It is here recommended that 'Map' is noted in headings in a combined book and map catalogue, as discussed earlier, so that a distinction is made for a proper dichotomy in arranging entries of books and maps under area, author and class/subject.

The size of sheets is given in centimetres, but note comment earlier in 'scale' regarding millimetres. Most published catalogues have in the past always given size measurements as height first and width second, in the form '20 × 30 cm', but in recent years it seems an unfortunate lack of uniformity has appeared and width has preceded height. It is to be hoped that the standards mentioned earlier will, when published, conform to the traditional *1* Height × *2* Width, to prevent any further confusion with the many published catalogues and cartobibliographies which have practised this method.

Maps of the most common physical format are measured from the outer lines of the border rules, unless a portion of the map proper juts beyond the border. Manuscript plans, and some printed maps, are not necessarily contained within any kind of border rules and the overall measurements of the drawn area are then used. Maps are presented in a variety of forms and useful notes are given on their measurement in AACR, but generally speaking the rule is to provide the overall measurements of the map proper, excluding any printed text, titles etc which may be printed or drawn beyond the area of the map proper.

Early maps and local maps may have been published folded, or dissected and folded to be stored in a box possibly made to look like a leather bound book, with author and title on the spine for shelving in, originally, a private library. In such cases note should be given of the overall and folded sizes, with 'boxed', 'dissected' etc being used in description.

Notes

All the details of title, author statement, scale, imprint and collation noted above must be considered as essential items to be included in the description of all early and local maps. Further information is equally important for different categories of users in different libraries and to some extent the number, arrangement and detail given in additional notes will depend on the map librarian's, not the general cataloguer's, estimate of the use made of the map library and the potential of the collection. The earlier notes to be given below are essential for every library, with others discretion is possible but the information not included on the catalogue card is to be recorded on the separate 'Map information file'.

Analytical note

A map not separately produced but which is part of a book or periodical is noted here as 'In', or in different cases another suitable descriptive phrase, and the brief author, title, date of the containing work is given. BOGGS (p 36) also notes the descriptive phrase 'Detached from' when the map or plan, originally part of a volume, is represented in the library by the detached map alone. AACR rule 212 L appears to be too permissive on this point stating 'If a map is known to be detached from an atlas or collection, it may be catalogued as an independent work, with a note to show its relationship to the complete work'.

The detached map is a common example of the early and local map in general libraries in Great Britain and probably throughout the world. The early popularity of English atlases of county maps has resulted in many such maps remaining extant in collected volumes.

Interest in early maps commonly being represented by private collectors and libraries, the broken atlas binding is better not repaired for sale but the individual maps are sold individually. It should be an essential item that the origin of such maps is stated in the catalogue entry as 'Detached from [the atlas or volume]'. Seldom is this very necessary information given in some libraries. Incidentally, this is a further example of the general library cataloguer cataloguing the map which comes before him, without reference to the map librarian who bought this map from a dealer's catalogue in which the origin of the map will be clearly stated with a lesser or greater degree of accurate information. Once the bookseller's bibliographical description of the map for sale is ignored and lost, a piece of possibly very difficult bibliographical detective work has to be undertaken. This is the position for many early maps in general libraries which are now inadequately catalogued because of the omission of this information. It is the duty of the map librarian to trace the necessary information and then to have the map recatalogued, and it is also the map buyer's duty for new maps to see that the examiner of the newly added maps for cataloguing and 'Map information file' purposes is provided with the bibliographical information which accompanied the map at the time of sale.

Of course many individual sheet maps are bought or presented to a library accompanied by no knowledge of their bibliographical history, they may have been previously in a collected volume, or they may have been published as and always remained a single map. The analysis of all incoming maps should establish if it has been extracted from a volume or not.

Authorship note
The early maps in any collection may all be seen as having a part to play in the understanding of the development of cartography, and, as in all historical subjects, a knowledge of the work of individuals, who may have been innovators, is essential for an understanding of the growth of the subject. Authors, in the widest sense, are therefore of much more significance for approach to the catalogue than they are for current maps. The various people involved in the production of early maps may, at different times, have been compilers, surveyors, draughtsmen, publishers, printers, engravers and mapsellers, and not a few of them occupied a number of these roles at the same time. Therefore in any collection of early maps all 'authors' have importance and should be given in a note unless it has been possible to note them appropriately in the author statement, or imprint. All recorded should be given added entries in the catalogue.

246

Date of situation

AACR rule 212 J8 'If the date of situation depicted by the map is known to differ from that shown in the imprint and has not already been given in the heading or the title, it is given in a note'. This is of vital importance for the historian/geographer's use of the content of the map. It is recommended that the date of situation is always added to the heading, as the arranging feature for entries of early maps under the same area, classification, author, and where necessary, subject headings, but a note here regarding the reason for the selected date, is desirable, unless the date was explicitly stated on the map. In a simple form, a nineteenth century map may have an imprint date much later than the railway network shown on the map.

Content notes

It is recommended that a clear brief description of the content of the map is given for the benefit of the historical and geographical interests of users. The content note is probably best commenced by the descriptive word 'Shows . . .' as used by PARSONS to introduce such a section in the ruled catalogue card used in that scheme. ADAMS (p x) uses 'Showing . . .' and '. . . shown' also which 'indicates functional details; further details, which although important are incidental to the main purpose, are "noted".' Usually the content note can have a brief general phrase to describe the category of map, if that is not self-evident from the title; British examples might be 'estate plan', 'turnpike map', 'county map', and more generally 'portolan chart'. From this phrase certain essential details of the content of the map can be assumed, an 'estate plan' delineates the owner's land, divided in closes, with boundaries clearly marked and adjacent landowners named, the area of each close given. The cataloguer will then add after 'shows' details which cannot be assumed, although they are common, such as field names, names of tenants, houses (in block plan, in elevation etc). If the ADAMS convention is followed additional contents, eg post-mill, mine-shaft, are 'noted'.

A list of items for description in the content of the different types of early map can be established by the map librarian, and probably in conjunction with the local history librarian, as an aid for future uniformity when maps are initially examined on addition to the library. Guidance on such matters can be obtained by examining works which are concerned with the description of the type of map and particularly published catalogues of maps which provide contents notes.

J B Harley *Maps for the local historian: a guide to the British sources* London, National Council of Social Service 1972, is invaluable as a general work in this connection, but catalogues of maps in libraries or record offices will give many examples of specific maps and plans which are probably matched in style and content in other collections. Among these catalogues might be noted: Essex Record Office *Catalogue of maps in the Essex Record Office, 1566–1855* Edited by F G Emmison Chelmsford, Essex County Council 1947, With three supplements, 1952–1968.

Headings

The main point of difference in the headings which will be used for catalogue entries for early and local maps compared with current maps is the greater importance of author entry in all the forms of cartographer, etc. The question by a user will sometimes be to see if the library possesses examples of maps by Jansson, Mercator, Saxton or Bowen, for example, and in some cases the map-maker may have been involved at times as draughtsman, sometimes as publishers etc and so added entries are required for all the people named as having some responsibility for the production of an early map. These names will all have appeared in the description on the unit card. In the case of local maps the same principle should be followed, added entries for all persons involved in the production of the map including firms of printers, engravers. These persons may not be major subjects of cartographic interest but because of their connection with the locality through at least a local map, although in many cases they will be found to have stronger connections, they warrant documentation as part of the library's accepted role in being a centre for all information concerning the locality.

Area heading for early maps should use the current form of name for the area if it is different in the early map. Local maps, in particular, will often be concerned with very small areas, some of which are not readily named as an individual unit and there should be entries for these areas under the name of a recognised administrative unit containing them. Areas smaller than a parish or village can be difficult to locate precisely. It should be done for cataloguing by an examination of large scale maps of an area, or if the area has been considerably developed since the early map was drawn, by examining old maps. In England and Wales the 1st Edition Ordnance Survey 1″ to 1 mile map is very useful for this purpose. The location must be recorded by establishing the National Grid reference number for the approximate centre of the plan and this Grid reference should follow a colon after the parish name in the heading. Direct entries therefore should only be made for areas of a certain administrative unit size, and larger areas. In England the smallest area to be

248

designated in a local collection would probably be parish. A catalogue devoted to maps in a local collection would find it acceptable to make direct area entry under parish or other areas covered by maps, but where the local map collection is amalgamated in a full map collection, or in a catalogue covering the whole of the contents of a general library it would seem of value to provide indirect entries so that entries for all local maps may be brought together for ready checking in the catalogue. If the library collected all maps for a metropolitan district and for the adjacent counties the maps might be entered under the names of the metropolitan district or the appropriate county followed by the name of the district or parish. This is relevant to a dictionary catalogue, in a classified catalogue the entries for local maps are already brought together by the classification scheme and the local extension created.

Subject entries will be made as necessary but as thematic maps they will be infrequent compared with those which would be required for the current map collection, however, geological maps for example begin to appear in early and local map collections from the late eighteenth century. There is need for a type of subject, or form entry. Categories of map, such as tithe maps, which are concerned with showing very much the same detail as would a general map of similar large scale but which are drawn for a particular purpose, should be identified by subject entry. Any enquirer wishing to see an example of an enclosure map, a T-O map, a canal map, should be able to approach them via the form or subject heading.

Additional entries should always be made in a catalogue for recording matters of interest, against the day when knowledge of the existence of the point of interest is needed. Within a local map collection there are so very many points of local interest contained in maps that a special index is required and this will be discussed later but early maps sometimes contain examples of points relevant to the development of cartography. Any student of cartography will know that early maps did not observe a convention of the north point of the compass being used as the top of the sheet, he should be able to see such a map in the collection. If anyone wishes to see a compass indicator with the east pointer, pointing to the Holy Land, in the form of a Christian cross, he should be able to do so. An early map may contain drawings of ships and whales in the seas, or mythical beasts in unexplored continents, the map curator or any of his staff, should be able to produce such a map when required. These, and many other examples could be made, should not require a long search, they should be recorded in appropriate entries, probably noted as examples. In a dictionary catalogue some such heading as 'CARTOGRAPHY—historical examples' may be appropriate, and a similar heading in a classified catalogue represented by the class number for 'historical cartography', followed by the written term 'example' in the heading. This heading will probably be directly used only by the library map room staff, but it will save a great deal of unnecessary searching on behalf of readers requiring this type of example.

BROWN (p 78) recommends that 'When space and time permit, it is well to make title cards for all maps'. For general libraries to follow this precept would be a misuse of effort, except of course for anonymously produced maps, or maps with no known authors or titles which have become well known under a given title, such as 'Vinland map'. If a map, with known cartographer, is thought to have become known through its title, a title entry ought to be provided.

Arrangement of entries. Headings of all types will include the date of survey, if known, otherwise the date of publication, as an aid for filing map entries chronologically under the heading. The card should also be prominently distinguished as bearing an entry for a map, as a guide to the person filing the card in the catalogue to put the card in the map section under the heading following the entries for books, if any, bearing that heading. The distinction is probably best made by including the word 'Map' at the right hand side of the card but in line with the heading.

Map information file

For a map library and the map users to obtain the fullest benefit from the early general and early local maps acquired in a general library collection, more information should be discovered and recorded for these maps than it is possible to do within the compass of an entry in a card or computer-produced catalogue. As already mentioned it is felt that the majority of users of maps in general libraries and university geography departments are concerned with the information that is contained in the maps within a collection, and for early maps this information may be of a historical as well as a geographical nature. As much as possible, recognition of this will guide the cataloguer in making descriptive notes in the catalogue.

The historian of cartography, the collector of early maps, the student of cartography etc will however rightly expect to examine maps from his point of view, and these interests demand a critical examination of the map by the map librarian/cataloguer and a record of the results of the examination to be entered in a 'Map information file'.

Mr Cooper's form for the inventory of local history maps at Chesterfield Library, Derbyshire names some of the items which ought to be recorded in a map information file, but providing a series of ruled compartments on a printed sheet may inhibit the addition of some useful information if the space allowed is found to be too small to include it. If a printed form is used the space allowance for each item should be generous. If a printed form is not used, a list of the categories of information to be recorded should be available to the map curator, and in recording, the information should be itemised under the same headings, and the headings retained in the chosen order. BROWN's suggestion referred to earlier that the 'sheet record' should be kept with the map may be followed by some libraries but it is usually preferable to have the record available, as a special catalogue, so that choice of maps to be examined can be made with its aid. This suggests that the sheets should be kept adjacent to the catalogue, along with published map bibliographies, catalogues of other map collections, bringing together for the user those cartobibliographical reference works which the historian of cartography might wish to use together. The sheets of the information file could in this case be put in a loose-leaf binder for shelving with the associated books.

The content of the information sheets can be grouped in three main divisions, identification, bibliographical, and cartographic, although other elements could be added which are either thought to be items of interest within that library, or are for administrative purposes, such as call numbers and source of acquisition. Not all maps will include all the items listed, in particular manuscript maps will obviously have no entries for matters concerning printing.

Identifying elements These will be the same as the similar section on the catalogue card, but no abbreviations or omissions would be used, wherever the information is written on the map itself it is copied here in full.

Cartographer or surveyor: The person stated to be or thought to be primarily responsible for the content of the map or plan. Give the name in full, even if only initials are used on the map.

Title: The title in full as on the map using the same punctuation and spelling, repeat the author statement, any scale statement etc if they are combined with the title statement on the map within a cartouche, label etc.

Scale: As on the map; any statement in words, the units of a bar rule and its measurement in millimetres. A representative fraction scale is not required.

Engraver, publisher, printer: As written on the map, with addresses and any other information, eg 'Published according to the Act . . .' which might be included in the appropriate statement on the map.

For manuscript maps any statement recording the date of survey, or of drawing can be recorded in this position.

Date of situation, date of impression: The dates should be identified as situation, or impression (ie printing date of the copy in the library) and every attempt should be made to gain as accurate a date as possible. Manuscript maps should be similarly dated for situation and drawing. The evidence used, the content of the map, the guidance of named reference books etc must be recorded.

Analytical note: If the map is in a volume, or containing work, the volume is to be recorded. If the physical appearance of the map suggests that it may have been extracted from a volume, every possible attempt must be made to establish the identification of the volume concerned. Record the evidence for the attribution.

Size: The size of an independent map, preferably in millimetres with height before width. Measure the same area as for the catalogue entry. The size should be in millimetres because variations of a few millimetres can be observed between apparently similar copies of a map, which may be due to different rates of shrinkage or because the apparently similar copies have been printed from slightly different plates, or the same plate in different states.

The size of a map in a volume or extracted from a volume should be included in the analytical note together with the size of the containing volume. For an extracted work the size of the containing volume may have to be taken from a reference work, and this should be clearly stated. A bibliographical reference to a map by cartographer, title, date etc may suggest that two maps are identical until the sizes are seen to be very different.

Text: Text printed on the face and reverse of the map should be identified as eg 'table of reference' etc. The listing of text should commence at the north west corner of the sheet and proceed in a clockwise direction, concluding with text on the reverse. In this way 'title' will be located but not given in detail as it has already been transcribed in full, a dedication not previously detailed should be given in full.

Bibliographical elements

Map curators should know the writings of cartobibliographers and writers on the history of cartography. An understanding of cartobibliography and the history of map and atlas publication in general terms will create an awareness of the problems which arise and the evidence to be checked and noted in this section, and to a lesser extent in the next section. The works of Sir Herbert G Fordham, R A Skelton, Walter W Ristow, Ir C Koeman, should be noted, and the periodical *Imago mundi* and publications of *Map collectors' circle*. Essential background information for recording early maps will be found in:

Leo Bagrow *History of cartography* Revised edition in English edited by R A Skelton. London, C A Watts 1964.

R A Skelton *Decorative printed maps of the 15th to 18th centuries* London, Staples Press 1952 and the stimulating R A Skelton *Maps, a historical survey of their study and collecting* Chicago; London, University of Chicago Press 1972.

For British local maps the works of J B Harley are, among others, essential reading, in particular: J B Harley *Maps for the local historian: a guide to British sources* London, National Council of Social Service 1972.

Of direct relevance to the writing of a bibliographical record for an early map in the library is: Coolie Verner, 'Cartobibliographical description: the analysis of variants in maps printed from copper-plates' *The American cartographer* 1 (1) April 1974, 77–87.

VERNER defines cartobibliographical description as 'the systematic study of early printed maps as objects which diffuse geographical knowledge,' and it should be the intention of the map librarian to produce in this section of the 'Map information file' an accurate description of these elements of a map in the library which will enable a cartobibliographer to assess the position of the map in a systematic study. Cartobibliography attempts to detect and elucidate changes which have been made in plates from which maps were printed. A plate found to have been used over many years with minor changes of content, but with regular changes of date and printers name, is obviously not showing the geographical situation which it purports to show. The systematic study of early printed maps in this way is largely by comparative methods, and if a library possesses similar copies of a map, the 'Map information file' record sheet should include the record of a comparison that has been made. Most maps will however be represented as single copies and the bibliographical elements of the record sheet should note carefully these items which would be compared if several copies were examined.

Imprint check: Record any variation in the imprint details compared with the entry for a similar map in cartobibliographies, map library catalogues or other reference books. If the details agree in every respect with a standard bibliography this should be recorded, giving the relevant item number in the bibliography, if any, eg Chubb, CCCXXXIII 41.

Medium check: Record any information for a printed map concerning the paper, including any watermark, and colouring. For a manuscript map the medium, paper and watermark, parchment/vellum can be recorded; the use of pencil, black or coloured ink is understood; the use of paint is noted.

Printing check: The map or plan should be checked for any evidence of content which might have been changed or which might be changed in a later impression of the map. The former includes evidence for erasure of words from a plate and the substitution of new ones, eg the removal of a publisher and map-seller's name and address and the substitution of one which does not properly fill the space cleared for it, or lines which could be scratches. The latter includes misspelled contemporary place names, and the wrong location of a village or geographical feature, obvious errors could be rectified easily for a new impression of the map and a copy recorded elsewhere as not having such misspellings or mis-locations would obviously be of later date. Comment on the quality of the impression should be made if it is noteworthy.

Cartographic elements
Information of this nature has received scant attention to date in map catalogues and bibliographies, but cartographic practices of an unusual nature should be recorded and included in the sheet, these may be of a technical nature or concerning draughtsmanship. At the time of writing, 1975, research is in progress on the development of conventional signs on maps, and a desiderata in the study of manuscript maps is a means of recording characteristics of style. The recording of unusual examples within these topics and many others will facilitate research, a librarian's prime duty, and possibly stimulate research in other cartographic topics.

Cartographic data: The prime meridian used must be recorded if different from Greenwich, established by the longitudes identified on the map. Accuracy of longitudes, early use of a graticule. The early recording of data, eg at different times—roads, types of roads, variation in land height, land use. These may also be present in large scale manuscript plans which may be found to include notes from the survey, and calculations of measurement.

Variations in cartographic format, eg top of sheet other than north, form of compass rose or compass indicator; use of local, customary, measurements of length or area, 'Bird's-eye view' drawings; presenting buildings in front elevation 'on their backs'; apparent accuracy of such representations.

Draughtsmanship data: Brief description of form of commonly drawn aspects of maps, eg scale bar, dividers, border, ornamentation, compass rose or indicator, cartouche frame etc.

Conventional signs not conforming to expected design for the period should be noted.

254

Idiosyncracy of style of any kind should be noted. This particularly concerns manuscript maps. When hand written, formation of capital letters could be included as well as eg unusual drawing to represent trees. Such recorded information may assist in the tentative attribution of an unsigned map to a particular map maker represented by signed maps in the collection.

Further information

Bibliography: Full citations to books, parts of books, etc which describe or refer to the map. Additional references may be made for writings on the cartographer, if he is of minor importance and not obviously recorded in major works of history of cartography.

Prices: Source and price paid for the library copy might be noted but as the sheet is to be placed on public access this is probably better recorded elsewhere. Published sale prices for the map might also be recorded here, giving the reference. This is of value for general insurance purposes and a ready guide for temporary special insurance if the map is loaned for exhibition. Again this information is best recorded only on the sheet filed for staff use, the public sheet, if it contained this information, could be a guide for informed theft.

Other information may be included according to the circumstances of a library. BOGGS (p 35–38) is particularly helpful in recording the notes which might be made in cataloguing a map but these do not include many topics of bibliographical or cartographic significance.

Index to local maps

A number of maps acquired for local interest will have been made to illustrate a particular facet of the contemporary scene for any one of a number of purposes, some of them being statutory requirements in the last two hundred years or so. The line of a new highway built under the powers of a town improvement act, the location of the chapels of a dissenting church as a guide to church members within the area, there is a large variety of possibilities. Currently produced maps such as those produced to identify for motorists one-way streets in a town, street parking areas, and car parks can be matched by victorian maps showing cab ranks and the radius for distances relevant to a fare from that rank. Where possible these thematic maps will be catalogued with an appropriate subject heading or classified heading. But many other maps which are general, or even topographical, may incorporate unexpected information; an English county map carefully marking the houses of 18th century gentry and naming owners, an estate map identifying crops, a town plan identifying the use of buildings and naming the owner or tenant. Sometimes a previous owner of a map has added information to the original such as a victorian local authority adding the lines of the new drainage system to an ordinary street map. The map librarian and/or the local history library must compile an index to such information which, being unexpected, cannot be readily traced otherwise. Such indexes repay many times the cost of the time spent in preparing them. If an enquiry involves knowledge of the field-names of a particular area prior to the urban development, and field-names of the past are known to have been used to name houses, roads, schools and public houses on the site today, then it should not be necessary to examine all maps. Those plans containing field-names should be indexed. If another enquirer wishes to locate all the wells which have existed in the area, one avenue of enquiry is through maps and it should be possible with the aid of an index to have immediate reference to the local maps which do identify the sites of wells. Map librarians concerned with local maps should read the two useful articles cited below which offer guidance on the practice of indexing local maps.

M A Walton 'Suggestions for making fuller use of local maps and plans' *Library Association record* 39, 1937, 354–357.

D M Norris 'Local collections, some problems of classification and cataloguing' *Library world* LXIX (Feb) 1968, 193–195.

Chapter references:
AACR; ADAMS; BAGROW; BOGGS; BROWN; BSI DRAFT; CARR; CHUBB; EDEN; HARLEY 1972; HULL; KOEMAN 1961; NORRIS; PARSONS; SKELTON 1952; SKELTON 1972; VERNER; WALTON.

13

Dating and identifying early and local maps

Too often early maps not bearing informative imprint information are inadequately or incorrectly described in the general library map catalogue. The errors most obviously seen are the absence of a date and the incorrect attribution or, more commonly, absence of attribution for the containing work from which the sheet map has been removed. Early maps have always to be viewed with some suspicion with regard to the information they purport to contain. Historians of cartography repeatedly warn map users that the evidence of historical detail obtained from an early map should always be checked with other documentary evidence if possible. It is not easy for a map librarian to authenticate the authority of a single copy of an early map, but no further errors introduced by an inadequate or inaccurate catalogue description should compound the inherent difficulties in using the evidence of a map. Every effort should be made not only not to err, but to establish as much information as possible about the map on receipt and a technique which might be of assistance can be followed.

Any information received with the map, such as a bookseller's catalogue entry should be retained. However, in the circumstances of a sale for example, this should be used as a guide for checking and not immediately accepted as correct in all details, a bookseller might have made errors. Important maps should always be accompanied with everything that can be traced concerning provenance and such information will be retained and recorded with the entry in the 'Map information file'. A map which has been extracted from an atlas or containing volume will usually show physical signs of this when examined. A map sheet may have a crease down the centre, possible evidence of having been folded in a volume for a long time. The fold on the reverse side of the sheet may be seen to have the remains of the guard strip which was sewn into the spine of the volume, so that the map could be fully opened within the bound volume without the centre of the face of the map being hidden from view in the curve of the binding. Early maps drawn on copper plates were engraved in intaglio, the line being incised in the metal plate. For printing, ink was

257

pressed into the incised line with the surface of the plate cleaned, and the printing press flattened damp paper on to the plate, forcing the paper into the lines to take up the ink. Pressure leaves the paper, which was between the press and the plate, with a smoothed finish compared with the paper sheet margin which was beyond the edge of the plate. Often the resultant plate line will be seen around the engraved area of a map, and sometimes a number will be seen just within the plate line, usually top right, which is found to be the plate number for the map in a collection of maps brought together in a volume. When individual sheet maps bear such signs it can be assumed that they have been extracted from a volume.

If no such evidence is visible and the map bears no imprint information an attempt must be made to date it from the internal evidence on the map. The map has to be examined very closely to establish all possible evidence. Helpful information might be somewhat hidden in a flourish of decorative line at the border, or within the extravagance of ornament of a cartouche in baroque style. Text printed on the map may refer to people, in dedications, in naming the owners of mansions drawn empaled on the map. With the aid of biographical reference sources the dates of such persons may be discovered and it could be found that all of them were living at the same time for only about ten years, which suggests the map was drawn during that decade. Other matters recorded will give some evidence as to the earliest possible date for the map, a copy of a plan recording the site of a battle must have been prepared after that battle, but, such is the difficulty with early maps, the plate from which the map is printed may have been drawn long before the battle and copies printed from it, but for a later impression the reference to the battle is added to the plate to up-date the map. It is therefore desirable, not only for the map librarian to achieve an accurate date for the library copy, but to attempt whatever comparative study is possible with the assistance of map library published catalogues and cartobibliographies which may describe similar copies. If possible the catalogue should make the user of the map aware that although this library copy is one of an impression made at date $X+$, the map was published with the same information, except for some updating details, at date X, and therefore the bulk of the general information given can be dated $X-$. The site of a battle is an example of a geographical/historical fact which cannot be anticipated, but man-made topographical details might be anticipated. A cartographer would be aware of the intention to build a canal in an area he had mapped, or later a railway. He would possibly have a copy of the map produced by the canal company or the railway company, either in a prospectus inviting the purchase of shares, or in a copy to be delivered to parliament for the needs of a private act giving permission to build. The cartographer may have used this information in order to put the line of the canal or of the railway on his map before the construction had taken place, in order to make the map as up-to-date as possible for better sales. Unfortunately sometimes the canal venture did not take place, or the railway line was directed to be built over an alternative route. In these latter cases it is shown that the map alone cannot be taken as proof that what it shows is necessarily correct, and it also shows that such evidence is not positive proof for dating an undated map. In both cases, for the canal and the railway other documents are mentioned, a canal company prospectus and a Private Railway Bill, and a map cataloguer should always take his quest for dating into the use of other documents for confirmation, if they are available.

Many books and more particularly periodical articles, give examples of the search and evidence discovered identifying categories of maps and particular maps of interest, some of them are to be mentioned below, and a map librarian should be aware of their publication. All general libraries have an interest in the history of cartography, all have examples of early maps or early local maps, as proof of this interest. If a library has an especial interest, in an English public library it would probably be English regional cartography, books concerning that special interest should be bought by the map librarian and periodical articles concerning the interest should be analytically catalogued in the map department catalogue. Obviously books and periodicals specifically concerned with cartography, or local history if that is the case, will be housed in the map library but many other relevant articles and chapters in books may be correctly filed elsewhere. The periodical covering an aspect of geography or of history may not be filed in the map library, arrangements should be made for the subject specialist concerned with history etc. to inform the map librarian of the publication of an article of interest which should then be analytically catalogued where it should be seen by map users. Often articles for cataloguing will come from further afield than the geography departmental library, as *Artscanada* XXXI (188/189) Spring 1974, which is an issue with the theme 'On maps and mapping' and has a useful article, John Warkentin 'Discovering the shape of Canada' pp 17–35, with numerous illustrations and sections on 'Completing the outline of Canada', 'Early topographic mapping', 'Surveys', 'Modern topographic maps', 'Thematic and special maps'. The map librarian cataloguing a newly received early map will also find this analytical information of assistance in the literature search he may have to conduct for evidence on the map. The literature search may have to be conducted, of course, beyond the material available in the general library itself, by the use of bibliographies, periodical indexes, etc.

Examples of primary literature which can be or is designed to be used in this way are traced similarly and no doubt exist for the regional cartography of most countries in the world. Selected works follow, based on a general and a British interest.

Selected literature on early maps.
A large proportion of early printed maps of value in the sixteenth and seventeenth centuries were published in the Netherlands and no basic collection of early maps would be complete without a representation of the landmarks in the development of Dutch or Flemish map publishing. Important atlases may be in the library but many more general libraries have sheets from atlases, by Blaeu for example, which have been broken up. In recent years an outstanding bibliographical tool has become available in:

Ir C Koeman *Atlantes Neerlandici* 5v Amsterdam, Theatrum Orbis Terrarum, 1967–1972. A bibliography of terrestrial, maritime and celestial atlases and pilot books, published in the Netherlands up to 1800.

Volumes 1–3 provide descriptions of over 1000 editions of terrestrial atlases entered under the names, alphabetically arranged, of the cartographer or publisher. Volume 4 lists and describes the remaining atlases and pilot books, whilst volume 5 contains four indexes. The indexes are

1 By author or publisher, alphabetical, the 1450 titles of all atlases.

2 By year of first publication.

3 Name index to the 4500 cartographers, engravers, etc.

4 Geographical names, to provide an index to the maps in the atlases.

The entry for an atlas gives a complete bibliographical description with a description of the contents, and to assist in the identification of detached maps, signatures and page numbering and notes on the text pages. Historical notes on variants and editions are given, with necessary references to establish historical continuity. The geographical name index has entries under the heading of the modern name, in bold type. This is followed by the name used on the map and all the entries for that area are in chronological order, giving year of publication, author, number of the bibliographic code [number for the atlas], map number, volume and page of *Atlantes Neerlandici*. Original names are entered in the index but reference is made to the modern name, eg Golfo van Venetion *see* Adriatic Sea. An example of the use of

the geographical name index is:
  Yorkshire (West Riding)
  Eboracensis pars occidentalis 1646 Mercator
  [Me] 152 [No map no] II 488.

The entry Me 152 in Vol II, p 488 being: Ioannis Ianssonii/Novus Atlas/Sive/Theatrum/Orbis Terrarum:/In quo/Magna Britannia,/ seu Angliae & Scotiae/nec non Hiberniae,/Regna/exhibentur/ Tomus Quartus.
  Amstelodami,/Apud Ioannem Ianssonium/Anno CIƆIƆCXLVI.
[Full bibliographical description of the atlas follows including eg] (41) Pars Orientalis Eboracensis Ducatus dicta East-Riding. Ducatus Eboracensis Pars Orientalis. The Eastriding of Yorkeshire. 42 × 50 cm. 1:225,000.
  The published catalogues of national and other important map libraries are also of obvious importance, eg.
  British Museum, Department of Printed Books *Catalogue of printed maps, charts and plans* Photolithographic edition. 15 vols London, British Museum 1967.
  This catalogue includes materials added up to 1964, after which *Corrections and additions* have been published. The main entry is under geographic area, or areas, but added entries are provided for all surveyors, compilers, editors etc. In addition to atlases, maps and globes, the catalogue includes literature on them.
  Library of Congress. Map Division *A list of geographical atlases in the Library of Congress, with bibliographical notes* 7v Washington, Government Printing Office 1909–1973. Vols 1–4 compiled by P Lee Phillips. Vols 5–7 compiled by Clara E LeGear.
  National Maritime Museum *Catalogue of the library; Vol 3 Atlases and cartography* 2 parts London, HMSO 1971.
  Early atlases pre-1840 are grouped according to national groups eg Dutch and Flemish, British, with a group 'Ptolemy', within each group the atlases are arranged by name of cartographer or publisher, a short bibliographical description is given for the atlas and the maps included and listed by plate number giving title in modern form with a note of any inset.
  Analytical entries for maps in all atlases in the library published before 1600, and for maps in world atlases before 1800 are included in The New York Public Library, Research Libraries *Dictionary Catalog of the Map Division* Boston, G K Hall and Co, 1970.
  The above reference works and others will assist in the identification of detached maps in many cases, given some imprint information on the map it is often possible to refer to the atlases it may have

been extracted from and by a comparison of all the known details, eg size, a reasonable attribution can usually be made. It is always possible however that an early map is printed from an altered plate not previously recorded in which case it should be catalogued as a variant from a published state. Use the accepted abbreviation for the bibliography and the entry number as a reference in a catalogue, eg Koeman, Me 152 (41).

English county maps
A significant feature of the development of map-making in England was the publication of county maps from Saxton in the sixteenth century until they were ousted by the Ordnance Survey sheet system of publication in the nineteenth century. Certainly in England therefore a collection of county maps, not merely the local county, will provide a mirror for English cartography during nearly three hundred years and include an example of the work of most of the famous English map-makers. LEE has produced a pamphlet largely devoted to the identification of English county maps, which can still be read with profit as a guide to technique and to the pitfalls which might beset the path of the bibliographer of English county maps but the bibliographical reference works he uses have been superseded by later publications which have created a new norm for scholarly work in cartobibliography, HARVEY, THORPE and HODSON, noted below, and SKELTON, unfortunately not yet completed by his successors.

Thomas Chubb *The printed maps in the atlases of Great Britain and Ireland; a bibliography, 1579–1870* Reprinted London, Dawsons of Pall Mall 1966.

A chronologically arranged list of atlases, firstly of England and Wales, secondly Scotland and thirdly Ireland, with full title and imprint for the atlas but not a full bibliographical description, with bibliographical notes both descriptive, comparative and historical. For each atlas the included maps are listed with plate number, title as on the map, scale as on the map, and notes such as arms included on the sheet. Notes on the imprint of each map, if any. The volume concludes with a list of map-makers, with notes on their life and work, and a personal name index. The atlases listed are mainly those known to Chubb in the Map Room of the British Museum prior to the first publication of the bibliography in 1927, and include atlases from different countries, their characteristic being they are concerned with the British Isles, wholly or in part.

In the fifty years or so since the Chubb bibliography was prepared a great deal of new information has been discovered about atlases of Great Britain and Ireland, and new volumes or editions have come to light. In order to incorporate all the new knowledge, Skelton began work on a bibliography to supersede Chubb which was published in parts by the Map Collectors' Circle, and later collected in the edition cited below. Unfortunately the volume only covers up to 1703 but continuation of the work is in active progress.

R A Skelton *County atlases of the British Isles, 1579–1850: a bibliography* [Volume one] 1579–1703. London, Carta Press 1970.

The atlases are all arranged in chronological order, irrespective of the individual country or countries covered. Another departure from Chubb is that all the different editions of an atlas are entered under their own date whereas in Chubb they were all arranged under the date of first edition. Copies from a selected number of collections are recorded and references in Chubb, STC [Pollard and Redgrave, *Short title catalogue* . . . 1475–1640] and Wing [D Wing, *Short title catalogue* . . . 1640–1700], Koeman (1967) etc. The information given is very full, the description of Speed *Theatre* . . . 1611 occupies some fifteen pages, and the headings in this entry can be taken as a guide to the general contents for all maps;

Title and imprint transcribed literally, line-endings shown; copies; collation [full bibliographical description]; contents; description; bibliographical history; later history; literature [on the atlas or one or more maps included]; list of maps. Skelton gives the fullest description of the individual maps in any bibliography.

To demonstrate the usage of these works by the cataloguer/bibliographer an example may be followed. A new map is added to the library, it is on paper, creased across the middle of the longest dimension, height; it shows signs of having been detached from an atlas volume. On the face of the map the surrounding plate line is clearly visible, and there is a small printed number outside the printed border but within the plate line. The number is 28, and it is assumed the map must have been plate 28 in a county map atlas. In the top left corner of the map there is a long title surrounded by a landscape vignette of woodland with deer and huntsmen with bows and arrows, one presumes it is representative of Sherwood Forest for it is: 'An Accurate Map of Nottingham Shire, Describing its Wapontakes and Divisions . . . By Eman: Bowen Geogr. to His Majesty'. Below the southern border there is an imprint: 'Printed for John Bowles in Cornhil, Carington Bowles in St. Pauls Church Yard, & Robt. Sayer in Fleet Street' but no date.

There is a scale statement 'British Statute Miles 69 to a Degree' [ie of longitude] and a scale bar of 12 [miles = 5.5/8"].

The size of the map, outer border, is $27\frac{1}{2}" \times 21"$; inches are used in this example as these are the units used by Chubb.

A dedication in an armorial cartouche is at top right, to Thomas, Duke of Newcastle, Lord Lieutenant . . . of Nottingham.

Compass rose, 8 star, marked only for North and East.

Text is printed in many places surrounding the boundary of the county, usually descriptions of towns and their trade but with a list of Earls of Nottingham, the seats of the nobility and an explanation of the conventional signs used.

The above is not a catalogue entry for the map in any way, but a listing of the information readily seen in the order and style it might be noted by the cataloguer. The cartographer, the title, publishers are known, but not the date of the publication nor the atlas from which it was detached. The last two items must be found if possible. The internal evidence of the map may give assistance with the date. The latest date mentioned on the map, in the text concerning Earls of Nottingham, is 1729 and so the map must be after that date and indeed the style of the map is obviously eighteenth century. The dates when Emanuel Bowen flourished as a map maker could obviously be useful and the dates when Thomas, Duke of Newcastle was Lord Lieutenant can be compared. But examine the possible entries in Chubb.

Checking the name index in Chubb it is found that there are many entries for the prolific Bowen and one starts with the earliest. A number are checked but quickly discarded usually because the publishers or printers of the map under examination bear no relation to the printers of the atlases first checked. Eventually an entry is seen which seems fruitful.

26. An Accurate Map of Nottingham Shire . . . By E. Bowen . . . British Statute Miles 12 [= 5.5/8"]. Printed for T. Bowles . . . John Bowles & Son . . . John Tinney, & Robt. Sayer

Arms: Duke of Newcastle.

Obviously this is not the same, correct title, correct scale and arms, but not the plate number, not the same form of Bowen's name, and not the same printers; but it does seem to be in the correct family. This entry is for a map in Emanuel Bowen and Thomas Kitchin *The Large English Atlas* . . . 1760. Another edition of an atlas first published in 1755.

Going back to the 1755 edition it is seen that a size, $17\frac{1}{2} \times 23$ inches is quoted, this was not given for the 1760 ed therefore it must be the same size in 1760 because Chubb does not repeat information unless changes occur in later editions. The size quoted is for the atlas, and this size would accommodate the detached map when it is folded, as it would be in the volume, but then it is noticed, in a description below, that the maps in the atlas measure $20\frac{1}{2}'' \times 27\frac{1}{2}''$, a reasonable agreement. Unfortunately the British Museum copy is imperfect and lacks the 1755 edition map of Nottinghamshire so the printers cannot be checked, but the maps which are quoted list printers not represented on the Nottinghamshire map being examined.

Checking through further editions of *The Large English Atlas* it is found that they do not agree fully with the library copy until the 1785 edition. Then the entry is:

28 Nottingham Shire . . . Printed for John Bowles . . . Carington Bowles . . . & Robt. Sayer etc.

Correct plate number, correct printers, and, from earlier entries, size, title, arms are in agreement. Perhaps however this is not the only edition of the atlas which agrees with these details. The next edition is of 1787, and this is found to agree in title and printers but the plate number has changed to 32. Checking further it is found that maps stated to be very similar to those in the *Large English Atlas* were being published from 1762, also by Bowen and Kitchin, in *Royal English Atlas* but the sizes and scales do not tally.

It is therefore reasonable to attribute the library's detached map to the 1785 edition and the catalogue entry will therefore include in the description:

[? Detached from: Emanuel Bowen and Thomas Kitchin, and others, *The Large English Atlas* . . . London, Robert Wilkinson, [1785]].

Robert Wilkinson is the successor to the business of John Bowles, who although his name remains on some of the maps had died before this edition was produced. The 'Map information file' entry would additionally bear the reference 'Chubb CXCIX'.

In many ways the descriptions in Chubb leave a little to be desired by their brevity and that, combined with the age of the bibliography, causes the bibliographer to look forward to the later volumes of SKELTON. The revised bibliography was of course of no assistance for the example as the map was later than the coverage date for SKELTON volume 1.

For some areas the cataloguer is fortunate in that a bibliography of printed county maps had been compiled and published, many by Sir Herbert G Fordham, Thomas Chubb and Harold Whitaker, they are named, and a map of their coverage of the country is included, in HARLEY (1972). These bibliographies have been prepared over many years and their date of publication reflects to some extent their current adequacy and comprehensiveness, but compared with the atlas bibliographies they offer the important advantage of identifying county maps which were individually published and did not appear in an atlas. Judicious use of the county map bibliographies can be made for maps of counties where no such bibliography exists or as a check on the editions of maps listed by CHUBB. Obviously in atlas volumes, and to a limited extent for other maps, there tends to have been what might be called 'kinship' groups in private map publishing, something of the nature of what would now be considered a publishers series. On this assumption a cataloguer with a newly received map to be identified, of an area for which no county bibliography exists, may examine published county bibliographies hopeful of finding that a similar map may have been published in other counties, which whilst being in no sense decisive, does offer an approach to identification and the correctness of the assumption could then be checked, perhaps in a major map library catalogue or by an examination of originals in a national map collection. Any county map bibliography could be of assistance in such a case, but the excellence of the latest publications in this field of carto-bibliography, HARVEY, THORPE for Warwickshire and HODSON for Hertfordshire would suggest that a start should always be made through these reference works.

One map commonly found, and frequently not identified, in the local collection of English public libraries, is a local map of the area prepared by Robert K Dawson, published in 1832. The map will be detached from *Plans of the cities and boroughs of England and Wales: showing their boundaries as established by the Boundaries' Act, passed 11th July 1832:* . . . 2v London, Hansard 1832. The two volumes contain 277 lithographic maps of the counties, cities and boroughs, and these are listed in CHUBB, but HARVEY, THORPE identifies the Warwickshire map with a more extensive description and HODSON the Hertfordshire map in five states.

As with all early maps it should be remembered that information about the map being examined may be found outside the standard bibliographies, in articles in journals, etc which are discovered by a literature search. This applies equally for manuscript maps, and discoveries are continually being made. K G Newton, 'The Walkers of Essex' *Bulletin of the Society of University Cartographers* 4 (1) December 1969, 1–6, with 15 pages of plates, states that these father and son surveyors, working in the late sixteenth and early seventeenth centuries, were virtually unknown until examples of their work were brought together in the Essex Record Office when it was founded in 1938. It is most probable that other Walker work will be awaiting full identification in a map collection and this article would be of great assistance. A new work which will be helpful in this and other ways is Peter Eden *Dictionary of land surveyors, 1550–1850* Pt 1 Folkestone, Wm Dawson and Sons, 1975, which will be completed in four or five parts.

Bibliographies and guides to many other British sources will be found in HARLEY (1972) and of course similar regional cartobib-liographical works are available for other countries.

One outstanding example is:

James Clements Wheat and Christian F Brun *Maps and charts published in America before 1800: a bibliography* New Haven and London, Yale University Press 1969, which is based on locations in a remark-able number of libraries in USA, and the BM and PRO in Great Britain.

An interesting narrative survey of early map making, printed and manuscript, in Australia has appeared in:

Paul Ballard 'Eighteenth and nineteenth century cartography in Australia' *Bulletin of the Society of University Cartographers* 7 (1) September 1972, 23–36.

Dating Ordnance Survey maps.

The accurate identification of early Ordnance Survey maps, primar-ily the first edition of the one inch to one mile map, is fraught with di-fficulties. The maps will be well used for historical and geographical purposes, and will be thought by most users to provide the most accurate information of their time and so it is incumbent upon the map librarian to provide as accurate a date as possible for the copies in the collection. Fortunately in recent years there have been a num-ber of publications to provide assistance.

Harvey and Thorpe *Printed maps of Warwickshire, 1576–1900* was pub-lished in 1959, and recorded the difficulties in identifying the early OS one inch maps for that county. The name 'edition' for Ordnance Survey maps is not bibliographically correct, and the name 'series' is often used instead. This is because although new editions do occur when the map appears in a new revised form for the whole set of sheets forming the map, there were seven such 'editions' prior to the publi-cation of the 1:50,000 map, there are many more printings in a revised form of individual sheets. In the first edition or old series the revised printings, based on the original copper plates to which additions and corrections had been made, were not named as a new edition etc and the original dates of publication were retained on the sheet. Sheets were not all revised together, but individually when revision was thought to be needed, and as often as it was required. The half century coincided with the major internal migrations of the industrial revol-ution, the growth of cities like Birmingham, and the rapid develop-ment of railways. Urban development and railway building were two reasons for the frequency of revisions and printings in Warwickshire as elsewhere, and these factors will be used as internal evidence of the date of situation, if not of printing, of the copies of the old series 1″ in a map collection. To assist in this process for Warwickshire an appendix was included in Harvey, Thorpe giving the dates of opening, and other factual information, of nearly eighty stretches of railway line in Warwickshire, and notes on some eleven railways projected but not built; an exercise which would be of benefit for knowledge of the local rail system in many libraries if it has not been published. Harvey and Thorpe also identified three categories of borders used on the Warwickshire Old Series maps which corresponded with three groups of printings, early, middle and late. The borders are illustrated in the cartobibliography and seemed capable of assisting in the dating of sheets elsewhere, or of suggesting a technique which might be adopted elsewhere. This is referred to in:

J B Harley and C W Phillips *The historian's guide to Ordnance Survey maps* London, National Council of Social Service 1964, which of course is also of importance with reference to Ordnance Survey maps of other dates and other scales.

Ian Mumford 'Engraved Ordnance Survey One-inch maps, the problem of dating' *The cartographic journal* 5 (1) June 1968, 44–46, records further examination of sheets in libraries which include embossed date stamps on the sheets for date of impression, and discusses the fact that 'margination', such as border design, was found to be completely variable as far as printings were concerned, at least after 1850. The examination was continued in:

Ian Mumford and Peter K Clark 'Engraved Ordnance Survey One-inch maps—the methodology of dating' *The cartographic journal* 5 (2) December 1968, 111–114, which reviews the methodology evolved to date, introduces the possible existence of watermarks in the map paper and concludes by usefully listing 'those positive indications of date that are to be found on copies of the maps'. The work is continued with:

R V Clarke 'The use of **wat**ermarks in dating Old Series One-inch Ordnance Survey maps' *The cartographic journal* 6 (2) December 1969, 114–129, in which to quote the journal abstract, 'the methods available for locating watermarks in Old Series maps [are discussed]. The watermarks found in over 2000 maps and their contribution to dating are analysed. The main conclusion is that the watermarks enable a particular sheet to be dated within a few years, especially in the period 1823–1836'.

The facsimile edition of the old series, edited by J B Harley *Reprint of the first edition of the one-inch Ordnance Survey of England and Wales . . .* 97 sheets. Newton Abbot, David & Charles Ltd 1969, is in print and each sheet contains notes on the publication history of that sheet. The reprint sheets can only be a facsimile of one of the impressions of the sheet of course, and so a library copy of an old series sheet cannot be identified by comparison. An article by J B Harley 'Error and revision in early Ordnance Survey maps' *The cartographic journal* 5 (2) December 1968, 115–124, is of obvious general interest but also includes a number of diagrams showing, for sheet lines within southern Britain, broad dates for major revision of sheets of the old series, and the range of dates for the date of survey of a sheet area. The field surveyors drawings for the topographical survey from which the old series one-inch maps were drawn are in the Map Library of the British Library. The field surveyors drawings are on a larger scale than the published map, being two, three or six inches to one mile and appropriate photocopies of them should be held in the local map collection of any British library, both for their own interest and in establishing the date of situation of the impressions of the published map.

Preparation of bibliographies of maps.
A library which has established a 'Map information file' on the guidelines indicated will have a wealth of information about the early and local maps in the collection which is primarily for better service to map users. As time passes further snippets of information and literature sources will be added to the file, and the number of maps so described will grow. The library authority should consider the publication of the 'extended' catalogue to the collection, or the map librarian should use the knowledge as a nucleus for a specialist bibliography, probably concerning the maps of a region, to which other entries for maps and editions of maps are added after their location and description in other collections, both regional and local.

Too often published catalogues of a collection are a pale shadow of what they might be, they ought to be an example of scholarly work in which the map curator and all concerned with the map library can take justified pride. The content of a printed catalogue may vary according to the potential use it is expected to have but if it is to be of a cartobibliographical nature, and the value of all other uses of early and local maps depends initially on the cartobibliographical research undertaken on them, then there are excellent models which should be taken into account by any other bibliographer as the standard at which he should aim. Two of them are English county cartobibliographies P D A Harvey and Harry Thorpe *The printed maps of Warwickshire, 1576–1900* Warwick, Warwickshire County Council and University of Birmingham 1959, and D Hodson *The printed maps of Hertfordshire, 1577–1900* 5 parts Map Collectors' Circle Publications Nos 53, 59, 65, 75, 83. London, Map Collectors' Circle 1969–1972.

The form of entry devised by Harvey and Thorpe, and the contents, is as follows; a similar arrangement is used by Hodson:

Order: The maps are listed chronologically by date of first appearance. Later editions are included in the entry. No references are given in the chronological sequence from the date of a later edition of the map to the date where it is entered.

Heading: Preference in the order—surveyor, draughtsman, engraver, publisher.

Size: Height by width in inches, but from the inmost frame lines of the map.

Scale of one statute mile: Bibliographies should now use the representative fraction, scale of miles will become to be out-of-date and rather meaningless. When the scale is not stated in words, it has been calculated by measuring two selected Warwickshire axes.

Inscriptions: Title, date, scale with measurement for scale-bar, name of cartographer or engraver as on map, imprint, given in full. Conventions indicate any inscriptions which are given outside the border.

Supplementary notes: Statistical or topographical notes, views, printing method etc.

Descriptions of editions: A note of any first edition inscriptions not already given, ie they are different in later editions; and alterations made in later editions.

Publication of maps: Title and imprint of every book, if any, in which a particular edition of a map was published.

Reproductions: Facsimiles known.

Lithographic transfers: State of the plate when the transfer was made, and alterations to the transfer.

James Clements Wheat and Christian F Brun *Maps and charts published in America before 1800: a bibliography* New Haven and London, Yale University Press, 1969, has maps initially arranged by area beginning with the world, in each group the maps are chronologically arranged and the form of entry is as follows:

Date: The first edition and all subsequent editions are entered separately at their own date of issue. If the map has more than one state, the state of the map entered is numbered, eg 'State II' and reference is then made to the entry numbers for the other states of the map.

Description: Given systematically but in a narrative form, to include details of title, imprint and author as given on the map and the location of these inscriptions on the map sheet. Information on the map's history, errors etc of a distinguishing nature, literature and other notes thought relevant, unless entered elsewhere.

Size: In inches, height before width.

Scale: Given as a brief numerical statement but using the units of measurement as on the map. Size and scale are only given for a first printing unless they are changed subsequently.

Published: Containing volume, if any, and selected reproductions.

References: Citing sources used, or bibliographical references.

Locations:

Chapter references:
BALLARD; BM CAT; HARLEY 1968; HARLEY 1969; HARLEY/PHILLIPS; HARVEY/THORPE; HODSON; HULL; KOEMAN 1967; LC LIST; LEE; MUMFORD; MUMFORD/ CLARK; NATIONAL; NEWTON; SKELTON 1970; STEER; WALNE; WARKENTIN; WHEAT/BRUN.

14

Care and preservation of maps

Any user of early maps is soon aware that many maps drawn or printed on paper and other materials four hundred or more years ago have survived in very good, almost perfect condition, and younger maps a mere two or three hundred years old in even greater numbers. The map user can only see the survivors however. Over the centuries owners have thrown away maps no longer needed or have allowed them to be in conditions where they have deteriorated and been lost. The early maps which remain have been filed, either intentionally or accidentally, in a suitable atmosphere and not in damp conditions, probably flat and slightly pressed by fellow documents which has kept dirt at bay, or rolled and adequately covered, but most importantly they have seldom been handled to any great degree and hand-made rag paper was used. Handling, even carefully, brings forward the deterioration of a document, and mis-handling is a rapid ageing process. The existence of well-used map libraries or collections, bringing together maps which have been preserved in a variety of sources to that date and the greater use then made of these maps helps to destroy them. Although some, previously housed in unsuitable conditions, will have a longer life after repair.

The British Library, and other institutions, will not allow the surface of a map to be touched by hand. At the other end of the scale one can find in some public libraries early local maps with half-moon shaped portions of the edge of a sheet torn away by the regular pulling of the sheet from the middle of a pile of sheets in a drawer. Mishandling is often by the library staff as well as by the user. Conditions for maps in some record offices, physically unsupported maps rolled in brown paper and tied with tape, dust abounding, suggest that if the map had as many consultations as an early map in a public library department of local studies it would be in an equally poor condition, and enclosure maps at least are probably beginning to approach that frequency of use.

Libraries, record offices, do not exist in order to prevent enquirers using the maps in the collection, so can they be used without handling? It has already been suggested that effective classification, cataloguing and information indexing will reduce handling by more closely identifying the individual sheet or sheets which will answer a user's expressed information need. Good storage, properly used, will allow a sheet to be removed from a file with the minimum disturbance of its fellows. But when the map is removed from the file it is handled. The assistant and the user must be aware of the dangers of mishandling an early map. The user must have a satisfactory table, one large enough to take the whole area of a sheet. The table must have good lighting to allow weaker and older eyes to have the best chance of reading detail at a distant point on the sheet. Magnifying glasses of large dimension, and reading torches carrying their own light source should be available in support, but even with these aids a user may need to pore over a map and will be tempted to lean on the map to keep balance. The face of the map should therefore be protected and a transparent plastic sheet is put over any map of an archival nature whilst it is consulted. Users must be advised that if they intend to take a tracing from any map, not just archival, it must be protected by a heavy gauge tracing screen. If the user of a large map feels unable to lean far over a table, it is tiring on the back muscles, he is tempted to pull the sheet towards him to allow the nearest edge to hang down the front of the reading table with the danger that the reader may lean against it and crease and crumple the sheet in the process. The reader may wish to make notes, this must be with pencil only, the early map would be thoroughly spoiled and a current map could lose information with the addition of an accidental blot of ink. All these points, and users soon find other ways of mishandling a map, are matters for user education and that is a role for the librarian or her assistant who supplies the reader with the map. The librarian must not only care how maps are handled but must be seen to care. The user will learn much from observation of the careful way in which a librarian handles the map, and for detail the assistant must give a few quiet words of advice on how that map is to be physically used. When the map has been returned to the library staff after use the danger has not finished. It is most unlikely that all maps can be refiled immediately on return, but they must not be negligently left on a convenient table with a lot of others. There must be a designated drawer, folder or box into which sheets are carefully placed for protection prior to filing. Any particularly valuable or fragile sheet will have appropriate separate storage and such sheets should be re-filed immediately after use.

Atlases can be difficult to use for a prolonged consultation. Many libraries have atlas cabinets in the public reading room, the atlases being filed horizontally on the shelves as all folio volumes should. The unit will have a sloping top for consultation but for more prolonged use the reader will wish to sit down. Then he will probably find it most convenient to slope the atlas volume by supporting it against the edge of the table, creating the possibility of damaging the lower part of the plates by catching them against clothing when turning the page. If it is an atlas with a fine binding, the surface of the binding will not be enhanced by rubbing against the table edge. A desk reading slope should be available for large volumes, one of variable angle and capable of being used at any available reading table.

For many maps in a collection, maps bought for current use which will be replaced when new issues appear, the reasonable care outlined above will be sufficient, but for maps which are intended to be permanently preserved other steps can be taken. The general policy should be to reduce map/user contact to a minimum, and as far as possible keep the map free from handling. Some British city libraries have photocopied all the early local maps housed in the library, and for all normal consultations a map-user is given the photocopy of the map, not the original. In the vast majority of cases this is quite sufficient, the enquirer needs the map for reference purposes to establish some information, to copy in whole or in part, or merely to check a location. The user can be given far more freedom with a photocopy, including perhaps the facility of rolling it up and borrowing it. Measured rules along the edges of the map, both height and width, should be included in the photocopy so that discrepancy between the size of the copy and of the original, and therefore discrepancy in scale, can be checked. CRITCHLEY has described the procedures adopted at Aberdeen city library where every early local map has been photographed commercially and for each has been prepared a 35 mm aperture card mounted negative; a 70 mm negative; a photo-reproduction on rough document paper, size A2 ($16\frac{1}{2}'' \times 23''$); a photo-reproduction on a lightweight projection document paper size A2; a translucent dye master on paper as distinct from a polyester film, size A4 ($8.1/4'' \times 11.3/4''$); and a dyeline copy. The A2 rough document paper copy becomes the file copy for all normal consultations. The other copies are shown to readers who require a personal copy of the map by purchase and the negatives are available in the aperture cards so that copies can be made available within 24 hours, by a local firm. The 35 mm and 70 mm negatives allow for the various sizes and type of reproduction. A photo-reproduction on A2 paper can be a very severe reduction in size of some early maps and in most cases a library should try to offer for consultation purposes a photocopy which is of the same size as the original except for slight changes in processing.

274

This implies the availability of a large bed photocopying machine in the general library's photographic department to provide the photocopy on one sheet. Strong document paper must always be used not the type of paper used for ordinary office copying. In some cases the original will not permit a good photocopy to be made, eg lack of contact between original and copy paper due to severe creasing, or the lack of flexibility in a vellum original, and in such cases a photographic copy will be made. A skilled photographer may also be able to improve the legibility of a photograph compared with a deteriorating original. For some purposes a 35 mm colour transparency should be made available. Whenever photography, as opposed to photocopying, is used a record should be made of the sheet dimensions of the original or the reduction factor introduced.

The original map will be available for consultation by the map user who requires it, for example a student of cartobibliography who would wish to make a close examination of the whole of the surface of the map, including the rear of the sheet and the paper it is printed upon. For these reasons the original map should not be mounted if that can be avoided, the photocopying takes the brunt of usage and so much of the need for mounting an original has been removed. A badly damaged map will have to be mounted in order to repair it, as also a fragile map for preservation, but with a mounted map the cartobibliographer is denied full opportunity to make his examination. Even if windows are left in the mount to show, for example, writing on the reverse, the scholar cannot be sure that the repairer has not covered other unobserved information such as a watermark.

Protection for an archival map may be of a nature which will both protect the map in handling and in its file. Libraries should consider the use of some form of transparent plastic pocket into which the map is placed during storage and kept there for protection during use. Map curators using this method usually leave one end of the pocket open or have a few holes punched towards one end in order, it is said, to keep the paper aired and prevent fungus growth. However as this is associated with dampness it would seem that a heat-sealed plastic pocket would be of defence against dampness. The transparent plastic cover is a fine defence against abrasion, and it needs to be, because of the dust which is so often present on the surface of such materials, another reason one would imagine for sealing the pocket. But the paper needs air to breathe: map librarians should perhaps experiment in their individual filing conditions on the best method for 'pocketing' maps. If more physical protection is required the polythene or polyester cover can be attached to a suitable weight card, larger than the area of the map, which will keep the map flat and protect it from any damage which might otherwise occur from bending or creasing. If the card is introduced, loosely, into the pocket with the map it must be of acid-free, or minimum acid content, material. Such a combination of pocket and 'stiffener', even if not used where appropriate for storage and handling, is a very useful means of protecting maps when they are on temporary public display on walls in the library or on tables during an exhibition, and it is suitable for suspension filing of early maps where the weight of the cover and map is taken by the cover and card. An alternative method for suspension filing is for the map to be 'mounted' on the inside of one side of the polyester 'pocket' by polyester film strips crossing over the map to hold it, the strips being fastened at their ends by special polyester adhesive tape. The transparent polyester sheet is folded over the map to create the pocket and support it in the suspension file from the fold. ICI Plastics Division, Films Group, Welwyn Garden City, Herts, make 'Melinex' polyester film for this kind of protection.

Map mounting, with edge binding, is useful protection for maps of a non-archival nature which are in frequent use. Expensive forms of mounting, laminating etc should not be used for sheets it would be possible to replace if they became seriously damaged, replacement or superseding with a later appropriate map would be cheaper. Self-adhesive transparent film can be used to cover well used non-archival maps, and for index maps which need both the physical rigidity of a card backing and the surface protection of a transparent film if they are not fastened to a display board.

'Tri-seal' is a self-adhesive transparent film from Trident Products, 63 Windermere Street, Gateshead NE8 1TX. 'Filmolux' and 'Filmomatt'—the latter being matt reduces light reflections, are available from Aga Standard Ltd, Aga House, 111 Church Road, London SE 19.

In any necessary mounting of archival maps the boards used must be acid free or of minimum acid content. The names of suppliers of boards, adhesives, etc as well as the general method of mounting is described in MUSEUMS ASSOCIATION Information Sheet No 12.

The mounting and the repairing of archival maps is work for a specialist craftsman; it is not within a librarian's professional competence. The role of the map librarian or curator in a general library in preserving maps is by proper storage and correct handling and the elimination of all factors which can cause deterioration of the maps. In Great Britain any university library and any public library system should have a document repairer, or conservationist, as a member of the staff of the library. The conservationist's work will include the repair of all archival documents, not just maps. The map curator should have a knowledge of what can be done to repair or prevent further deterioration in an early map and there is an ample literature to provide the information, but that is rather different from being able to practise the craft. This is not to say that the librarian's role in the matter is quite passive. As well as the actions already suggested, she has to ensure that the atmospheric conditions are as required for the preservation of paper, etc. ROYAL GEOGRAPHICAL SOCIETY recommends a steady temperature of between 55°F and 60°F, relative humidity not exceeding 65%, and good ventilation preferably by air conditioning. The curator has to recognise the need for the repairer's attention to a map, and this is probably at its most acute when early maps are newly received in a collection, particularly from a donation. Each should be thoroughly examined for sources of decay which must be corrected by the conservationist's techniques. Plain dirt, quite common, can be removed by the librarian, and other straightforward commonsense actions. Old roll maps, for example, may arrive attached to wooden rollers, they could originally have been an estate map to grace a landowner's study wall, as much a status symbol as a working record. Over the years, whilst the map has been rolled, dirt has penetrated along the inner rod and the map at that end has to be cleaned. Then it is found that the map is fastened to the wooden roller by tacks, and rust from them has already rotted parts of the borders of the map. The rollers are removed, the map edges are repaired by the document repairer. If the map is too big to be stored flat or hung in a suspension file, it has to be rolled again around a former, possibly using the method followed in the British Library, Map Library, and described in ROYAL GEOGRAPHICAL SOCIETY p6.

Document repair is based on a technology which of course progresses, and in one aspect much of the literature on conservation has probably been overtaken by events and that is in lamination. It is possible to laminate an early map using archival restoration tissue with an acrylic adhesive, which in order to return to the original is removable at any time by soaking in water. Ademco Ltd, Lincoln Road, Cressex Estate, High Wycombe, Bucks, HP12 3QU, make 'Lamatec' archivists laminating tissue which is reported to have shown no discolouration of tissue or adhesive and little deterioration, in artificial ageing tests. The map is laminated by the tissue being applied in a heated Ademco laminating press.

Chapter references:
ALONSO 1973–1; ALONSO 1973–2; CRITCHLEY; EHREN-BERG; LaHOOD; MALING; MUSEUMS ASSOC.; RGS REPORT; SMITH 1972; SNYDER; WARDLE.

15

Envoi

Whatever theories, techniques and practices are evolved, the library and library information services of the world always depend on two things for their existence and their success. The service is to provide the materials of record, including maps, which are needed now and in the future, and to ensure that the appropriate document or information is made available in answer to the expressed requirement of an individual library user.

Although collections of current maps in general libraries have been developing in the last few decades they are still comparatively small collections when measured in the light of the map output of the world. All map librarians in general libraries are well aware of geographical regions for which their map collection has little to offer, and of the paucity of thematic maps elsewhere. Readers' use reflects the map holdings of a collection, and the librarian is not often asked to supply maps which he has not got, but the reader is often disappointed with the atlas map that has to be used in lieu of the larger scale sheet map which would have been preferred, whilst the potential user is left unaware of the riches that a major map collection could offer. It is impossible for a general library to have coverage for the world on 1:50,000 scale, but any sheet in such a set might be valuable to some library user. At present he has to do without in most cases. Map librarians must develop methods of attempting to overcome this difficulty, as librarians in general book collections have.

In following the history of general libraries this would appear to suggest the further development of individual map collections with an emphasis of a chosen area of particular interest and presumably current strength, so that for a particular geographical region, for example, the library has a reasonably comprehensive collection of up to date materials which must include associated reference works. These holdings must then be made available nationally on a cooperative basis by lending to other libraries as requested. In general libraries the administrative machinery for this exists already but not the willingness to lend nor a knowledge of holdings. A directory of map libraries is of assistance but it is very difficult to codify the extent and value of the contents of an individual map library of a general nature. It is very different, however, if the library can note that all current series covering a particular area or region are available there. No doubt it will be economically possible at some time in the future to consult a map by distant visual transmission, but for the time being maps would have to be lent. Copies could not be made of current material because of copyright law and the time factor involved would often require the sheet to be borrowed even if a copy was being purchased, particularly from abroad.

Early maps can only be reasonably recorded nationally by their inclusion in published map catalogues or in map bibliographies giving locations. Such material would not be lent to other libraries, but often the student or scholar is quite happy to travel to see such maps, if he is sure that the material he requires is available, most users of national map libraries have made their visit with such knowledge or expectation. The general libraries of Great Britain and no doubt elsewhere, can add a tremendous volume of early local maps to the national stock, one suspects the number would easily surpass the total for this category of map in national map libraries. This wealth should be recorded by all libraries for publication and either catalogues produced of the local maps in the library, or better still bibliographies of the local maps in the combined libraries of any area with, if possible, the relevant contents of libraries elsewhere which have some appropriate maps for the area. These catalogues and bibliographies should be as accurate and as descriptive in identification as possible but they will only exceptionally be true carto-bibliographies. They would in fact include manuscript maps and plans and their purpose would be to provide an accurate knowledge of the holdings of local maps in libraries, so that they are fully used. These published catalogues would not become out of date, although other maps would be discovered later and supplements may have to be issued, so they would have a permanent value in giving the map user the knowledge he might require. In many cases this would result in the user buying a photographic copy of the map for his use.

A computer-based catalogue covering a university library or public reference library would, if comprehensive, include the maps within the library as well, and it is probable that knowledge of holdings of current maps in a library will be made public in this way in future. In a general library it is most probable that a computer-based catalogue including maps, will only occur as part of a policy decision for the production of such a catalogue for all materials. Some university geography department libraries however, have produced map catalogues using a computer and ALONSO (1972) is a very interesting feasibility study for such a project. Usually in general libraries however the role of the map librarian will be to ensure the adequate cataloguing of maps in a computer produced general catalogue initiated elsewhere, and this could imply the eventual production of a separate map catalogue. For local and early maps the wealth of detail which is ideally required, the comparatively static nature of such a collection, the catalogue not requiring frequent revision, suggests a traditional publication would then be far more appropriate.

Computerised and automated techniques will make their presence felt in other ways in the map collection. Increasingly maps will be in the general library which owe their production to digital techniques and other non-conventional methods, and copies will be supplied from microfilm masters. The director general of the Ordnance Survey wrote in the *Annual report* 1972–3, 'The Ordnance Survey no longer has any general obligation to supply maps of 1:1,250 and 1:2,500 scales printed on paper. Instead it has full discretion as to the form in which the survey at these scales will be made available. Large scale survey information will continue to be supplied but the department will take account of the variety of possible techniques of publication and will be free to decide how best to produce and market it having regard to the needs of users, to income and to proper economy'. The sheet map on paper has a long life ahead of it but the map library will be increasingly concerned with the storage and exploitation of cartographic information recorded in microfilm or on tape.

Chapter references:
ALONSO 1972; ORDNANCE SURVEY; PHILLIPS/ROGERS; RISTOW/CARRINGTON.

Reading list

In addition to the references listed below readers are recommended to see two collections of papers on map librarianship:

Drexel library quarterly 9 (4) 1973. Graduate School of Library Science, Drexel University. 'Map librarianship' issue. Issue editor, J B Post.

Special Libraries Assoc, Geography and Map Division *Recent practices in map libraries* Proceedings of a Map Workshop Panel . . . 1969 at the Special Libraries Association Annual Conference in Montreal. Reprinted from *Special libraries* New York, SLA 1971.

A bibliography on map librarianship was recently published: Alan E Schorr 'Map librarianship, map libraries and maps; a bibliography 1921–1973' Special Libraries Association, Geography and Map Division *Bulletin* No 95 1974, 2–35, 39.

The following list of works in one alphabetical sequence according to the abbreviations used, provides full citations for the references included within, and at the end of, each chapter.

AACR *Anglo-American cataloguing rules, British text* London, Library Association 1967.

ADAMS Scottish Record Office *Descriptive list of plans* Ian H Adams, comp 2v Edinburgh, HMSO 1966–70.

ADMIN Great Britain, Department of the Environment 'Maps of administrative areas'. Review note *Society of University Cartographers' bulletin* 9 (1) 1975, 78.

AGS R Drazniowsky *Cataloguing and filing rules for maps and atlases in the Society's collection*. Revised and expanded edition. New York, American Geographical Society 1969.

ALA Pauline A Sealy ed *ALA rules for filing catalog cards* 2nd ed Chicago, American Library Association 1968.

ALONSO 1972 Patricia A G Alonso 'Feasibility study on a computer produced map catalogue' *Australian library journal* 21 (July) 1972, 245–252.

ALONSO 1973–1 Patricia A G Alonso 'Map collections in public libraries; starting, building, maintaining them' Library Council of Victoria, Public Libraries Division *Technical bulletin* 1/73. 1973.

ALONSO 1973–2   Patricia A G Alonso 'Map storage and conservation' Map Keepers' Seminar and Workshop, Canberra, 1973 *Proceedings* pp 9–12. Canberra, National Library of Australia 1973.

AVICENNE   Paul Avicenne *Bibliographical services throughout the world, 1965–1969* Paris, Unesco 1972.

BAGROW   Leo Bagrow *History of cartography* Rev ed in English by R A Skelton London, C A Watts 1964.

BAHN   Catherine Bahn 'Map libraries—space and equipment' Special Libraries Association, Geography and Map Division *Bulletin* 46, 1961, 3–17.

BALLARD   Paul Ballard 'Eighteenth and nineteenth century cartography in Australia' *Society of University Cartographers' bulletin* 7 (1) 1972, 23–36.

BDT   *Bibliography, documentation, terminology* Bi-m. Unesco, Place Fontenoy, Paris.

BERESFORD   M J Beresford *History on the ground: six studies in maps and landscapes* Rev ed London, Methuen 1971.

BKS   BKS Surveys Ltd 'Maps of the Channel Islands' Reviews by G B Lewis *Society of University Cartographers' bulletin* 5 (1) 1970, 107–108.

BM CAT   British Museum, Department of Printed Books *Catalogue of printed maps, charts and plans* 15v London, British Museum 1967.

BM CAT-MSS   British Museum *The catalogues of the manuscript collections in the British Museum* Rev ed London, British Museum 1962.

BM MSS   British Museum *Catalogue of the manuscript maps, charts and plans and of the topographical drawings in the British Museum* 3v 1st ed 1844–1861. Reprint London, British Museum 1962–3.

BM NAT-HIST   British Museum (Natural History) *Catalogue of books, manuscripts, maps and drawings* . . . 8v Trustees of the British Museum 1903–4. Reprint. Codicote, Herts, Wheldon and Wesley Ltd, and Verlag J Cramer, 1964.

BM RULES   *Rules for compiling the catalogues of printed books, maps and music in the British Museum* Rev ed London, British Museum 1936.

BOGGS   Samuel W Boggs and Dorothy C Lewis *The classification and cataloguing of maps and atlases* New York, Special Libraries Association 1945. Facsimile, by microfilm/xerography. High Wycombe, England, University Microfilms Ltd.

BONSER   Kenneth J Bonser and Harold Nichols *Printed maps and plans of Leeds, 1711–1900* Leeds, Thoresby Society 1960.

BROWN   Lloyd A Brown *Notes on the care and cataloguing of old maps* (Reissue of 1st ed 1941) Port Washington, NY, Kennikat Press 1970.

BSI   DRAFT   British   Standards   Institution.   Panel

OC/20/10/9—Maps and charts, Sub-committee OC/20/10—Document preparation *Draft British Standard recommendations for bibliographical references to maps and charts in accession lists* Document 73/80194 DC. London BSI [1973].

BUFFUM Charles W Buffum 'On the final report, part 1' SLA Geography and Map Division *Bulletin* 24 (April) 1956, 10–12.

CAMERON K Cameron 'Maps in the study of place-names' *Society of University Cartographers' bulletin* 4 (2) 1970, 1–9.

CANADA Canada, Department of Energy, Mines and Resources, Departmental Map Library *List of map sources* 3rd ed Ottawa, Dept of Energy . . . 1972.

CANADIAN L A Jean Riddle Weihs, and others *Nonbook materials, the organisation of integrated collections* First ed Ottawa, Canadian Library Association 1973.

CARR A P Carr 'The growth of Orford Spit; cartographic and historical evidence from the sixteenth century' *Geographical journal* 135, 1969, 28–39.

CHUBB Thomas Chubb *The printed maps in the atlases of Gt Britain and Ireland: a bibliography 1579–1870* 1st ed 1928. Reprinted London, Dawsons of Pall Mall 1966.

CLARKE R V Clarke 'The use of watermarks in dating Old Series One-inch Ordnance Survey maps' *Cartographic journal* 6 (2) 1969, 114–129.

CNRS Service de Documentation et de Cartographie Geographiques (CNRS) et l'Union Geographique Internationale. *Bibliographie cartographique internationale* Annual. 1949–

COBB David A Cobb 'Selection and acquisition of materials for the map library' *Drexel library quarterly* 9 (October) 1973, 15–25.

CRITCHLEY W E Critchley 'Old maps, photocopying helps in using them' *Microdoc* 9 (3) 1970, 68–9.

CRONE G R Crone and E E T Day 'The map room of the Royal Geographical Society' *Geographical journal* 126 (1) 1960, 12–17.

CURRENT C E Current 'Acquisition of maps for school and other small libraries' *Wilson library bulletin* 45, 1970–1971, 578–583.

DARLINGTON/HOWGEGO I Darlington and J L Howgego *Printed maps of London, circa 1553–1850* London, G Philip 1964.

DDC *Dewey decimal classification and relative index* 18th ed, 3v New York, Forest Press, Lake Placid Club Education Foundation 1971.

DES Great Britain, Department of Education and Science, Libraries Division *The public library service; reorganisation and after* (Library information series, No 2) London, HMSO 1973.

DE VRIJ Y M de Vrij *comp The world on paper; catalogue of an exhibition* 3rd International Conference on Cartography, Amsterdam,

Amsterdams Historisch Museum, 1967.

DRAZNIOWSKY R Drazniowsky 'Cartography' [a bibliography of bibliographies etc] *Library trends* 15, 1966–67, 710–717.

DREWITT Betty Drewitt 'The changing profile of the map user in Great Britain' *Cartographic journal* 10(1) 1973, 42–48.

EDEN Peter Eden *Dictionary of land surveyors, 1550–1850* Pt 1. Folkestone, Wm Dawson 1975.

EHRENBERG Ralph Ehrenberg 'Reproducing maps in libraries and archives; the custodian's point-of-view' *Special libraries* 64 (January) 1973, 18, 20–24.

FERRAR A M Ferrar 'The management of map collections and libraries in university geography departments' *Library Association record* 64 (5) 1962, 161–165.

FETROS John G Fetros 'For the smaller collection'. Special Libraries Association, Geography and Map Division *Bulletin* 92, 1973, 52–54.

FINK Mary E Fink 'A comparison of map cataloguing systems' Special Libraries Association, Geography and Map Division *Bulletin* 50, 1962, 6–11. Comments on 'A comparison . . .' SLA, Geography and Map Division *Bulletin* 51, 1963, 7–10.

GALNEDER Mary Galneder 'Equipment for map libraries' *Special libraries* 61 (July–August) 1970, 271–274. and in: Special Libraries Association Annual Conference, Montreal, 1969 *Recent practices in map libraries* Proceedings of a Map Workshop Panel. New York, SLA 1971.

HAGEN 1970 Carlos B Hagen 'Survey of the usage of a large map library' Special Libraries Association, Geography and Map Division *Bulletin* 80, 1970, 27–31.

HAGEN 1971 Carlos B Hagen 'The establishment of a university map library' Western Association of Map Libraries *Information bulletin* 3 (1) 1971, 2–15.

HARLEY 1963 J B Harley 'The Society of Arts and the survey of English counties' *Journal of the Royal Society of Arts* 112, 1963–1964. Studies in the society's archives, 43–46, 119–124, 269–275, 538–543.

HARLEY 1965 J B Harley 'The re-mapping of England 1750–1850' *Imago mundi* xix, 1965, 56–57.

HARLEY 1968 J B Harley 'Error and revision in early Ordnance Survey maps' *Cartographic journal* 5 (2) 1968, 115–124.

HARLEY 1968–1 J B Harley 'The evaluation of early maps; towards a methodology' *Imago mundi* XXII, 1968, 74–

HARLEY 1969 J B Harley ed *Reprint of the first edition of the one-inch Ordnance Survey of England and Wales . . . 97 sheets. Newton Abbot, David and Charles 1969.

HARLEY 1972   J B Harley *Maps for the local historian; a guide to British sources* London, National Council of Social Service 1972.

HARLEY 1975   J B Harley *Ordnance Survey maps, a descriptive manual* Southampton, Ordnance Survey 1975.

HARLEY/PHILLIPS   J B Harley and C W Phillips *The historian's guide to Ordnance Survey maps* London, National Council of Social Service 1964.

HARRIS   Chauncy D Harris *Bibliographies and reference works for research in geography* Chicago, Department of Geography, U of Chicago, 1967.

HARVEY/THORPE   P D A Harvey and Harry Thorpe *The printed maps of Warwickshire, 1576–1900* Warwick, Warwickshire County Council and University of Birmingham 1959.

HIGHWAY   'Highway maps and tourist offices—a source list' Special Libraries Association, Geography and Map Division, *Bulletin* 92, 1973, 16–21, 34.

HODSON   D Hodson *The printed maps of Hertfordshire, 1577–1900* 5 pts, Map Collectors' Circle publications Nos 53, 59, 65, 75, 83. London, Map Collectors' Circle 1969–1972.

HORNER   John Horner *Special Cataloguing* London, Clive Bingley; Hamden, Conn, Linnet Books 1973.

HULL   F Hull *Catalogue of estate maps, 1590–1840, in the Kent County Archives Office* Maidstone, Kent County Council 1973.

HYDE   Ralph Hyde *Printed maps of Victorian London, 1851–1900* Folkestone, Wm Dawson 1975.

IGU   International Geographical Union, Commission on the classification of geographical books and maps in libraries. Chairman: A Libault *Final report* XIth General Assembly and XXth International Geographical Commission, London 1964 Bad Godesberg, Germany, Institut für Landeskunde 1964.

IMW   UN Department, of Economic and Social Affairs *International map of the world on the millionth scale Report for 1969* New York, United Nations 1970. Further reports, latest seen (ST/ECA/SER D/15) dated June 1974, are supplements of 1969 report only.

IUGS   International Union of Geological Sciences *Geological newsletter* Each issue has an 'Inventory of available geological maps' for one nation.

IYC   *International yearbook of cartography* IX, 1969, 74–194. London, George Phillip 1969. Contains: International Cartographic Association, 4th Technical Conference, New Delhi; December 1968, reports by national organisations on 'Activities in the field of cartography in various countries 1964–1968'.

KIRBY   R P Kirby 'A survey of map user practices and requirements' *Cartographic journal* 7 (1) 1970, 31–39.

KOEMAN 1961   Ir C Koeman *Collections of maps and atlases in the Netherlands, their history and present state* (Imago mundi, supp III) Leiden, E J Brill 1961.

KOEMAN 1967   Ir C Koeman *Atlantes Neerlandici* 5v Amsterdam, Theatrum Orbis Terrarum 1967–1972.

KUNZ   E F Kunz 'Maps for small and medium size municipal and shire libraries' *Australian library journal* 9 (April) 1960, 56–60.

LaHOOD   Charles G LaHood 'Reproducing maps in libraries; the photographer's point-of-view' *Special libraries* 64 (January) 1973, 19, 25–28.

LAWRENCE   G R P Lawrence *Cartographic methods* London, Methuen 1971.

LC   Library of Congress, Subject Cataloguing Division *Classification: Class G; geography, anthropology, folklore, manners and customs, recreation* 3rd ed, Washington, Library of Congress 1954.

LC LIST   Library of Congress, Map Division *A list of geographical atlases in the Library of Congress, with bibliographical notes* 7v Washington, US Government Printing Office 1909–1973. Vols 1–4 compiled by P Lee Phillips, Vols 5–7 compiled by Clara E LeGear.

LEE   R J Lee *English county maps: the identification, cataloguing and physical care of a collection* (Library Association pamphlet No 13) 1st ed 1955. Reprinted London, L A 1970.

LE GEAR   Clara E LeGear *Maps, their care, repair and preservation in libraries* Washington, Library of Congress, Division of Maps, 1956.

LOCK   C B Muriel Lock *Modern maps and atlases* London, Clive Bingley; Hamden, Conn, Linnet Books 1969.

McGECHAEN/VERNER   Alexander McGechaen and Coolie Verner *Maps in the Parliamentary Papers by the Arrowsmiths* (Map Collectors' Circle Publications Nos 88, 89) London, Map Collectors' Circle 1973.

MALING   D H Maling 'Some thoughts about miniaturisation of map library contents' *Cartographic journal* 3 (1) 1966, 14–17.

MARGARY   Harry Margary 'The facsimile reproduction of early engraved maps' *Society of University Cartographers' bulletin* 7 (2) 1973, 1–7.

MARTIN   E L Martin 'Select regional list of geological maps and map series' pp 122–150 D N Wood ed *Use of earth sciences literature* London, Butterworths 1973.

MUMFORD   Ian Mumford 'Engraved Ordnance Survey one-inch maps, the problem of dating' *Cartographic journal* 5 (1) 1968, 44–46.

MUMFORD/CLARK Ian Mumford and Peter K Clark 'Engraved Ordnance Survey one-inch maps—the methodology of dating' *Cartographic journal* 5 (2) 1968, 111–114.

MUSEUMS ASSOCIATION E G Harding *The mounting of prints and drawings* (Museums Association Information Sheet, No 12) London, Museums Assoc, 1972.

NATIONAL Great Britain, National Maritime Museum *Catalogue of the library; vol 3, Atlases and cartography* 2 pts London, HMSO, 1971.

NEWTON K G Newton 'The Walkers of Essex' *Society of University Cartographers' bulletin* 4 (1) 1969, 1–6.

NOKES Elizabeth M Nokes *The provisions for the storage of maps in libraries* Unpublished MA thesis, Loughborough University of Technology 1970.

NORRIS D M Norris 'Local collections, some problems of classification and cataloguing' *Library world* LXIX (February) 1968, 193–195.

ORDNANCE SURVEY Ordnance Survey *Annual report 1972–3* London, HMSO 1973.

O'REILLY R N O'Reilly 'Expansion of class 993.1; New Zealand classification schedules revised (1963) edition.' *New Zealand libraries* 27 (6) 1964, 133–153.

PANGBORN Mark W Pangborn 'Geologic maps' pp 352–436 In: Dederick C Ward and Marjorie W Wheeler *Geologic reference sources* Metuchen, NJ, Scarecrow Press 1972.

PARSONS E J S Parsons *Manual of map classification and cataloguing, prepared for use in the Directorate of Military Survey, War Office* London, War Office, 1946.

PARSONS/FATHERS E J S Parsons and Betty D Fathers 'Map room, Bodleian Library' *Society of University Cartographers' bulletin* 2 (2) 1968, 1–7.

PHILLIPS/ROGERS B Phillips and G Rogers 'Simon Fraser University computer produced map catalogue' *Journal of library automation* 2 (September) 1969, 105–115.

PRESCOTT Dorothy Prescott 'Map classification' *In* Map Keepers' Seminar and Workshop, Canberra, 1973 *Proceedings* pp 26–38 Canberra, National Library of Australia, 1973.

PRO Great Britain. Public Record Office *Maps and plans in the Public Record Office 1. British Isles, c 1410–1860* London, Public Record Office 1967.

RADO Sándor Radó 'World map, scale of 1:2,500,000' *International yearbook of cartography* VI, 1966, 94–99.

RGS REPORT Royal Geographical Society 'The storage and

conservation of maps; a report prepared by a committee of the Royal Geographical Society, 1954'. *Geographical journal* 121, 1955, 182–189.

RICS 1955   Royal Institution of Chartered Surveyors (Yorkshire branch) and Leeds City Libraries *Surveyors and map makers; catalogue of an exhibition* Leeds, Leeds City Libraries 1955.

RICS 1956   Royal Institution of Chartered Surveyors (Surrey branch) *The story of Surrey in maps; catalogue of an exhibition* Esher, RICS 1956.

RISTOW   *Facsimiles of rare historical maps: a list of reproductions by various publishers and distributors* Washington, Library of Congress [1969].

RISTOW/CARRINGTON   W W Ristow and D K Carrington 'Machine readable map cataloguing in the Library of Congress' *Special libraries* 62 (September) 1971, 343–352.

RODGER   E M Rodger *The large-scale county maps of the British Isles, 1596–1850: a union list* 2nd ed Oxford, Bodleian Library 1972.

SKEAT   T C Skeat 'The catalogues of the manuscript collections in the British Museum' *Journal of documentation* 7, 1951, 18–60.

SKELTON 1952   R A Skelton *Decorative printed maps of the 15th to 18th centuries* London, Staples Press 1952.

SKELTON 1970   R A Skelton *County atlases of the British Isles 1579–1850: a bibliography* V1, 1579–1703. London, Carta Press 1970.

SKELTON 1972   R A Skelton *Maps, a historical survey of their study and collecting* Chicago and London, U. of Chicago Press 1972.

SLA   Special Libraries Association, Committee on map cataloguing, *Final report* SLA, Geography and Map Division, *Bulletin* 24 (April) 1956, 3–9.

SMITH   T R Smith *Map collection in a general library; a manual for classification and processing procedures* Lawrence, USA, U. of Kansas 1961.

SMITH 1972   Richard Daniel Smith 'Maps, their deterioration and preservation' *Special libraries* 63 (February) 1972, 59–68.

SNYDER   D L Snyder 'Lamination as practised in the California State Archives' *Western Association of Map Libraries Information bulletin* 1 (3) 1970, 8–12.

SPIESS   Ernst Spiess 'Proposals for definitions of "Map Author"' *International yearbook of cartography* XIII, 1973, 52–57.

STANDARDS   Extract, '4, Maps and plans' (p 24) from: Appendix; standards for provision of reference material, *in Basic stock for the reference library* Edited by A J Walford and Charles A Toase. 3rd ed London, Library Association, RSI Section 1973.

STEER   Francis W Steer *A catalogue of Sussex estate and tithe award maps* Sussex Record Society, LXI. Lewes, the society 1962. *A catalogue of Sussex maps* Sussex Record Society, LXVI. Lewes, the society 1968.

STEPHENSON   R W Stephenson 'Published sources of information about maps and atlases' *Special libraries* 61 (February) 1970, 95–98, 110–112. And in: Map Workshop Panel, 3rd June, 1969; SLA Conference, Montreal, Proceedings *Recent practices in map libraries* New York, SLA—Geography and Map Division 1971.

TATE   W E Tate 'The (18th century) enclosures of the townships of (Sutton) Bonington St Michaels and Sutton St Annes' Thoroton Society *Transactions* 31, 1931. Nottingham.

TAYLOR   W R Taylor 'The Ordnance Survey of Northern Ireland, an outline of its history and present mapping tasks' *Cartographic journal* 6 (2) 1969, 87–91.

UDC   *Universal decimal classification; UDC 9, geography, biography, history* English full edition. (FID publication, No 179) BS 1000 (9): 1972. London, British Standards Institute 1972.

USGS   US Department of the Interior, Geological Survey *Topographic maps* Washington, Geological Survey 1969.

US—NAT ARCH   US National Archives *Guide to cartographic records in the National Archives* Washington, Government Printing Office 1971.

VERNER   Coolie Verner 'Cartobibliographical description: the analysis of variants in maps printed from copperplates' *American cartographer* 1 (April) 1974, 77–87.

WALLIS   Helen Wallis 'The rôle of a national map library' *Cartographic journal* 3 (1) 1966, 11–13.

WALLISCH   Hans Wallisch 'Review' of Jean Riddle and others, *Nonbook materials* . . . Prelim ed Ottawa, Canadian Library Assoc, 1970 *Library resources and technical services* 16 (1) 1972, 106.

WALNE   Peter Walne *A catalogue of manuscript maps in the Hertfordshire Record Office* Hertford, Hertfordshire County Council 1969.

WALTON   M A Walton 'Suggestions for making fuller use of local maps and plans' *Library Association record* 39, 1937, 354–357.

WARDLE   D B Wardle *Document repair* London, Society of Archivists, 1971.

WARKENTIN   John Warkentin 'Discovering the shape of Canada' *Artscanada* XXXI (188/189) 1974, 17–35.

WEAR   Angela Wear 'The departmental map collection and its management' *Society of University Cartographers' bulletin* 3 (1) 1968, 17–23.

WEST   J West *Village records* 'Printed editions of county maps' pp 70–72 London, MacMillan 1962.

WHEAT/BRUN   James Clements Wheat and Christian F Brun *Maps and charts published in America before 1800: a bibliography* New

Haven and London, Yale University Press 1969.

WINCH   Kenneth L Winch ed *International maps and atlases in print* London, New York, Bowker Publishing Co 1974.

WOLTER   J A Wolter 'The current bibliography of cartography, an annotated collection of serials'. Special Libraries Association, Geography and Map Division *Bulletin* 58 (December) 1964, 9–13.

WOODS   Bill M Woods 'Map cataloguing; inventory and prospect' *Library resources and technical services* 3 (Fall) 1959, 257–273.

Index

292

294

International Geographical Union, Commission on classification . . . *report* London, 1964 151–52
International map of the world 1 : 1M 23, 81, 187
. . . *Series 1301* 23, 25, 81
International maps and atlases in print K L Winch, ed, 1974 33–42, 44
International Standard Bibliographic Description for maps 236
International topographic map of the world, Series 1404 23–25
International yearbook of cartography 60–61
Inventory file 165
Iran
Sahab's catalogue of publications 42
Ireland
medium scale maps 82
official mapping services 74
Irish geography 57
Islands
place-name catalogue entry 179
Isle of Man
official mapping services 73
Istituto Geografico Militare, Italy 74–75
Italy
Bibliografia nazionale italiana 47
medium scale maps 82
official mapping services 74

Johnston & Bacon Ltd
agency 43

Kansas University, map library 135, 150, 171, 197, 212
Karta mira 22, 25
Koemann, Ir C *Atlantes Neerlandici* 5v 1967–72 260–61

Laminating tissue, 'Lamatec' 277
Lamination 276–77
Lancashire Record Office 99
Land capability maps
Canada 64
Land use maps
Great Britain 16, 17, 72, 85
Northern Ireland 73
Leeds
City Library 81, 217
University, Harold Whitaker collection 99
Leiden University early maps collection 87–88

Libraries
accessions lists 49–54
collections of early maps 87–91
collections of local maps 98–111
see also under names of individual libraries and map collections
Library Association; Reference Special and Information Section, *Standards for reference service in public libraries*, Approved, 1969 16–22, 81
Library of Congress, *Catalog of copyright entries, third series, Pt 6, maps and atlases* 52–53
Library of Congress, Subject cataloguing Division *Classification: Class G . . .* Washington, 1954 150, 160–63, 171
Local maps (British)
acquisition 98–111
cartobibliography 102–111, 232–34, 252–54, 269–71
cataloguing 229–56
pre-cataloguing examination 235–238, 245–46
classification 215–28
dating 257, 262–69
preservation 272–77
Location symbol 139, 154–55
Lock, C B Muriel, *Modern maps and atlases*, London 1969 22, 31–33, 39, 60
Luxembourg
medium scale maps 82

Manuscript maps, plans 107–11
Map author, definition 185
Map assessment 27
Map cataloguing rules
AACR 175, 184–86, 189–93, 205–12, 234–35, 238–39, 242–45, 247
AGS 178–80, 183–85, 189–91, 209, 212
BM 178, 183, 185
Boggs 178–80, 183–85, 187, 189–93, 197, 203–205, 235, 238, 240, 244–45
Parsons 146, 178–79, 183–84, 189–90, 193, 210, 247
printed catalogue card 193–95, 210
RGS 178, 184
see also Cataloguing
Map classification schemes
AGS 166–69, 171, 209
Boggs 152–55, 171–72, 201–205
DDC 155–58, 171, 182, 211–12
IGU 151–52
LC 150, 160–63, 171

295

296